FAMOUS KENTUCKY TRAGEDIES AND TRIALS

FAMOUS

Kentucky Tragedies and Trials

A collection of important and interesting tragedies and criminal trials which have taken place in Kentucky

BY

L. F. JOHNSON

HENRY CLAY PRESS
LEXINGTON
1972

ISBN 0-87642-008-0

HENRY CLAY PRESS/BOX 116/LEXINGTON, KY.

To

Judge Patrick U. Major

a great criminal lawyer, my preceptor and law partner,
who was born in 1822 and died in 1903,
this work is dedicated

TABLE OF CONTENTS

Preface and Introduction 1
The Rowan-Chambers Duel 7
The Jackson-Dickinson Duel 16
The Holman-Waring Duel 27
The Assassination of Francis Baker by Isaac B. Desha, in 1824 34
The Assassination of Solomon P. Sharp by Jeroboam O. Beauchamp 44
The Richardson-Waring Tragedy 58
The Wilkinson Trial 68
Speech of the Hon. S. S. Prentiss 79
Speech of the Hon. Benjamin Hardin 126
The Trial of Matt F. Ward 163
Hon. John J. Crittenden—closing remarks in speech. 171
The Execution of Sue Mundy 180
Thompson-Daviess Tragedy 191
Assassination of Judge John M. Elliott 205
Judge Geo. M. Curtis—remarks in part 212
The Grandson of Gov. John J. Crittenden 224
Thompson-Davis Tragedy 233
Judge Richard Reid, Cowhided by J. J. Corneilison. 246
The Tolliver-Martin or Logan Feud 257
The Goebel-Sanford Killing 272
Swope-Goodloe Tragedy 282
The Colson-Scott Tragedy 292
The Goebel Assassination 301
The Hargis-Cockrell Feud and the Death of Judge James Hargis 320

FAMOUS KENTUCKY TRAGEDIES AND TRIALS

This book is a collection of trials and tragedies involving the politically prominent in Kentucky during the nineteenth century. The tragedies include duels, murders, and assassinations. The trials are accounts of judicial proceedings in several circuit courts in criminal cases, which attracted great public interest. The author, an attorney at law who practiced at the capital city during the late nineteenth and early twentieth centuries, researched court records, newspaper accounts, and other sources. He was a defense counsel in some of the criminal trials spawned by the Goebel assassination. His selection of events for inclusion was fortunate, but it was his choice of material for verbatim or paraphrased repetition that placed the book a considerable notch above the average local history of ancient blood and thunder incidents.

The last decade has developed a current of despair over our failure as a nation to eliminate violence as a means of seeking redress of real or claimed wrongs. This book, however, shows that the attraction to violence is neither new nor a monopoly of the poor or disadvantaged—at least as far as the border state of Kentucky is concerned. The accounts in this volume range from the famous duel between Andrew Jackson and Charles Dickinson in Logan County, Kentucky, in 1806 to the still-discussed Swope-Goodloe tragedy that occurred in the post office in Lexington, Kentucky, in 1889.

To social observers who theorize that political assassinations are usually the work of a single demented psychoneurotic, the events before, during, and after the murder of William Goebel should prove disquieting. It is interesting to compare the author's account and analysis with the apologia of Caleb Powers in his *My Own Story* (1905). The fierce partisanship that influences both writings is evident; the same partisan zeal appears to have openly influenced the courts when they handled the cases. Perhaps modern courts really are more objective than some of their predecessors despite recent complaints to the contrary.

Some authorities believe that a critical deficiency in the adversary system of American justice is the loss of the art of advocacy. According to these students of the system, we are simply not training the trial advocate who can speak effectively and persuade. The final arguments made to the jury in Wilkinson-Murdaugh trial by S. S. Prentiss and Ben Hardin represent trial advocacy at its best. Modern lawyers would surely be entertained, and, with adaptation of style of expression to fit today's audience, could possess no better models of effective jury persuasion than Johnson includes here.

Places and institutions fade in and out of the current of tragedies in an intriguing manner. The Galt House in Louisville, Kentucky, was the scene of the murder that resulted in the Wilkinson-Murdaugh trial in 1839 at Harrodsburg. The Galt House was the scene of an abortive peace meeting between Republican and Democrat leaders as the state lapsed into temporary anarchy in 1900 as the result of the Goebel assassination.

In 1801, a judge of the Court of Appeals fought a duel with a son-in-law of a judge of the same court. Another judge of that court acted as one of the seconds. In 1879, Judge John M. Elliott of the Court of Appeals was assassinated on a public street in Frankfort by a disappointed litigant. The so-called "old court - new court" dispute that was caused by the depressed financial conditions in 1824 played a definite part in the trial and subsequent disposition of Isaac Desha, son of the then Governor Joseph Desha for the murder of Francis Baker. Finally, the voting record of the judges of the Court of Appeals in the decisions of the several appeals of convictions by various defendants in the Goebel cases demonstrated remarkable partisan consistency.

The author's style is the ornate and moralizing means of expression of the Victorians. The subject matter is not difficult; the style, therefore, lends an air of authenticity rather than presents a barrier to enjoyment. One may privately play the satisfying role of the amateur historian and yet not be required to pay the price of wading through too many laboriously fashioned pompositieS.

Read the book? I would have been afraid not to. After all, the nineteenth century poet Shelley wrote,

> **"Forget the dead, the past? Oh, yet there are ghosts**
> **That may take revenge for it, . . ."**

But then I am a judge of the Court of Appeals of Kentucky, and have a greater need than many of remembering the past and of securing protection from ghosts bent on revenge.

Scott Reed

Lexington, Kentucky
June 16, 1972

Prefatory.

MEN form their judgment of the true nature of the human mind from the expressed sentiments and desires of men; these sentiments and desires are often more forcibly expressed by actions than by words; the ruling passion of a man will find expression in some way.

It matters not how skillful a man may be in producing false impressions, the actual condition of his mind and the innermost thoughts of the man are known, to the expert reader of men.

We know of no way to judge the future except by the past. We judge ourselves by what we think we are capable of doing, but we judge other men by what they have done and by what they have been and not by what they might have been.

Psycology is a great science, it treats of the mind; a study of the mind is a study of mankind.

The most opportune time in which to study man, is when some great crisis in his life causes him to act according to the natural impulses of his nature.

The world is a comedy to him who sees only the frivolous and ludicrous side of life, but it is a tragedy to him who feels the weight of its cares and responsibilities.

Tragedies are the most striking events in history. Some might be termed world tragedies: such as the fall of man and his expulsion from the Garden of Eden. The flood,—that great cataclysm which brought death and destruction to the nations of the earth so that, "All in whose nostrils was the breath of life, of all that was in the dry land, died."

After this God made a covenant with man and as a perpetual token of such covenant, He set His bow in the clouds and this covenant was between Him and every living creature of all flesh.

The greatest of all the tragedies known to the world was

the trial and suffering and crucifixion and death of Him who died for men.

For nearly two thousand years this event has been the subject of constant discussion; the suffering in Gethsemane, the perspiration of blood, the nails through His hands and feet, the riven side, the crown of thorns and the death on the cross, have awakened the sympathies of men and have brought the world to realize the infinite compassion of a God.

Christian people in every country delight to tell, in story and song, the details of this the greatest of all tragedies.

The government of the Hebrew people was a theocracy, it was the only pure type of that form of government known to men. God walked and talked with men. The Old Testament is a history of this government: it gives an account of many tragic events: God's dealing with man and man's rebellion against God and man's wicked and cruel dealings with his fellowmen are its constant theme. The history of no other people is so fraught with human interest, because the history of no other people has given to the world the motives and impulses and sins of men.

Some of the strongest characters in the Old Testament committed great sins. Moses, the great law-giver and leader, was the meekest of men; he was the adopted son of a princess; he was unknown to himself and his people until he arose in his wrath and slew the Egyptian; after that he was God's agent in bringing the plagues upon Egypt, and he walked and communed with God and he became God's instrument in the deliverance of his people, and the Lord gave to him two tables of stone upon which were written, "with the finger of God," the ten commandments, and in a fit of anger he threw these priceless tables down and broke them.

King David's life was filled with tragic events; the life of the shepherd boy and his adventures, his duel with Goliath, his success as a military leader and elevation to the throne are not more interesting facts than his love affair with Bathsheba, the wife of Uriah; the death of Uriah by order of the king; the death of their first born, the fruit of their sin, and Nathan's parable of the ewe lamb which caused David to be his own judge, and in his anger he said, "As the Lord liveth the man that has done this thing shall surely die," and Nathan said to David, "Thou art the man."

There is not a more pathetic incident in all history than David's lamentation over the death of his handsome and wayward son Absalom. Though at the head of an army in open rebellion against his father, when David sent Joab with an army to subdue him, his command was, "Deal gently, for my sake, with the young man, even with Absalom." After the battle, when told that Absalom had been slain, the king was much moved and went up to the chamber over the gate and wept, and as he went, thus he said, "O my son Absalom, my son, my son Absalom; would God I had died for thee, O Absalom, my son, my son."

The love affair between Hamor and Dinah and its tragic ending resulting in the death of Hamor from the hands of Simeon and Levi; and the love affair of Amnon and Tamor which was terminated in the death of Amnon by the command of Absalom; portray the same characteristics of head and heart, and they disclose the same passions which dominate and control the actions of men, of like passions, at the present day.

"Cain rose up against his brother and slew him." This incident has been repeated over and over again in the history of men. Some of the strongest characters spoken of in the Old Testament were the most frequent violators of the law. Joab was one of the great generals of the world but his family was in a feud with that of Abner and Joab slew Abner, though he knew that he was transgressing the law of God and that he would incur the anger of the king. Joab also slew Absalom, after he had been directed by the king to " deal gently with the young man."

And Joab took Amasa by the beard with his right hand and smote him in the fifth rib so that he died and thereupon Solomon, who had succeeded to the throne, commanded that Joab should die and Joab fled to the sanctuary and caught hold of the horns of the alter, but even that did not save him from the wrath of the king.

Jepthah's rash vow brought death to his beautiful daughter and she was offered up as a burnt offering.

Samson was a victim to the blandishments of a deceitful woman.

A just retribution was meted out to the wicked Jazebel and she was thrown from an upstairs window and her body was eaten by the dogs.

Hayman was hung upon the gallows which was eighty-seven and a half feet high and which he had prepared for his enemy.

The Moabites and the Amonites were conceived in sin and born in iniquity and every period of their existence as a nation or a tribe was marred by the same ignoble and vicious spirit which marked their infamous beginning.

Many strong characters of the New Testament illustrate the idea, that some men have been willing, " To acquit themselves like men " and give their lives as a sacrifice for the cause which they thought just; they have demonstrated, on many occasions, the truth of the statement made by the poet who said:

"But whether on the scaffold high
Or in the battle's van
The fittest place that man can die
Is where he dies for man."

By the command of King Herod, John the Baptist was beheaded. Paul, the greatest of all Jews, was also beheaded.

Peter was crucified with his head downward. Judas went out and hanged himself. John was thrown into a kettle of boiling oil. James was killed by a sword thrust. It is a tradition that all of the remaining diciples met violent death.

These tragic events teach lessons. These men were martyrs; they suffered persecution for a principle; they taught men how to die for a just cause.

Tragic events in the history of our own State ought to serve a good purpose. Every event detailed in this work is given as a matter of history. Some allowance may be made for the ordinary exaggeration of the newspaper reporter who may have colored his story for the purpose of adding zest to it, but practically all the dates and a large part of the evidence have been taken from court records and the reports of the Court of Appeals.

A few " skeletons " in the closets of prominent Kentuckians are exhibited to the present generation for the first time. These disclosures are not made for the purpose of humiliating any person; they are given as historic facts in order that this and succeeding generations may upon the one hand emulate the acts of patriotism and upon the other be warned by the examples of sin and folly and tragic deaths of men, known as men of affairs.

The tragedies and trials of prominent Kentuckians should be of interest to every citizen of the Commonwealth. The cases cited are confined to the families of Governors and other State officials, lawyers, judges and men of affairs, socially, politically and intellectually.

Many of them are incidents which have occurred in our midst. Some of us have participated in them and have been a part of them and we know by observation, and some by actual experience, the motives, the impulses and the interests which have caused men to act. We know that a man in a normal condition often acts differently from what he does when in the extremity of death or when threatened by some great catastrophe.

Three straight lines, forming a triangle, give the key to many of the greatest scientific facts which have been revealed to men; the properties of the triangle give the sciences of geometry, surveying, architecture, navigation and mathematical astronomy, and they give a glimpse of other scientific facts which only the infinite mind can fully understand. Man in extremity gives an insight into human nature; into the strongest passions of men: passions which may be reeking with lust, avarice or sordid interests and which may often times disclose the human heart fatally bent upon mischief, but yet, of intense interest to the student of human nature because they are intensely human.

This is not a history of an imaginary people, nor is it told only to those who listen with credulity to the whispers of fancy, nor who pursue with eagerness the phantoms of hope, nor who expect that age will perform the promises of youth. This work is made up of historic incidents; actual facts in the lives of real men, many of whom have acted well their part in the development and government of a great Commonwealth. Some have acted important parts in the government of the Nation and some have played ignoble parts in the great drama of life, but every act performed shows the intensity of human feelings and discloses the inspiration of human action.

These lives teach great lessons to all who will get close to the human heart and listen to the warnings which a history of man's weaknesses and passions and failures discloses.

FRANKFORT, KY., November 1915.

The Rowan-Chambers Duel.

On February 3, 1801, there was a duel between John Rowan, afterwards Judge of the Kentucky Court of Appeals, and Doctor James Chambers, son-in-law of Judge Benjamin Sebastion, who was also a Judge of the Supreme Court of the State.

On account of the social and political prominence of the parties connected with this affair, and because of the high positions held by Judge Rowan and Judge Geo. M. Bibb, who was Judge Rowan's second " on the field of honor," this incident has become one of the most noted duels which was ever fought on Kentucky soil.

Prior to this time, dueling had become a very popular way of settling personal difficulties; many prominent men in different sections of the United States became victims of this unfortunate and vicious code of honor.

It was only a short time after this tragedy, that one of the Nation's greatest statesmen lost his life in a duel. It was on Wednesday, July 11, 1804, at Weehawken Heights, about three miles above Hoboken on the Jersey side of the Hudson river, that General Alexander Hamilton was killed by Col. Aaron Burr. Following this killing, a wave of indignation spread over the United States. Several States, among them was Kentucky, enacted laws prohibiting the practice; but little or no attempt was made to enforce them, and it was not until after the adoption of the constitution of 1849, which prohibited any one from holding any office of honor or profit in the Commonwealth, who had sent or accepted a challenge to fight, or who had assisted any one else in so offending, that the anti-dueling law became effective. It seems that the Kentuckian's innate love for office has been strong enough, in recent years, to effectually eradicate the desire he has to wantonly kill his fellow man.

The personal difficulty which led to the Rowan-Chambers duel occurred at Bardstown on the night of January 29, 1801. Judge Rowan, Doctor Chambers and some other gentlemen were engaged in a game of cards at McLean's tavern. Judge Rowan said something which offended Doctor Chambers, and after several words passed between them they came to blows, but in a short time they were separated. Doctor Chambers said at the time, that he would challenge Mr. Rowan. The challenge was sent on January 31, 1801.

Judge Bibb, who acted as Judge Rowan's second, on that fatal occasion, wrote a letter to the editor of the *Palladium,* in which he gave the details connected with the tragedy. This letter can be found in a bound volume of the *Palladium,* now in the custody of the State Librarian, and it is as follows:

To the Editor of The Palladium:

Sir: For the benefit of those who loving truth, have been or might be mislead by the many false reports which have been industriously circulated respecting a duel between Dr. Chambers, deceased, and Mr. Rowan, I request you to publish this letter together with the enclosed certificates, etc., referred to herein.

This publication would not have been made until the return of Major Bullock from New Orleans, but for the manner in which the subject has been introduced into your paper of the 28th of April, (1801).

For the cause of the quarrel between the Doctor and Mr. Rowan, I refer to the certificates Nos. 1 & 2, as also the copy of the Doctor's letter No. 3.

On the first of February Mr. Rowan and myself returned from Bullitt County where we had been the preceding week. The next morning Mr. Rowan showed me a note from Dr. Chambers of the 31st of January, requesting Mr. Rowan to make known his time and place of meeting, as well as his friend's name; to which he returned an answer the same day, by me, as his friend, appointing the next morning, and also naming a place.

In the evening of the 2nd of February, Major Bullock and myself met at Wilson's tavern where we had a conversation, in which Major Bullock expressed a desire that an accommodation to the satisfaction of both might be reached. I supposed that could not be unless the Doctor would withdraw his note of the 31st of January. We then had some conversation about the manner of firing. Major Bullock proposed that they should stand with their backs towards each other, in that position wait for the word, then face and fire at pleasure. Nothing of the distance was proposed that evening, but that and the manner of firing was postponed, to be agreed on in the morning. Accordingly, when the parties alighted from their horses, Major Bullock and myself were apart from the Doctor and Mr. Rowan, to agree upon the subject postponed from the preceding evening.

Major Bullock again spoke of an endeavor to accommodate the differences. I still thought it could not be made unless the Doctor's note should be withdrawn, to which the Major would not assent. The distance was then mentioned. Major Bullock said he supposed the usual distance; I requested him to mention it; he said ten steps, to which I agreed immediately, but said he might add two steps which he did not choose to do, the distance remained as agreed upon. We then agreed that they should, at that distance stand with their backs, each towards the other and wait for the word 'fire' after which they should face and fire when they pleased. To prevent doubt, it was particularly mentioned and agreed that each might hold his pistol as he pleased, and use in firing one or both hands. No other propositions than these, as to distance or firing were made or signified to me, and these at such a distance, and in such a voice, that I do not hesitate to say that they were not heard by the Doctor or Mr. Rowan.

The Doctor and Mr. Rowan had ridden out in their great coats, which they took off before the pistols were handed to them. As agreed upon they fired, each long after they had faced; Mr. Rowan first and then the Doctor. Mr. Rowan rested his pistol on his left hand —the Doctor his on the left arm above the elbow. The deliberate and long aim of each prompted each of their friends to ask if they were hurt; Doctor Chambers said first, " No," Mr. Rowan also said, " I am not," to which the Doctor replied, " I am sorry for it; " Mr. Rowan said, " Well, try it again," the Doctor said, " Agreed." As agreed upon from the first they fired the second round, the Doctor first, the interval between their fires just distinguishable, and shorter than before, each resting his pistol as formerly and taking deliberate aim. The Doctor fell. Major Bullock and myself ran to his assistance; we searched, but searched too low for the wound. The Doctor was unable to tell us, not knowing where. Major Bullock then opened the Doctor's waist-coat, raised his left arm and found it. I saw the wound, but little blood had issued. I went to Mr. Rowan and told him I thought the wound was mortal; he answered, " I am sorry " and going to the Doctor he said he supposed there was no further use for him. Major Bullock replied, " No." Mr. Rowan was going, but turned to the Doctor, with the pledge of his, Mr. Rowan's honor, to serve him, and offered to send his carriage for the Doctor.

Major Bullock had bound up the wound and was supporting him. The Doctor was restless and requested me to extend his left leg and unbound the joint of the knee, in doing which my head was near Major Bullock's, which opportunity he took of requesting me to go to town and tell Mr. Caldwell to send for the doctor. I hastened to my horse and on him was passing to see the doctor, Major Bullock desired me to hasten. Mr. Caldwell was absent from the town, I informed Mr. McClean of my business. The news spread and the whole town was in haste to see the Doctor. I returned as soon as possible with Doctor Chapieze. In the interview at Mr. Rowan's home a few hours after we had parted from the Doctor Mr. Rowan observed that Major Bullock had taken whiffs at his words to the Doctor when wounded, for which he was sorry, and they were spoken without any intention of giving offence, under the impression that having been called there to satisfy the Doctor, it was proper to have his leave to depart, not judging the wound would prove so quickly mortal. Major Bullock told me he thought Mr. Rowan was wrong, I then told the Major of what Mr. Rowan had said, in the interview above, of his answer to my telling him of the wound mentioned his last words to the Doctor, which seemed to change the Major's opinion, but he still expected Mr. Rowan to mention the subject. When I saw Mr. Rowan next, he had discussed with the Major and satisfied him completely, of which, had I doubted Major Bullock's conduct to Mr. Rowan would have been ample proof. Major Bullock never sent any challenge to Mr. Rowan by me.

Whether it be criminal in men to suffer their prejudices and passions to gain ascendency over their reason or judgment, I have not leisure to discuss. But Mr. Printer; I believe, had the enemies of Mr. Rowan opposed to their prejudices a small exertion of reason and dispassionate inquiry about this unfortunate single combat, the certificates on that subject would not have differed from those I herewith transmit to you marked Nos. 4, 5, 6, 7, 8 and 9, except that some of them would have been rendered unnecessary.

For myself, I say they fought bravely and honestly. The wound was in the left side, so that the arm, if suffered to hang at ease would have covered it, and here let me refer to a certified copy of the inquisition marked No. 10 and also the certificates marked Nos. 11, 12 and 13. These, it is hoped, Mr. Printer, will wipe the stain from the honor of the deceased which the report of his having been shot in the back would seem to impart and which he so little deserved. And now sir, through this medium I beg forgiveness of the real friends of the deceased. Should this remind them of his brave yet modest and unassuming worth, renew their sorrows, let me plead the sacred majesty of truth. The respect due the sacred memory of the dead, and the importance of his good name to the living. Counting myself in the number of his friends, it is with pleasure I say, we never had a single jar, and with consolation I remember, after he was sensible of death's approach, my hands administered drink at his request and my ears heard him express it.

Your fellow citizen,

Geo. M. Bibb.

Bardstown, May, 1801.

The exhibits filed with Judge Bibb's letter were evidently intended to corroborate his statements. They contained the affidavits of several men to the effect that Judge Rowan and Doctor Chambers were engaged in a game of cards and there were several gentlemen in the room at the time. The first evidence of trouble between them, was thought to be a harmless exchange of epithets, until blows followed.

One of the exhibits referred to by Judge Bibb was the sworn statement of Thomas Hubbard and is as follows:

"I was at McClean's in this town (Bardstown), late in the evening, Mr. Rowan came in about sunset and called for beer and asked help to drink it. After that Mr. Crozier and Doctor Chambers came in. In a short time I missed the Doctor and Mr. Crozier. Mr. Rowan went up stairs and called me; I went up. Messrs. Rowan and Bibb were sitting near the fire; Crozier, Hilton, McClelland and the Doctor were playing at whist. Mr. Rowan asked me if I would be one of the party, to which I agreed, but a full pack of cards could not be made. I went after some cards; when I returned, Mr. Rowan and the Doctor had by this time engaged in *Vigutun,* near the fire. I looked on, and they disputed their game and required me to sit and keep it for them, which I did. They played sometimes for money. Mr. Rowan said several times, 'Damn you Doctor, give me a card,' or words to that effect. The Doctor replied, 'I will Mr. Rowan, as soon as I can.' A conversation soon arose as to which understood some of the dead languages the best. Mr. Rowan observed that the Doctor was not able to dispute with him on such subjects. The Doctor said he thought he was, with him or any man. Mr. Rowan then said, 'I'll be d—d if you are,' and the Doctor answered, 'I'll be d—d if I am not.' Mr. Rowan said, 'Doctor you know you are inferior to me on such subjects.' The Doctor said he thought he was his superior. Mr. Rowan said, 'You are a d—d liar.' They both arose; Mr. Rowan lifted his hand as if to strike; the Doctor caught hold of him on the breast near the neck, either to evade the blow or to choke him. At that moment they were separated; Mr. Rowan was taken to the other end of the room; the Doctor stood still where he was near the fire; they continued to quarrel. Mr. Rowan was let go and he returned near the Doctor and engaged him; the Doctor gave way until he was near the head of the stairs, when they were again separated and the Doctor was taken down stairs."

Doctor Chambers said that he would challenge Mr. Rowan and if he did not accept he would publish him as a coward in every paper in the State. Judge Rowan's reply was in very strong and emphatic terms; the outcome of which resulted in the challenge and duel. It is set out in one of the certificates that the duel and the incidents connected with it took place in or near Bardstown, Kentucky.

The verdict of the Coroner's inquest was signed by twelve jurors and was as follows:

"At an inquest taken and held over the body of James Chambers, deceased, at the home of said decedent on Thursday, the 5th day of February, 1801, taken before Joe Lewis, a Justice of the Peace for said county, and Christian Bringle, Sheriff of said county (the coroner being absent), the jury on their oaths do say that they are of the opinion that the wound in the body of James Chambers, deceased, was by a ball shot out of a pistol or gun, that the ball entered the body about four inches below the left arm; that the ball went into the hollow of the said decedent's body, and that it remains in the body, and that the wound was the occasion of the death of said decedent; that the accident happened on Tuesday the 3rd instant, in the woods, near Jacob Yoder's plantation on the Beech-fork, about one mile and three-quarters southwardly of Bardstown.

"Given under our hands this 6th day of February, 1801."

The following affidavit was also filed as an exhibit with Judge Bibb's letter:

"On the morning of the 3rd of February last, I was at Mr. Rowan's in company with Messrs. Barry and Bibb when Major Bullock came there; about an hour or so after Doctor Chambers was carried into town. Major Bullock breakfasted there and talking of the affair, mentioned that it was either the third or fourth of the kind in which he had been engaged as principal or second, but in all his life had never witnessed anything more determinedly brave, gentlemanly and honorable. While we were at Mr. Rowan's the sheriff with a guard came in to the meadow; the Major expressed great indignation at the idea of a prosecution, and instantly mounted and set off for the town, in order, he said, to prevent it getting to the Doctor's ears, which he said he knew would hurt his feelings extremely and also said he thought he could put a stop to it. I have many times since heard Major Bullock express himself to the same purpose both to myself and others."

Signed "JOHN CROZIER."

Bardstown, May 7, 1801.

This duel was like many others which were fought in Kentucky during its early history. What emphasized it more than others, was the prominence of all the parties engaged in it. All of them were young men at that time; Judge Rowan was twenty-eight years old, Judge Bibb was twenty-five, and Doctor Chambers about the same age; Major Bullock was the oldest one of the four and Doctor Chambers was the most prominent professionally and socially. He married the daughter of Judge Benjamin Sebastion of the Kentucky Court of Appeals and he was regarded as the most promising young physician in the State.

Judge John Rowan, the surviving principal was born in 1773, his father was a Revolutionary soldier who moved to Kentucky in 1783 and settled at Louisville, Ky., where Judge Rowan received the chief part of his education, later however he attended Doctor Priestly's classical school at Bardstown, Kentucky. Judge Rowan was admitted to the bar in 1795, and commenced the practice at Elizabethtown, Kentucky. He was a member of the constitutional convention of 1799; removed to Frankfort in 1800 to practice in the Court of Appeals; was appointed Secretary of State by Governor Greenup in 1804, and was elected to Congress in 1805. He served several terms in the Kentucky Legislature from Nelson county and he was the recognized leader of the New Court or Relief party in Kentucky. He was commissioned Judge of the Court of Appeals in 1819 and served one year. He was especially active in the Kentucky Legislature in 1824 and while serving in the House he was elected to the United States Senate for six years. Later he represented the United States in adjustment of some claims against the Mexican Government. He was one of the great criminal lawyers of Kentucky. He defended Isaac B. Desha for assassinating Francis Baker in 1824 and he defended the Wilkinsons at Harrodsburg on a change of venue, for killing several men at Louisville in 1838. For nearly half a century he was regarded as one of the greatest lawyers in Kentucky. He was one of the most illustrious men Kentucky has produced. He died at Louisville, Kentucky, July 13, 1843.

Judge Geo. M. Bibb was born and educated in Virginia; he came to Kentucky in 1798 and located at Lexington. He was appointed one of the judges of the Court of Appeals in 1808 and was made chief justice the following year. He resigned from the bench in 1810, but was reappointed by Governor Desha in 1827. He was elected to the United States Senate in 1811 and was elected again in 1829 and served until 1835. He was Secretary of the Treasury in the cabinet of President Tyler and he was recognized as one of the very great men of that day. He died in 1859.

There have been very few Kentuckians more prominent in the law or politics than Judge John Rowan or Judge Geo. M. Bibb.

The Jackson-Dickinson Duel.

On Red river in Logan county, Kentucky, on the 30th day of May, 1806, was fought the famous and fatal duel between Major General Andrew Jackson, afterwards President of the United States and Charles Dickinson, attorney-at-law, of Nashville, Tennessee.

The trouble which led up to the fatal meeting on " the field of honor " has been " variously " stated. Ill feeling had existed between them for several years. General Jackson was a very high tempered, over-bearing and determined man who had incurred the ill-will and hatred of several prominent people. His friends declared that there was a plot upon the part of his enemies to get Dickinson to kill him or drive him out of that section of the country. It was claimed that Dickinson was the best shot in the United States and the general idea was that a duel between them necessarily meant the death of General Jackson. It was generally understood that the duel was to be fought and many bets were made upon the result, the odds were always against Jackson. Dickinson himself had a bet of five hundred dollars that he would " get him " at his first fire.

The ill feeling between the two men, which culminated so fatally, originated from statements made or reported to have been made by Dickinson in reference to General Jackson's wife, a subject upon which he was at all times exceedingly sensitive.

About the year 1790 General Jackson was boarding with the widow of John Donelson; her daughter Rachel had married a man by the name of Lewis Roberts who was later known as Lewis Robards. In that year Robards petitioned the Legislature of Virginia to divorce him from his wife, Rachel, and in his petition he filed an affidavit setting out the fact that his wife had deserted him and that she was living in adultery with General Jackson. On December 20, 1790 the Legislature passed an act granting to Robards the right "to sue out of the office of the Supreme Court of the district of Kentucky a writ against Rachel Robards, etc."

Section 2 provided for a commission to take depositions.

Section 3 provided for the publication of notice, etc.

Section 4 provided for a jury to try the issue, etc., and "If the jury should find that the defendant hath deserted the plaintiff and that she hath lived in adultery with another man since such desertion, that said verdict shall be recorded and thereupon the marriage between the said Lewis Roberts and Rachel Roberts shall be totally dissolved." After this act was passed, Roberts took no action for two years; in the meantime General Jackson and Mrs. Roberts or Robards were married in July, 1791. In September, 1793, the Supreme Court of the district of Kentucky, at Harrodsburg, granted the divorce and in January, 1794, the second marriage ceremony was performed. These circumstances caused a great deal of scandalous talk; the prominence of General Jackson magnified these mistakes. His enemies soon found that any reflections upon the regularity of his marriage or any disparaging remarks about his wife, who was not fitted for the high station to which she was raised, would incense him more than anything else. He was ready to challenge any man "to meet him upon the field" who dared to state the truth about his marriage. His enemies, not a few in number, and not lacking in influence, seem to have agreed that Charles Dickinson was the proper man to seek a quarrel with him. When the report came to General Jackson that Dickinson had uttered disparaging statements in reference to Mrs. Jackson, the General called on Dickinson and asked him if he had used the language attributed to him, Dickinson replied, that if he had, it must have been while he was drunk. This statement was accepted and the two men separated in a friendly manner. A second time Dickinson uttered offensive words respecting Mrs. Jackson in a tavern at Nashville, which were duly conveyed to General Jackson and he thereupon went to Capt. Ervine, the father-in-law of Dickinson, and advised him to exert his influence over his son-in-law and induce him to restrain his tongue and comport himself like a gentleman in his cups. He said: " I wish no quarrel with him, he is used by my enemies in Nashville who are urging him on to pick a quarrel with me, advise him to stop in time." In January, 1806, the most deadly enmity existed between the two men and a trivial event was sufficient to bring them into collision.

For the autumn races of 1805 a race was arranged between General Jackson's race horse " Truxton " and Capt. Joseph Ervine's " Plowboy ; " the stakes were two thousand dollars, payable on the day of the race, in notes which were to be due of that date. The forfeit was eight hundred dollars. Before the day for the race arrived Ervine and Dickinson decided to pay the forfeit and withdraw their horse which was amicably done and the affair was supposed to be at an end.

A young lawyer in Nashville, named Swan, misled by false information, circulated a report that General Jackson had accused the owners of " Plowboy " of paying their forfeit in notes other than those agreed upon—notes less valuable because not due on the date of settling. Following this report several open letters were published in the newspapers of that date, in one of which General Jackson said that Dickinson was " A base poltroon and cowardly tale-bearer." In one of Dickinson's publications he said: " I declare him, notwithstanding he is a Major General of the militia of mero district, to be a worthless scoundrel, a poltroon and a coward," etc. This letter was published in the *Impartial Review.* General Thomas Overton rode out to General Jackson's store at Clover Bottom with the information that Dickinson had written this scurrilous attack upon General Jackson and within a few hours thereafter General Overton placed in Dickinson hands the following letter:

Charles Dickinson:

Sir: Your conduct and expressions relative to me of late have been of such a nature and so insulting that it requires and shall have my notice.

You have disturbed my quiet, industriously excited Thomas Swan to quarrel with me, which involved the peace and harmony of society for a while.

You, on the 10th of January, wrote me a very insulting letter, left this country, caused this letter to be delivered after you had been gone some days, and viewing yourself in safety from the contempt I held you, have now in the press a piece more replete with blackguard abuse than any of your other productions. You are pleased to state that you would have noticed me in a different way, but my cowardice would have found a pretense to evade that satisfaction if it had been called for, etc.

I hope, sir, your courage will be an ample security to me that I will obtain, speedily, that satisfaction due me for the insults offered and in the way my friend who hands you this will point out. He waits upon you for that purpose, and with your friend will enter into immediate arrangements for this purpose, etc.

ANDREW JACKSON.

During the same day a reply to the challenge was delivered through Doctor Hanson Catlet and was as follows:

" Your note of this morning is received, and your request shall be gratified. My friend who hands you this will make the necessary arrangements."

The seconds immediately conferred and they agreed upon the time and place of meeting; this agreement was in writing as follows:

" On Friday, the 30th inst., we agree to meet at Harrison's Mills, on Red River, in Logan Co., State of Kentucky, for the purpose of settling an affair of honor between General Andrew Jackson and Charles Dickinson. Further arrangements to be made. It is understood that the meeting will be at the hour of seven in the morning.''

General Jackson was not pleased with the arrangement which postponed the meeting for a week and he insisted on an earlier date but Doctor Catlet would not agree to a change. Later in the day this further agreement was made:

'' It is agreed that the distance shall be twenty-four feet; the parties to stand facing, each with his pistol down perpendicularly. When they are ready, the single word, ' Fire,' to be given, at which they are to fire as soon as they please. Should either fire before the word is given we pledge ourselves to shoot him down instantly. The person to give the word to be determined by lot, has also the choice of position. We mutually agree that the above regulations shall be observed in the affair of honor pending between General Andrew Jackson and Charles Dickinson, Esq.''

These stipulations were signed by the seconds on Saturday, May 24, 1806.

In order to be on the battle field at the appointed hour it was necessary to leave Nashville at an early hour on the day preceding. A considerable company of friends went with each of the principals, all of whom were on horseback. Parton, in his life of Jackson says of Dickinson: '' He mounted his horse and repaired to the rendezvous, where his second and half a dozen of the gay blades of Nashville were waiting to escort him on his journey. Away they rode, in the highest of spirits, as though they were upon a party of pleasure. Indeed, they made a party of pleasure of it.'' When they stopped for rest or refreshment, Dickinson is said to to have amused the company by displaying his wonderful skill with the pistol. Once at a distance of twenty-four feet, he fired four balls, each at the word of command, into a space that could be covered by a silver dollar. Several times he cut a string with his bullet from the same distance. It is said that he left a severed string hanging near a tavern, and said to the landlord as he rode away: "If General Jackson comes along this road, show him that." Dickinson never seemed to realize that he was to meet in deadly combat a man of great courage and who most heartily despised his antagonist.

General Jackson believed that Dickinson had done him great injustice and he fully made up his mind, that if it was possible, he would kill him. He fully realized the gravity of the situation he was to meet the best shot in the United States and perhaps the best in the world. It was a fight to the death. He well knew that Dickinson would use his utmost skill, not merely to disable him by shooting him through the hips, which was the usual way of the professional duelist of that day, but the life of one, and perhaps of both was to be the forfeit of the meeting. The great question with him was, whether he should try to get the first shot or permit Dickinson to have it. He knew that Dickinson was an expert and that it was scarcely possible for any one to be quicker in movement; he required no time to take aim and that he would have a better chance in a quick shot and any precautions which Jackson might take could not prevent Dickinson from getting the first fire. After a long consultation with his friend and second, Major General Overton, they agreed that it would be better to let Dickinson have the first fire.

Each of the parties, with their attendants, found lodging in the neighborhood of the battle field, and before breakfast on the morning of May 30, 1806, they repaired to the designated spot. In a letter dated Adairville, Ky., September 5, 1914, the Hon. J. B. Grubbs said:

"Answering your questions relative to the location of the Jackson-Dickinson dueling ground, would say the duel was fought on the north side of the middle fork of Red river and about one hundred and fifty feet from its banks; one mile west of this place and thirteen miles from Russellville. It can still be identified by a slight depression in the otherwise level river bottom. It is now in cultivation and owned by Mr. R. J. Burr, and near the line dividing it from the land of Mr. W. B. Taylor, the owner of the old Keller homestead to which Dickinson was carried and where he remained for a short time before his removal to Nashville. The blood stained floor was only replaced by a new one a few years since. I have obtained this information from Mr. James I. Rice whose grandfather heard the shots and hastened to the scene and assisted in removing the wounded man to the Keller home.

"The old log springhouse from which Jackson procured his drink of buttermilk withstood the ravages of time until two years since when the decaying wood was torn away leaving the stone foundation intact. This spring and the adjacent dwelling was owned by one Harrison who was the host of Jackson the night before the duel. It was situated on the south side of the river, about three-fourths of a mile from the scene of conflict and is now the property of Mr. W. S. Gambill. The land where the duel was fought is now in cultivation."

Parton's life of Jackson gives the following account of the duel:

The horsemen rode about a mile along the river; then turning down toward the river to a point on the bank where they had expected to find a ferryman. No ferryman appearing, Jackson spurred his horse into the stream and dashed across, followed by all his party. They rode into the poplar forest, two hundred yards or less, to a spot near the center of a level platform or river bottom, then covered with forest, now smiling with cultivated fields. The horsemen halted and dismounted just before reaching the appointed place. Jackson, Overton and a surgeon who had come with them from home, walked on together, and the rest led their horses a short distance in an opposite direction.

"How do you feel about it now, General?" asked one of the party, as Jackson turned to go. "Oh, all right," replied Jackson, gaily, "I shall wing him, never fear."

Dickinson's second won the choice of position and Jackson's the office of giving the word. (Under the agreement referred to above, "the person to give the word, to be determined by lot, has also the choice of position.")

The astute Overton considered the giving of the word a matter of great importance, and he had already determined how he would give it, if the lot fell to him. The eight paces were measured off and the men placed. Both were perfectly collected. All the politeness of such occasions were very strictly and elegantly performed. Jackson was dressed in a loose frock coat, buttoned carelessly over his chest, and concealing in some degree the extreme slenderness of his figure. Dickinson was the younger and handsomer man of the two. But Jackson's tall, erect figure and the still intensity of his demeanor, it is said, gave him a most superior and commanding air, as he stood under the tall poplars on this bright May morning silently awaiting the moment of doom. "Are you ready," said Overton. "I am réady," replied Dickinson. "I am ready," said Jackson. The words were not sooner pronounced than Overton, with a sudden shout, cried, using his old country pronunciation "*Fere.*" Dickinson raised his pistol quickly and fired; Overton, who was looking with anxiety and dread, saw a puff of dust fly from the breast of his coat and saw him raise his left arm and place it tightly across his chest. He is surely hit, thought Overton, and in a bad place too; but no, he does not fall. Erect and grim as fate he stood, his teeth clenched, raising his pistol. Overton glanced at Dickinson, amazed at the unwonted failure of his aim and apparently appalled at the awful figure and face before him, Dickinson had unconsciously recoiled a pace or two. "Great God," he faltered, "Have I missed him?" "Back to your mark, sir," shrieked Overton, with his hand upon his pistol. Dickinson recovered his composure, stepped forward to the peg and stood with his eyes averted from his antagonist. All this was the work of a moment, though it requires many words to tell it. General Jackson took deliberate aim, and pulled the trigger. The pistol neither snapped nor went off. He looked at the trigger and discovered that it had stopped at half cock. He drew it back to its place and took aim a second time. He fired. Dickinson's face blanched; he reeled; his friends rushed towards him, caught him in their arms and gently seated him on the ground, leaning against a bush. His trousers reddened. They stripped off his clothes. The blood was gushing from his side in a torrent. And alas; here is the ball, not near the wound, but above the opposite hip, just under the skin. The ball had passed through the body below the ribs. Such a wound could not but be fatal. Overton went forward and learned the condition of the wounded man. Rejoining his principal, he said, "He won't want anything more of you General," and conducted him from the field. They had gone a hundred yards, Overton walking on one side of Jackson, the surgeon on the other and neither speaking a word, when the surgeon observed that one of Jackson's shoes was full of blood. "My God! General Jackson, are you hit?" he exclaimed, pointing to the blood. "Oh, I believe," replied Jackson, "That he has pricked me a little, let's look at it, but say nothing about it there," pointing to the house. He opened his coat. Dickinson's aim had been perfect. He had sent the ball precisely where he supposed Jackson's heart was beating. But the thinness of his body and the looseness of his coat combining to deceive Dickinson, the ball had only broken a rib or two and raked the breast bone. It was a somewhat painful, bad looking wound, but neither severe nor dangerous, and he was able to ride to the tavern without much inconvenience.

Upon approaching the house, he went up to one of the negro women who was churning and asked her if the butter had come. She said it was just coming. He asked her for some buttermilk; while she was getting it, she observed him furtively open his coat and look within it. She saw that his shirt was soaked with blood, and she stood gazing in blank horror, at the sight, dipper in hand. He caught her eye and hastily

> buttoned his coat again. She dipped out a quart measure full of buttermilk and gave it to him. He drank it off at a draught, then went in, took off his coat, and had his wound dressed. That done, he despatched one of his retinue to Doctor Catlet, to inquire respecting the condition of Dickinson, and to say that the surgeon attending himself would be glad to contribute his aid towards Mr. Dickinson's relief. Polite reply was returned that Mr. Dickinson's case was past surgery. In the course of the day General Jackson sent a bottle of wine to Dr. Catlet for the use of his patient. But there was one gratification which Jackson could not, even in such circumstances grant him. A very old friend of General Jackson writes me thus:
>
> "Although the General had been wounded, he did not desire that it should be known until he left the neighborhood, and had therefore concealed it at first from his own friends. His reason for this, as he once stated to me, was, that as Dickinson considered himself the best shot in the world, and was certain of killing him at the first fire, he did not want him to have the gratification of even knowing that he had touched him."

Poor Dickinson bled to death. The flowing of blood was stanched, but could not be stopped. He was conveyed to the house in which he had passed the night and placed upon a mattress, which was soon drenched with blood. He suffered extreme agony and uttered horrible cries all that long day. At nine o'clock in the evening he suddenly asked why they had put out the lights. The doctor knew that the end was at hand; that the wife, who had been sent for in the morning, would not arrive in time to close her husband's eyes. He died five minutes after, cursing, it is said, with his last breath, the ball that had entered his body.

The *Impartial Review,* of Nashville, in commenting on the tragedy said:

> On Tuesday evening last the remains of Mr. Charles Dickinson were committed to the grave, at the resi-

dence of Mr. Joseph Ervine, attended by a large number of citizens of Nashville and its neighborhood. There have been few occasions upon which stronger impressions of sorrow or testimonies of greater respect were evinced than on the one we have the unwelcome task to record. In the prime of life, and blest in domestic circumstances with almost every valuable enjoyment, he fell a victim to the barbarous and pernicious practice of dueling. By his untimely fate the community is deprived of an amiable man and a virtuous citizen. His friends will long lament with particular sensibility the deplorable event. Mr. Dickinson was a native of Maryland, where he was highly valued by the discriminating and good; and those who knew him best respected him most. With a consort that has to bear with this, the severest of afflictions, and an infant child, his friends and acquaintances will cordially sympathize. Their loss is above calculation. May Heaven assuage their anguish by administering such consolation as is beyond the power of human accident or change.

General Jackson's wound proved more severe than he had at first thought. It was more than a month before he could move about without great inconvenience. The wound did not heal properly. Twenty years afterward it caused him great trouble and it is believed that it ultimately caused his death.

The Holman-Waring Duel.

THE HOLMAN-WARING DUEL, IN WHICH FRANCIS G. WARING WAS KILLED AND WILSON P. GREENUP, SON OF GOVERNOR CHRISTOPHER GREENUP, WAS JACOB HOLMAN'S SECOND AND WAS JOINTLY INDICTED WITH HIM.

THE past century has brought many changes in the ideals of men. For four hundred years prior to the year 1800, dueling was not only considered honorable, but the man who refused to accept a challenge was regarded as a coward who did not deserve to live.

The Anglo-Saxons " allowed an appeal to the judgment of God " by single combat.

After the Norman conquest this became a regular part of the jurisprudence of the country, and it was regulated by fixed and solemn forms. In civil cases, personal combat was the usual and common way of settling disputes. A party to a law suit who was dissatisfied with the judgment, might throw down his glove and challenge the judge to defend himself. But dueling is of much greater antiquity than the Norman conquest. The duel between David, the Hebrew, and Goliath, the Philistine, and in which the Philistine was slain, is familiar to every Bible student. The Greeks and Romans recognized it as a proper way to settle disputes. The combat between the three Horatii brothers and the three Curatii brothers is familiar to every school child.

For hundreds of years, and especially under the feudal system of Great Britain, the chief education of a man was to teach him how to overthrow his opponent in personal combat; with such training, with such ideals, and with such ancestry it is not strange that the people of the United States were ready to follow the example of their fathers.

During the colonial period and the early history of the United States, many great men of this country were engaged in dueling, not a few of whom became victims of the cruel, inhuman and to the present generation, inexcusible custom. General Alexander Hamilton who fell by the hand of Col. Aaron Burr in 1804, and Commadore Stephen Decatur who was slain by the hand of Capt. James Barron in 1820, were among the greatest of the nation.

Kentucky, perhaps, furnished more duelists than any other State. The ideal Kentuckian, General John C. Breckenridge, had a personal difficulty with Hon. Francis Cutting in 1854 which resulted in a challenge, but the intervention of friends prevented the fight.

In 1858 the Hon. William J. Graves, a Congressman from Kentucky, killed Hon. Jonathan Cilley, a Congressman from Maine. The Hon. John J. Crittenden and Richard H. Menifee were present to witness the duel.

Hon. Henry Clay fought two duels and he was the challenger in both of them. The first was in 1808 with Humphry Marshall, a fellow member of the Kentucky Legislature; they met and exchanged two shots each and retired from the field, each of them slightly wounded. The second was in 1826, with Senator John Randolph, on the banks of the Potomac near Washington, D. C. Mr. Clay was, at that time, Secretary of State in the National Cabinet and Mr. Randolph was a Senator in Congress from Virginia. Mr. Clay fired without effect; Mr. Randolph discharged his pistol in the air, as he had previously stated to his second that he would. Mr. Clay immediately dropped his pistol and approached Mr. Randolph and said with emotion, "I trust God, my dear sir, you are untouched; after what has occurred I would not have harmed you for a thousand worlds."

In 1830 Gen. Conway and Hon. Robert Crittenden met on the field of honor in Arkansas. Ben Desha, son of Governor Joseph Desha, was Mr. Crittenden's second. Mr. Crittenden was slightly wounded and General Conway was shot through the heart.

The duel between Francis G. Waring and Jacob Harrod Holman was fought in Franklin county, about three miles from Frankfort, in the early morning of July 16, 1819. Francis G. Waring was a wealthy young Virginian who had recently come to Kentucky. He was a practiced duelist who had been engaged in several affairs of honor in the old dominion.

On the 4th of July, Waring attended a muster of the county militia which was drilled on the Peak's mill road about four miles from Frankfort. Jacob H. Holman was an officer of the company and during the maneuvers a dog which belonged to Waring was killed by a thrust from Holman's saber. This killing brought on a fist fight between the two men, but they were separated before any material damage was done to either of them and it was thought by those present that the incident was closed. The following day Waring sought his friend, Doctor Joe Roberts and after talking the matter over between them, Doctor Roberts became the bearer of a challenge.

Mr. Holman selected Wilson P. Greenup, son of ex-Governor Christopher Greenup, as his second in the coming affair of honor. Mr. Greenup and Doctor Roberts met the following day and agreed that since Holman had received the challenge he had the right to name the weapons to be used and Waring was given the right to select the ground, and the day fixed was the 16th of July, at the hour of six o'clock in the morning. Holman named the dueling pistols as the weapons to be used and Waring selected the beautiful woodland on the Rev. Silas M. Noel's farm as the place of meeting. This farm afterwards became famous for being the home of Theodore O'Hara, the author of "The Bivouc of the Dead." It was further agreed that the principals were to stand ten steps apart and at the words, one, two, three, Fire! they were to fire simultaneously. If either party fired before the command, " Fire " was given, the seconds agreed to shoot down the one so offending. If either party failed to fire at the command, his opponents second was to count, one, two, three, and if he failed to fire on the call of the last number he was to lose his shot.

The party met promptly at the time arranged and at the place named; all of the arrangements previously made were carried out. The principals took the places assigned them. The question was asked, " Are you ready," both of them answered in the affirmative. Doctor Roberts then counted, one! two! three! and each of them raised and presented his pistol, taking deliberate aim at his opponent, when he gave the command " Fire! " both shots were so nearly simultaneous, that only one report was heard. Holman's bullet took effect in Waring's right breast, ranging to the left and passed through his heart causing his death instantly. Waring's bullet took effect in Holman's right hip causing him to fall, he was carried from the battle field to his home where he lingered for many months. He finally recovered so that he could walk but he remained a cripple for life.

Niles' Register for August 1819, said:

> " A pair of dunces agreed to shoot at each other a few days ago near Frankfort, Ky. One was a young Virginian, the challenger, the other a printer. The first was instantly killed on the spot, and the other very badly wounded."

The Franklin county grand jury indicted Holman and Greenup for the murder of Waring, and Doctor Roberts was also indicted charged with aiding, abetting, etc., the felonious shooting of Holman by Francis G. Waring.

The indictment against Holman and Greenup jointly charged that:

"Jacob H. Holman and Wilson P. Greenup, not having the fear of God before their eyes, but being moved and seduced by the instigation of the devil, on the 16th day of July in the year of our Lord eighteen hundred and nineteen, with force and arms, in the County aforesaid in and upon Francis G. Waring, in the peace of God and of the said Commonwealth then and there being feloniously, wilfully and of their malice aforethought, did make an assault, and that the said Jacob H. Holman, a certain pistol, then and there loaded and charged with gun-powder and one loaded bullet, which pistol the said Jacob H. Holman in his right hand then and there had and held to, against and upon the said Francis G. Waring then and there feloniously, wilfully and of his malice aforethought, did shoot and discharge in the right pap of him the said Francis G. Waring then and there being in the Peace of God, and of the Commonwealth, from the effect of which the said Francis G. Waring then and there instantly died. And that the aforesaid Wilson P. Greenup, then and there feloniously, wilfully and of his malice aforethought was present, aiding, helping, abetting, comforting, assisting and maintaining the said Jacob H. Holman, the felony and murder aforesaid in the manner and form aforesaid to do and commit. And so the jurors aforesaid upon their oaths aforesaid, do say that the said Jacob H. Holman and Wilson P. Greenup, him the said Francis G. Waring, then and there in the manner aforesaid, feloniously, wilfully and of their malice aforethought did kill and murder against the statutes in such cases provided and against the peace and dignity of the Commonwealth of Kentucky.

"W. ANDERSON, Atty for Com."

On Saturday, July 24, Wilson P. Greenup surrendered himself into the custody of the court and bail was fixed at two thousand dollars. John J. Marshall (author of J. J. Marshall's Reports), and Thomas Loofborro went on his bond for his appearance at the October term of court. The method of selecting jurors differed from that of a hundred years later. The order to the sheriff was:

"You are hereby commanded to summons twelve good and lawful men of your county, being housekeepers, by whom the truth may be better known, residing as near as may be to the place where a certain murder is supposed to have been committed on the body of Francis G. Waring, late of your county, to appear before the Franklin Circuit Court immediately for the trial of Jacob H. Holman who stands indicted in the Circuit aforesaid for the murder aforesaid.

"Francis P. Blair,
Circuit Court Clerk."

On October 19th, Jacob H. Holman and Wilson P. Greenup appeared in the court and being arraigned, plead "Not guilty," and for their trial put themselves upon their country and the attorney for the Commonwealth likewise, and the prisoners having consented to be tried by the same jury and at the same time, thereupon came a jury to-wit: George Baltzell and eleven others, who being elected, tried, sworn the truth of and upon the premises to speak, and there not being time to go through the trial this evening, by consent as well of the attorneys for the Commonwealth as the prisoners at the bar, the jury is adjourned until to-morrow morning at nine o'clock and the jurymen permitted to go to their respective places of abode to return at the time aforesaid.

October 20th: "Jacob H. Holman and Wilson P. Greenup, who stand indicted for murder, were again led to the bar in custody of the sheriff, and the jury empaneled and sworn for their trial also appeared and took their seats, and having heard the evidence upon their oaths do say the prisoners at the bar not guilty as charged in manner and form as in the indictment against them alleged, and proclimation being made as the manner is, and nothing further appearing or being alleged against the said Jacob H. Holman and Wilson P. Greenup; it is therefore considered by the court that they be acquitted and discharged from the charge aforesaid and go thereof hence without day."

The indictment against Joseph Roberts, physician, for aiding, etc., Francis G. Waring in shooting Jacob H. Holman in the lower part of the right hip, was on motion of the Commonwealth's Attorney, dismissed.

Jacob Harrod Holman was public printer of Kentucky for many years. At one time he was editor of the "*Commentator*" and later was the editor of "*The Spirit of 76*" and "*The Kentuckian,*" all of which were published in Frankfort. He was a man of good reputation and of fine ability.

Francis G. Waring was a brother of the notorious John U. Waring, who killed Samuel Q. Richardson in 1835, and brother-in-law of Rev. Silas M. Noel, of Frankfort, a noted Baptist preacher and associate Circuit Judge of pioneer days. Doctor Joseph Roberts practiced his profession at Frankfort for more than fifty years. He had charge of the federal hospital at Frankfort during the civil war. He died about the close of the war. His son John Roberts was in the Confederate army and Joe Roberts, Jr., another one of his sons was an officer in the Federal army.

Wilson P. Greenup was the son of Governor Christopher Greenup, who discharged the duties of Governor with honor and credit and who died in the year 1818. Inscribed on his monument, by the Commonwealth of Kentucky, which was erected in the Frankfort cemetery, is the following:

> "His capacity, fidelity and usefulness in civil service is amply proven by his repeated elevation to and long continuance in offices, executive, legislative and judicial of the highest grade. He served repeatedly in the State and federal legislatures, filled the office of judge in several courts, inferior and superior, and was elected Governor of the Commonwealth in August, 1804. Patriot, soldier and statesman, through a long life of public service he distinguished himself in war and peace and died in the full enjoyment of the confidence of his countrymen, in the sixty-ninth year of his age."

The Assassination of Francis Baker by Isaac B. Desha, in 1824.

In order to understand the condition of affairs in Kentucky in the year 1824, it is necessary to consider a few things which caused the formation of the Relief and the Anti-Relief parties of that period. These two parties grew out of the disturbed conditions of the financial affairs of the country prior to the year 1818, which resulted in the withdrawal of gold and silver, to a large extent, from circulation, and an inflated currency having taken their places.

Kentucky had chartered about forty banks, with an aggregate capital of more than ten million dollars. During the summer of this year the State was flooded with paper of these independent banks, all kinds of speculation were engaged in and the people became very extravagant in their manner of living. Within the next two years nearly all of these banks had failed and the pressure of debt was greater than was ever known before in the history of the country. The legislature of 1819-20, passed a twelve months replevy law; and that of 1821, chartered the Bank of the Commonwealth. This bank was not required to redeem its notes in specie, though made receivable for taxes and all debts. Lands owned by the State west of the Tennessee river were pledged for the final redemption of these notes and if a creditor refused to receive their paper for his debt, the law permitted the debtor to replevy for two years. This new bank issued such an immense quantity of paper money that it sank to less than half of its nominal value, and creditors had to take it at its nominal value in full payment of their debts, or wait two years and risk the bankruptcy of their sureties on the replevying bonds.

The power of the Legislature to pass such an act was

held by Judge Clark of the Circuit Court to be unconstitutional. The Legislature was convened in extraordinary session which resulted in nothing being done. The case was then passed on by the Court of Appeals, and the opinion of the lower court was upheld. The opinion of the Court of Appeals created great excitement throughout the State. The financial interest of almost every man in the State was effected. This was the condition of affairs in 1824, when General Joseph Desha was elected Governor. The election was in August and in the following November his son, Isaac B. Desha, was charged with having committed one of the most atrocious assassinations which was ever committed in the State. Governor Desha was elected by the New Court, or Relief party. The Old Court, or Anti-Relief party was using all means it could to destroy the influence of the Governor and this gave some color to the contention of Desha's friends that the murder was charged against Isaac B. Desha because of the political bitterness against the Governor. The facts proved by the Commonwealth were as follows:

"Francis Baker, the man who was murdered, was an educated and talented gentleman, who formerly lived in New Jersey. He was educated for the law, but in the year 1815, he went to Natchez, Mississippi, where he became the editor of a monthly magazine. In September of the year 1824, he started on a return trip to his old home for the purpose of marrying a lady in New Jersey, to whom he had been engaged several years. There were no steamboats or steam cars of that date and the only mode of traveling was on horseback or on foot. Baker owned a beautiful gray mare which attracted general attention and the facts concerning which led to the apprehension and conviction of Desha. When the deceased reached Lexington, he was forced to remain there several days on account of an attack of fever, and when he had recovered from the disease to some extent, but still being very much enfeebled from the effects of his illness, he concluded that he would spend a few days with his friend Captain Bickley, who lived in Fleming county near the home of Isaac B. Desha. He left Lexington on the first day of November and spent the night at Blue Lick Springs. The next day he arrived at Doggett's tavern where he met Desha. The deceased made inquiries in reference to his friend Captain Bickley and Desha professed to be well acquainted with him, but he said that the Captain lived some distance from the main road. Desha said that he was going to ride that way himself and he offered to show him where his friend lived. This offer was accepted, and they rode off together, each of them on a horse; several men were present at Doggett's tavern at the time the two men left. At that time Desha had on a jacket with no coat or overcoat and with nothing about him except a horse whip which was heavily loaded with lead. In about two hours after he left Doggett's tavern, in company with Baker, he was seen in the possession of the gray mare, saddle bags and pocketbook, of the deceased. A man by the name of Lesborn Ball lived about two miles from the house of Desha. The horse of the deceased ran up to Ball's residence and one of his sons got on it and rode off in search of the owner. In a short time he met Desha, who was walking and who was very much agitated, his hands and clothes were stained with blood and he was carrying a pair of saddle packets on his arm. The same were afterwards found in the woods with the ends cut open and it was proven that they belonged to the deceased or were in his possession when he left Doggett's tavern. Desha claimed the horse as his property and said that he had just bought it from a man who owed him some money. He got on it and took the boy up behind him and rode off. In a few moments after he left his horse, the one on which he had left Doggett's tavern, ran up to the same house, without a briddle. Another son of Ball's put a briddle on it and went in pursuit of Desha, whom he knew to be the owner. He had not gone far when he met him and his brother on the gray mare. A pocketbook was in Desha's pocket; it dropped out and one of the boys got off the horse and handed it back to him. This pocketbook was afterwards found in the woods cut to pieces. The proof was conclusive that it was the same with which the deceased left Doggett's and the same which had been seen in the possession of Desha. When Desha left Doggett's tavern he had neither saddlebags nor pocketbook. He had been married about one year to a fine young woman, who belonged to a good family; she was so terrified at his manner and appearance that she left him the next morning and she refused to live with him again."

The day after the assassination, one of the deceased's gloves was found and the following day the saddle bags were found in the woods, empty and the ends were cut open. This led to further search of the woods where the pocket book was found, cut to pieces. In a hollow tree near where the pocketbook was found, there were found eight shirts with marks or name cut out, a vest, a hankerchief and four pairs of stockings. Desha's briddle was also found tied to a tree where his horse had, evidently, slipped it. The spot where the murder was committed was identified by the appearance of the ground. The body was found six days after the killing, in a gully, where it had been dragged about two hundred yards down a hill. The skull was fractured by the repeated blows of a heavy instrument, supposed to have been the loaded whip. There was a stab in the breast, two bruises on the shoulder and the throat was cut from ear to ear; there was a deep cut on the thumb from which it would appear that there had been an attempt to ward off the knife thrusts; the body was stripped of everything except the shirt which was marked "Francis Baker" with indelible ink, a vest, stockings and one glove which was on his right hand. The next day the trousers were found, very bloody, the watch was gone, and at the distance of two hundred yards the coat and hat were found; the hat was broken and near it was Desha's loaded whip, the butt end of which was shattered to pieces. The discovery of the horse in Desha's possession led to his arrest and the facts and circumstances which were proven as above set out, led to his conviction. The verdict of the jury was "death." Desha claimed that he was innocent of the charge and that his enemies and those of his father had conspired to convict him, with the evidence, which, he claimed, had been prepared by them.

Francis Baker was killed in Fleming county. Isaac B. Desha lived in Fleming and his father, Governor Joseph Desha, lived in Harrison county. On November 24, 1824, Judge John Rowan introduced a bill in the Kentucky Legislature providing for a change of venue in the case. The bill provided that the judge of the Fleming Circuit Court should hold a term of court on the second Monday in December, 1824, for the trial of Desha, and it further provided that on the calling of the case Desha should have his election to be tried either in Fleming or Harrison. In the event he selected Harrison it provided for the transfer of the papers, indictment and all records; also for Desha under a sufficient guard, to the jail of Harrison county. All of the original papers in the Fleming court were to be transferred but the transfer was not to be made until after the grand jury brought in an indictment in Fleming county. Governor Desha appeared before the committee to which this bill was committed on November 26th, and asked that the bill be favorably reported. The Act was duly passed and was approved by Governor Desha on December 4, 1824.

Isaac B. Desha elected to be tried in Harrison county and the case was transferred and set for trial at the January term, 1825. Judge John Trimble was the Circuit

Judge of that district, but he was appointed a judge of the Court of Appeals and he thereupon selected Judge George Shannon to try the case. Judge Trimble went to Lexington on Sunday, prior to the day on which the case was set for trial. Judge Shannon at first refused to preside. Judge Trimble went to see him again the next morning and Judge Shannon at that time, consented to try the case. He rode horseback from Lexington to Cynthiana that day, opened court at eight o'clock at night and adjourned over until the next day.

The next morning after the jury had brought in a verdict fixing the punishment at death, Judge John Rowan, senior counsel for the defense, filed a motion and grounds for a new trial.

The grounds for setting aside the verdict and granting a new trial were as follows:

1. The jury had intercourse with parties not on the jury; both day and night, some persons were in their room.

2. Threats had been uttered against the jury and a note was conveyed to the jury room, in some way, in which there was a threat made in these words: "If the jury do not bring in a verdict against the prisoner, Isaac B. Desha, they shall be hung in effigy and burnt."

3. On a pole of the jury, one Joshua Jones, when called by counsel to say if he entertained any doubt of Desha's guilt, answered that he did believe there were grounds to doubt it, and that he thought there were reasonable grounds to doubt his guilt.

4. The judge himself thought the evidence was calculated to raise a doubt of defendant's guilt.

On February 10, 1825, Judge Shannon set the verdict aside and granted a new trial.

Many charges were made against Judge Shannon by the press of the State accusing him of partiality to the defendant. The second trial was held in February, 1826. The proof was practically the same and the jury brought in a verdict of guilty and fixed the punishment at death. At that time there was no appeal to the Court of Appeals in a murder case.

The date for the execution was fixed for Friday, July 14, 1826. The scaffold was erected and the arrangements were made for the execution.

The defendant insisted that he would never consent to his father granting him a pardon, stating that he had rather die than to have his father do anything for which his official conduct could be criticised; that he would not accept a pardon, but firmly said that he would abide by the law of his country.

A short time before the day fixed for the execution, the defendant undertook to commit suicide by cutting his own throat. The windpipe was severed and his death was momentarily expected and he was in that condition when the Governor issued a pardon for him.

It is a tradition that the Governor pardoned his son and immediately thereafter resigned. The archives of the State show that he served his full term.

It is also a tradition that his son recovered from the severe self-inflicted wound and that he went to Central America where he changed his name and married a second time and that his descendants became and are now prominent and influential citizens of Honduras.

Amos Kendall, in his issue of "*The Patriot*" dated Monday, July 17, 1826, gives the defendant's side of this case. The article is headed "The Governor's Son," and is as follows:

> "This unfortunate young man has terminated his existence by cutting his throat. The windpipe was entirely cut off with a razor. After he committed the act, he made this declaration: 'I am innocent of the charge made against me.' The writing was presented to him while struggling for life and breathing only

through the wound. He recognized the paper and signed his name to it. He, in the same manner of communication, for he has never been able to utter a word, expressed great anxiety with regard to the distress his fate would give to his mother.

" Our informant who left him still breathing, stated, that but a few days before he made way with himself, he had a conversation with a gentleman of Cynthiana, to whom he said, that he never would consent to leave the jail by a pardon—protesting his innocence, but admitting that he was so involved by the artful management that he never would be able to acquit himself satisfactorily to the public. He, therefore, intimated an intention to end his existence, declaring that he would not live to disgrace his friends. When the first verdict was given, he declared that he would not allow his father to dishonor himself by granting him a pardon, but firmly said he would abide by the law of his country. There have been many cases in which all the circumstances have conspired to fix guilt on a particular person. Many cases in which such innocent persons convicted on circumstantial proof, have been actually executed, when after a series of years, the real criminal who was never suspected, has, when about to die, confessed the whole matter and exonerated the first sufferer from the charge. Every country has furnished many instances of this sort. May not young Desha's be one of these unfortunate cases? The possession of the murdered man's horse is the strongest circumstance against him. He had always declared that he bought it of a stranger. Is it not possible, that if a conspiracy was laid to fix the guilt on young Desha that this would have been one of the means of effecting it? Might not this account for the careless way in which Desha rode this horse of the dead man about the neighborhood? Might not the clothes of the unfortunate Baker have been scattered on the way to Desha's house, half hid and half exposed, on purpose to lead suspicion to the person who was put in possession of the horse? Might not the persons have obtained possession of Desha's bridle and hung it up near the dead body, and have got the whip and broke and cut it into pieces, scattering it along the road for the same purpose? The body was found eight days after Desha and the deceased left Doggett's, the throat cut from ear to ear, a deep stab in the breast and five cuts upon the head; there was no blood in the road from whence the body seemed to have been dragged about fifty yards; no blood even on the collar of the shirt; none on the glove worn on the right hand, the fellow to which was found on the way to Desha's; there was no blood along the trial and none about the body, except a little that had oozed out on the shirt from the wound on body. During the eight days, hunters and other persons had been by the place, and had seen none of the signs that appeared afterwards when the body was found. Is it not possible that this man was murdered elsewhere and brought to this place, as that he should have been killed eight days before by young Desha, should have laid in the woods for that length of time, three days of which were sultry, Indian summer, and the rest frosty mornings and hot suns; that he should be taken up yet quite limber, without bad smell, without being swelled, without ever having been touched by animals of prey, in a neighborhood full of hogs? The facts connected with this case are stranger and inscrutable. They are doubtless exceedingly strong against young Desha, as sworn to in court, and the jury were probably justified in their verdict; but still, without a miracle, it is impossible that the murder could have been committed on the day fixed in the testimony of Lisban Ball. All human experience, proves that the condition of the body of Baker, was not that of a person who had been dead eight days. Col. Sharp was killed a few days later in November than Baker, and although his corpse was kept in a cool apartment of his house, yet it became quite offensive to the smell in two days, and all the appearances greatly altered.

"It is singular that Ball, the principal witness against Desha, drowned himself a few weeks since. He went to a mill pond and was seen to swim to the middle of it, where he sunk without a struggle. He was a good swimmer and the person from the neighborhood, who brought the intelligence to Frankfort, said that it was believed, it was his purpose to drown himself, and a little while before this event, young Desha's houses were burnt by some incendiary. Whatever be the sentence, which public opinion may fix on the unhappy young man, who, even if guilty, has made atonement to public justice by a long and dreary confinement, and inflicting the last of human punishment on himself with his own hand, it is now to be hoped that political adversaries will cease to persecute the wretched father on his account. Never has any man's conduct been more exemplary than the Governor's under the trying circumstances to which he has been subjected. With power to put aside the law in favor of his son, he has bowed himself in humble submission to their most painful exactions.

"At every court he has placed himself by the side of his unfortunate son, to support him with his countenance and assist him with his counsel. He believed him innocent, but instead of employing his executive power to exempt him from punishment, he has spent thousands in employing counsel to defend him, and in expenses incident to his confinement. During the intervals of the court he has paid almost weekly visits to the prison, riding the distance of forty miles to console and support his child in his afflictions. When his public duties have prevented him from going, he has made it a point to write to him, and to send him papers to amuse him. No one has ever sustained, with more propriety than Governor Desha, the duties of a magistrate and a father. The public can allege no charge of delinquency against him and there never was a parent who gave stronger proofs of tenderness and attachment than he has done to his wretched son. In his intervals of absence at Frankfort, to his friends, he has made his unfortunate situation the theme of his conversation, asserting his conviction of his innocence and expressing the hope that some circumstances would yet come to light to satisfy the world of it."

"P. S. From accounts brought yesterday, it seems that young Desha is not yet dead, but the persons who attended him, and Dr. Dudley, the most eminent surgeon, who has been consulted, declare there there are no means to save him. The ends of his windpipe are contracted and stand apart an inch and a half."

The Assassination of Solomon P. Sharp by Jeroboam O. Beauchamp.

THE campaign for State offices in 1824, was very exciting and acrimonious; the result was favorable to the Relief party, though the majority was not sufficiently large to give that party the two-thirds majority which was necessary in order for it to remove the incumbent members of the Court of Appeals; not being able to impeach the court, it passed a bill repealing the act by which the Court of Appeals had been organized; and after which, an act was passed, reorganizing the court. The debate on these questions continued for several days; the most intense excitement prevailed, the lobbies were crowded to suffocation, visitors from all sections of the State were present, State officials were on the floor of the house, lobbying for the Relief party. Great disorder prevailed, and the Governor himself was heard to urge the calling of the previous question. The bill was passed through both the House and Senate; it was signed by the Governor as soon as it was presented to him and in a short time thereafter a new Court of Appeals was organized. The old court claimed that these proceedings were irregular, unconstitutional and void; each professing to be the court of last resort. This was the condition of affairs when the race for the Legislature was made in 1825. Never before, in the history of the State, had the passions of men been raised to such an intense heat and the political storm center was at Frankfort.

The Relief or New Court party was dominant in Franklin county, and in order to overcome this majority, the Old Court or anti-Relief party selected as a candidate for the Legislature John J. Crittenden, who had represented the State in the United States Senate and had held many other important positions; he was a man of international reputation and the idol of Franklin county, as a lawyer, statesman and orator, he was the greatest this country possessed. The New Court party thereupon, realizing the situation, selected a man who also had a national reputation, in the person of Col. Solomon P. Sharp, who was a noted orator, and who, President Madison had said, "was the ablest man of his age who had represented the west." Col. Sharp had served two terms in the Kentucky Legisalture and two in the lower house of the United States Congress, and was then holding the position of Attorney General of the State. He resigned this important and lucrative office for the purpose of making the race for Representative. It was thought that he was the only man in Franklin county who had a chance to defeat Mr. Crittenden. The contest between these two eminent men soon became of State and almost national interest; all the methods known to modern politics were used in that day. The contest stirred the county from center to circumference. The principal irritant causes of these exciting times, were the five newspapers which were ably edited and published in Frankfort. *The Argus* and the *Patriot* were advocates of the New Court. *The Spirit of Seventy Six, The Commentator* and *The Constitutional Advocate* were for the Old Court. Threats were openly made, that if Col. Sharp was elected, he would never take his seat. John U. Waring, the most deperate and dangerous man who ever became prominent in the politics of the State, was an ardent supporter of the Old Court; he and Patrick H. Darby became the most active and bitter partisans against Col. Sharp. Waring wrote him two letters threatening his life and in which he boasted that he had stabbed to death six men. He also took up the story in reference to Miss Ann Cook and gave it to the public in flaming hand bills. Patrick H. Darby also took up these charges through his paper and gave them to the public in an exaggerated form. Darby was heard to say, on several occasions that if Col. Sharp was elected that he would never take his seat, and that he would be as good as a dead man.

Col. Sharp was elected by a small majority and it was conceded by his opponents that he would be the presiding officer of the House when it was organized.

The Legislature was to convene on Monday morning, November 7, 1825. On Sunday evening prior thereto Col. Sharp, in the interest of his candidacy for Speaker, went to the Weiseger House, where the Capital Hotel now stands, and met several members of the Legislature. He later came down to the Mansion House, at that time the chief hotel in Frankfort, and remained there until about twelve o'clock, after which he went to his home on Madison street. About two hours later he was called to his door and assassinated. The killing created the wildest excitement in the city. The Legislature convened that day, and authorized the Governor to offer a reward of three thousand dollars for the apprehension and conviction of the assassin. The trustees of Frankfort were convened in extraordinary session and they too offered a reward of a thousand dollars for the same purpose. After some days, suspicion rested on Jeroboam O. Beauchamp, a young attorney located at Glasgow, Ky. A warrant was sworn out and Beauchamp was arrested and brought to Frankfort. He was tried before an examining court and released from custody. He at the time asserted his innocence and volunteered to stay in Frankfort for ten days, in order to give the Commonwealth ample opportunity to investigate the case and formulate a new charge. The Commonwealth first asked for fifteen days and at the expiration of that time fifteen days longer were granted, in which to secure sufficient evidence.

In the meantime John U. Waring and Patrick H. Darby

had come under suspicion. Mrs. Sharp stated that the voice of the assassin had sounded to her like that of Waring, a warrant was issued for him and sent to Woodford county, and from there to Fayette county, but an investigation revealed the fact that Waring had been shot through both hips, on the Saturday preceding the Sharp tragedy. Beauchamp became very active in helping to manufacture sentiment against Patrick H. Darby, and Darby having heard that he was suspected of the murder, in order to relieve himself from that suspicion, undertook to investigate the facts in the case, and it was through his efforts that Beauchamp was again arrested, and afterwards convicted. The indictment, still on file in the Franklin Circuit Court clerk's office, charges that: Jeroboam O. Beauchamp, attorney at law, on the 6th day of November, 1825, in the night of the same day, at Frankfort, Franklin county, Kentucky, with a certain dirk, which he held in his right hand, stabbed upon the front side of the body of Solomon P. Sharp, and two inches below the breast bone of the said Sharp, a mortal wound of the breadth of one inch, and of the depth of six inches, from which he instantly died, etc.''

Darby was one of the chief witnesses against Beauchamp. In the fall of 1824, Beauchamp had applied to him to bring a suit against Col. Sharp, for certain claims which are not specified in the record on file in the clerk's office. In this conversation Beauchamp stated that he had married Miss Cook and spoke of Col. Sharp's bad treatment of her and he swore that if he ever saw him he would kill him, and said if he could not see him in any other way he would ride to Frankfort and shoot him down on the street.

Darby went to Simpson county, the home of Beauchamp and while there he found a man by the name of Capt. John F. Lowe, who had received a letter from Beauchamp, in which there were some very damaging admissions against himself. (Letter is still on file in Franklin Circuit Court clerk's office.) Lowe stated that Beauchamp gave him, on Thursday evening, within a few hours after his return from Frankfort, a detailed account of the assassination, and in conclusion said: "Don't speak of this before Ann, you know what a talk has been about Sharp and her, none of the people about here talk to us about him, they all think he was the cause of her leaving society."

A large number of witnesses were introduced giving in detail the circumstances connected with the killing, the measurement of tracks, the presence of Beauchamp in the city at that time, and his suspicious conduct and statements. There was nothing but circumstantial evidence, which convicted him of the crime.

On Monday, May 15, 1826, the evidence was completed and on Tuesday the argument for the Commonwealth was opened by Mr. C. S. Bibb, who took about three hours, in which to make his argument to the jury. Mr. Daniel Mays for the Commonwealth also took about three hours. He was followed by Mr. J. Lacy in an hours argument for the defense in the afternoon and six hours the following day. Mr. Samuel Q. Richardson for the defense took twelve hours to make his argument. Mr. John Pope took the remainder of Thursday and a part of Friday. He became so personal against Darby, that Darby attempted to assault him with his cane; this incident caused great excitement, and resulted in a stampede from the court room. Mr. James W. Denny concluded the argument for the prosecution on Friday.

After an hours consultation the jury brought in a verdict of guilty and fixed his punishment at death. On Saturday Mrs. Beauchamp was taken before the justices on a charge of being accessory to the murder, but she was discharged.

On May 22, Judge Davidge overruled the motion for a new trial and pronounced the sentence upon the accused;

he fixed the time for execution on Friday, the 16th day of June. The defendant asked to have the time extended in order to give him time to write up the facts in the case; he observed that he did not ask time for the paltry consideration of a few days of life, when his country had demanded his sacrifice, but wanted time for the reason above stated and the court thereupon extended the time of execution until the 7th day of July.

There has been a doubt in the minds of some as to whether or not the alleged confession of Beauchamp was made by him; but it is perfectly evident from the facts disclosed in the damage suit of P. H. Darby v. Jeroboam Beauchamp, uncle of the assassin, that he made the confession, which was given to the public at that time. Darby not only sued Col. Beauchamp but he also brought suits for libel against Dr. Leander Sharp, Mrs. Eliza T. Sharp and Amos Kendall, editor of the *Argus*. The three last named cases were tried in the Woodford Circuit Court on a change of venue.

The confession of Beauchamp, is in substance as follows:

He was the second son of a man who owned a small farm and a few slaves, his father gave him a good English education. Beauchamp tried merchandising and afterwards school teaching, and at the age of eighteen commenced the study of law at Glasgow, Ky., where he became acquainted with Col. Sharp. While he was at Glasgow, Miss Ann Cook purchased a small farm in Simpson county about a mile from the home of Beauchamp's father. After his return to his home he persisted in calling on her, and in a short time he was desperately in love with her. She, at first, refused to marry him, but she afterwards said she would, upon the condition that he would kill Col. Sharp. He agreed to her proposition and he came to Frankfort for the purpose, in the fall of 1821; his plans failed and he did not get a chance to do the killing at that time.

In speaking of Col. Sharp on page 119, he said: " Col. Sharp was guilty of the most base dishonor and ingratitude, in the seduction of Miss Cook of which the villiany of man is capable. When he first set out in life the Cook and Payne family and connections were wealthy and in great affluence. He was then in poverty and obscurity. They patronized and supported him in his whole career, until at length the scale was turned, misfortune had followed each other in a train upon the Cook family until Col. Sharp had risen above them in wealth and influence. He had prostrated their pride and seduced one whom he should have protected as a sister."

In the year 1824, Beauchamp became of age and in a short time thereafter he was admitted to the bar; in June of the same year he and Miss Cook were married.

In November, 1825, in order to comply with the terms of his agreement with his wife in reference to the assassination, he came to Frankfort, he arrived there after dark on Sunday night, November 6th. After considerable search he found a room at Joel Scott's, who was at that time warden of the State penitentiary. He brought with him a mask, two pairs of yarn socks and some old clothes.

In his confession he tells about the arrangements he made as follows:

" After supper I was conducted to a bedroom above stairs and took out a book, observing to Mr. Scott, I believe I would read awhile. So soon as he had left me I accoutred myself for the deed. I had provided myself with an old ragged surtout coat which I had procured long before, and which no human being could have proved to have been in my possession. I had provided me a large butcher knife several months before, the point of which my wife had poisoned, which no one could ever have proved I ever owned or had in my possession. When traveling in Tennessee, I had passed a clearing where a negro had left his old wool hat on a stick. I took the hat, and splitting the end of the stick left a silver dollar in place of the hat. I put on a mask of blue silk which gave me, at five steps distant, in the clearest moonlight, the exact appearance of a negro, so well had my wife fitted it to my face. I put on two pairs of yarn socks to preserve my feet in running and to avoid my being pursued by the direction I might be heard running in the dark if I had worn my shoes. Besides in this way my tracks could not possibly be identified anywhere. But I took my shoes, my coat and my hat and hid them down near the river where I could run and get them after the deed should be done. I had learned from a source, which the offer of life would scarcely wring from me, where Col. Sharp's house was. It was the nearest house to the State house, for it stands only the width of the street from the (then) State house, and almost right across the street from it. I put on my mask with this design: That if a candle should be lit before Col. Sharp approached me, I would keep it on and as he approached I would knock the candle out with one hand and stab him with the other, but if he approached me without a light, I intended to draw down my mask as he approached, from over my face, for it was so constructed and fastened on as to be easily drawn away from the face or placed over it again. There was no moonlight but the stars gave light enough, wherewithal to discern the face of an acquaintance on coming near him, and closely noticing his face."

His account of the murder is in these words:

"I put on my mask, drew my dagger and proceeded to the door, I knocked three times loud and quick; Col. Sharp said, 'who's there,' 'Covington,' I replied; quickly Col. Sharp's foot was heard upon the floor. I saw under the door, he approached without a light, I drew the mask from my face, and immediately Col. Sharp opened the door, I advanced into the room and with my left hand I grasped his right wrist, the violence of the grasp made him spring back, and trying to disengage his wrist, he said, 'What Covington is this?' I replied, 'John A. Covington; 'I don't know you,' says Col. Sharp, 'I know John W. Covington.' Mrs. Sharp appeared at the partition door and then disappeared. Seeing her disappear, I said, in a persuasive tone of voice, come to the light Colonel, and you will know me, and pulling him by the arm, he came readily to the door, and still holding his wrist with my left hand, I stripped my hat and handkerchief from over my forehead, and looked into Col. Sharp's face. He knew me, the more readily I imagine, by my long bushy curly suit of hair. He sprang back and exclaimed in a tone of horror and despair, 'Great God it is him,' and as he said that he fell on his knees. I let go his wrist, and grasped him by the throat, dashing him against the facing of the door, and muttered in his face, 'Die you villain;' as I said that I plunged the dagger to his heart."

The next morning Beauchamp left Frankfort, "when the sun was about half an hour high." He traveled through the country on horseback. He reached his home on Thursday afternoon, and was arrested the afternoon of the next day.

Beauchamp said that during the political campaign he received several anonymous letters with printed hand bills inclosed and that he had been informed that the story of the black child was being employed by Col. Sharp to repel the charges made against him during the canvass. He said: "I have since seen the man who gave me the information and conversed with him. He informed me that Sharp had told him, with his own mouth, that the child charged to him by my wife was a colored child, and that he had then slapped him on the shoulder and told him he would die for that story."

Some days prior to the time fixed for the execution, Mrs.

Beauchamp had secured a vial of laudanum which was divided between them, each of them took a dose, but it failed to have the desired effect. She then secured a case knife and about ten o'clock in the morning on the day of the execution, upon the urgent request of Mrs. Beauchamp, the guard went up the ladder and turned the trap door. When Beauchamp called to him, he immediately returned, Beauchamp said to him, "We have killed ourselves." The guard then saw that Mrs. Beauchamp had a knife in her hand which was bloody half way up.

It was found that Mrs. Beauchamp had a stab a little to the right of the center of the abdomen, which had been laid bare for that purpose. She did not sigh or groan or show any symptoms of pain. The guard asked Beauchamp if he was stabbed, he said "yes," and raised his shirt which had fallen over the wound. He was stabbed about the center of the body, just below the pit of the stomach, but his wound was not so wide as that of his wife. Beauchamp said that he had stabbed himself first and that his wife had taken the knife from him and plunged it into herself. It may have been a mere co-incident, but it is a fact, that each of the three victims of this tragedy had a wound located at almost the same point in the body.

Beauchamp stated that there was no one implicated in the crime except his wife and that he had killed Sharp because of the wrong which he had done her. He was in a dying condition when he was taken to the gallows. He was too weak to stand; while the rope was being adjusted he was held up by two negro men.

The Patriot of July 17th said: "It was now half past twelve o'clock." The military was drawn up along Lewis street and the alley in continuation, which passes by the jailor's house, surrounded by an immense crowd, all of whom were listening with intense interest to every rumor from the dying pair.

As Beauchamp was too weak to sit on his coffin, in a cart, a covered dearborn had been provided for his convenience to the gallows. He was now brought out in a blanket and laid in it. At his particular request Mr. McIntosh (the jailor), took a seat by his side. Some of the ministers of the gospel had taken leave of him. Just as they were ready to start he said in a severe tone, "I want to see Darby." He was asked why he wished to see Darby, he said, "I want to acquit him."

Darby soon made his appearance beside the dearborn, and Beauchamp, smiling, held out his hand to him; but Darby declined taking it. "Mr. Darby," said Beauchamp, "I felt as if I wanted to acquit you to your face, before I die. You are certainly innocent of any participation in the murder of Col. Sharp; but you were guilty of base perjury on my trial. I do not believe you would take a bribe, but certain it is, you were guilty of a vile perjury and I can not conceive your motive."

"Beauchamp," said Darby, "You have endeavored to do me all the injury you could; I was prepared to prove the falsehood of your charge that I participated in the murder of Col. Sharp, but this charge I cannot disprove, because no person was present at our conversation—it is the last injury you could do me."

"Mr. Darby," said Beauchamp, "You never saw me at Duncan's well nor any other person, I presume, who told you he had married Miss Cook, nor did you ever see me, anywhere, until you saw me a prisoner at Jackson's in Frankfort."

Darby was beginning to reply, hoping that he would retract this new charge before he reached the gallows, when Beauchamp waived his hand to him, indicating that he wanted to hear no more, and said, "Drive on." The drums beat and the military and crowd moved up Clinton street to Ann street, along Ann street to Montgomery (now Main) street to Weisinger's tavern, and up Montgomery street to the place of execution.

He was publicly hanged on Friday, July 7, 1826. At an early hour the drums were beating and a large crowd of people, from all sections of the country filled the street and thousands surrounded the gallows, which was erected near where the Glen's creek road intersects the Versailles pike, on what is known as the Feeble Minded Institute ground.

Mrs. Beauchamp remained with him until just prior to his removal to the scaffold. Beauchamp and his wife died the same hour and they were buried in the same grave at Bloomfield, Ky. A marble slab has been placed over them, on which is inscribed the poem, written by Mrs. Beauchamp for that purpose. Preceding the poetry is the following inscription: "In memory of Jeroboam O. Beauchamp, born Sept. 24th, 1802, and Anna, his wife, born Feb. 7th, 1786, who both left this world July 7th, 1826." Then followed the poem of eight stanzas, of inferior merit. The confession of Beauchamp, (of 144 pages), is well written and it shows that he was a man of more than ordinary education and intelligence. Mrs. Beauchamp was sixteen years older than her husband and one year older than Col. Sharp.

Beauchamp and his wife, Col. Sharp and his wife were all members of prominent families in Kentucky.

Col. Jeroboam Beauchamp, the uncle of the assassin, had represented his district in the State Senate and was, at that time prominent in the political and social circles of the State. Jeroboam Beauchamp was about twenty-four years old, with a bright promise for the future. Under different influences and conditions he might have made a good citizen and a successful lawyer.

Prior to her misfortune, Miss Anna Cook and her sister were noted belles, they traveled in elegant style with their servants and a team of four horses, and outriders. They were educated, vivacious and fascinating and notwithstanding they were known as great gamblers, they were leaders in the society of the "Four Hundred." They were frequent visitors at Frankfort, and they never failed to visit the city during the legislative sessions.

Dr. Leander J. Sharp's description of Miss Ann Cook, in his vindication of his brother, is not very complimentary to her, and it does not accord in any way with the traditions concerning her. He said: "Miss Ann Cook was then (1820), according to the most accurate information I can obtain, thirty-three or thirty-four years old, she was small in stature, probably not exceeding ninety pounds in weight, had dark hair and eyes, dark skin, inclined to be sallow, a large forehead, slender nose, large mouth, large chin, face tapering downward and lost her fore teeth, was stoop shouldered, and in no way a handsome or desirable woman."

Col. Sharp was thirty-eight years old when he was assassinated; he was raised on a farm, commenced to practice law at Bowling Green when he was nineteen years of age; four years later he was elected to the Kentucky Legislature and from 1813 to 1817, was a member of Congress. 1818 and 1819, he was again in the Kentucky Legislature and was married to Miss Eliza T. Scott, daughter of a prominent Frankfort physician, during that term, and moved to Frankfort. He was appointed Attorney General of Kentucky in 1821, and resigned in 1825, to make the race for Representative of Franklin county. He was one of the great men whom his State produced and he had scarcely reached the prime of life when the tragic end came.

Col. Sharp and his wife are buried in the Frankfort cemetery; a square marble shaft about ten feet tall and each side about ten inches broad, mark their last resting place. On the west side of the shaft is this instruction: "Eliza T., wife of S. P. Sharp, died, January 4, 1844, in her 46th year," under which is the following: "Precious in the sight of the Lord is the death of his saints." On the east side is: "Solomon P. Sharp was assassinated while extending the hand of hospitality on the morning of November 7th (it should be the 6th), 1825," and beneath this is: "What thou knowest not now, thou shalt know hereafter."

The Richardson-Waring Tragedy.

THE most prosperous and peaceful decade in the history of Kentucky was from 1830 to 1840. It was a period of internal improvement, macadam roads, slack water navigation, railroad construction and traffic, and a general awakening of all kinds of industries, trades and commerce. Political strife and excitement had been allayed. The old Court of Appeals was recognized as the court of last resort. Party lines had been obliterated to a great extent, peace and prosperity were enjoyed throughout the Commonwealth. But peace and prosperity cannot bring happiness to the man whose heart is fatally bent upon mischief. He who has not the fear of God before his eyes, but is moved and seduced by the instigation of the devil can at all times find a way to bring sorrow and bitterness to the man who has incurred his displeasure and in so doing he usually brings upon himself a corresponding amount of trouble and sorrow.

There were few, if any, more wealthy men in Kentucky in 1835, than John U. Waring, and perhaps at that time there was no better lawyer in the Commonwealth than Samuel Q. Richardson. The prominence of these two men, and the ability and standing of the lawyers who were employed to prosecute or defend the accused, makes the case of the Commonwealth of Kentucky v. John U. Waring one of the most noted that was ever tried in this State.

On Sunday afternoon, February 8, 1835, Mr. Samuel Q. Richardson walked over to the Mansion House, where the McClure building now stands. At that time it was the leading hotel in the city of Frankfort. He started up the steps, which led from St. Clair street to the second floor; he had gotten nearly to the top of the steps when he met John U. Waring. After a few words had passed between them, Waring drew a small pistol from his pocket and presented it at Richardson. Several men were present at that time and prevented Waring from shooting. Richardson went to the room of Judge Robins, who was rooming on the second floor of the hotel, and after staying there for only a few minutes he left Judge Robins' room and started down the steps where he had met Waring only a few moments before. In the meantime Waring had been taken to his room where he exchanged his small pistol for a large one and returned to the steps where he again met Richardson and renewed the trouble. Waring ordered Richardson from the building. Richardson then said, "What, what?" and told Waring to put his pistol up and at that time Waring fired two shots both of which took effect in Richardson's breast, and from the effects of which he died the next day.

A warrant having been issued for Waring, he was taken into custody by J. C. Clark, sheriff of Franklin county, on February 9th. He was presented to two magistrates for examining trial and they entered the following order: "The within named John U. Waring having this day been brought before us, Benjamin Lucket and Henry Wingate, two of the justices of the peace in and for said county of Franklin, and he having for the present consented to the truth of the charge set forth in the warrant, we are of the opinion that he ought to be tried for said offense in the Circuit Court of Franklin county, and that he be committed to the common jail of said county without bail or main prize, to await said trial." The order was signed and dated February 11, 1835.

The indictment charged: "That John U. Waring, late of the county of Franklin, attorney at law, not having the fear of God before his eyes but being moved and seduced by the instigation of the devil, on the 8th day of February, 1835, with force and arms, at Frankfort, in the county of

Franklin, aforesaid, in and upon one Samuel Q Richardson, in the peace of God, and of the Commonwealth then and there being, feloniously, wilfully and of his malice aforethought, did make an assault, and that the said John U. Waring a certain pistol of the value of $20.00 then and there loaded and charged with gun powder and with two leaden bullets weighing half an ounce each, which pistol the said John U. Waring, in his right hand and, etc., in and upon the right side of the body of him, the said Samuel Q. Richardson, about four inches below the right pap of him, the said Richardson, etc., two mortal wounds, from the effect of which he died the following day, etc.''

Waring petitioned the Legislature, which was in session at the time, for a change of venue to Woodford county, but the relief was not granted.

When the case of the Commonwealth v. Waring was called in the Franklin Circuit Court, the array of counsel on both sides, consisting as it did of the best legal talent in the State, was a guarantee that every point in the legal battle would be strongly contested.

Waring was prosecuted by John Mason Brown, Lewis Saunders, Jr., W. D. McHenry and J. M. Huett. He was defended by Francis Johnson, J. J. Crittenden, Thomas F. Marshall, Mr. Levins, Mr. Woods and Benjamin G. Burks.

The first test was a writ of habeas corpus, which was sworn out to test a question as to whether or not bail should be granted to the defendant, which was decided against him.

On June 15th, he filed his affidavit and moved the court to direct the coroner to summons a jury in his case. In the affidavit he said: '' That the cause of objection to the high sheriff is that your petitioner is informed and believes his information to be true that Mr. J. C. Clark the high sheriff did, near the mouth of Flatcreek in this county, very recently state, that it was a case of outrageous murder, but as your petitioner had plenty of money and was rich, he would get clear by that means."

At the succeeding term of court, David Waits had become sheriff. Waring was still anxious for Andrew Williams, the coroner, to summons the venire and he made an affidavit that he believed David Waits, sheriff of Franklin county, was prejudiced against him by reason of his suit which Waring had instituted against him and his half-brother Joseph LeCompt (at one time Congressman), for a valuable tract of land in LeCompt's bottom and that defendant believed that Lewis Saunders, Jr., attorney for the prosecution, and James Haggin, deputy sheriff, had entered into an agreement to convict him and he did not believe that they would spare pains or money to injure him in any way.

On the other hand John Mason Brown, M. D. McHenry and John C. Richardson made affidavits in reference to the coroner, Andrew Williams. John C. Richardson was the brother of Samuel Q. Richardson. He stated that " Andrew Williams, coroner of Franklin county, is an old and infirm man and that said Williams would not be an impartial officer between the Commonwealth and the accused, that the partialities are for said Waring, superinduced as he fears and believes by the employment of indirect means. That said Williams, in mind as well as body, is infirm. That he is of undecisive character and could be easily operated upon, if approached, and that there are persons in Franklin county who would employ money or other means, so to operate, if occasion should present itself in the selection of a venire in said case."

On March 26, 1836, Waring stated in an affidavit " that under color of this prosecution against him he has been confined within the jail of the county of Franklin for nearly fourteen months; that his confinement has been rigid for the whole time and especially so since early in November last. That from the time of his confinement his health has been bad, and for the past four months it has been very much on decline, and he has been sinking for some time past most rapidly under direct debility and emaciation, that his condition is such that it is with great difficulty he is enabled to get from his jail to the court room even with the assistance of another. That he has no doubt a continuance of his confinement will wholly undermine the remnant of his constitution and terminate his existence even before the next term of court. That the jailor, Mr. Buford, knows that the accused would not ask of him a cup of cold water if it would save his own life; that he has not been on speaking terms with the said jailor since 1816. He further stated that the room over the dungeon in which he is confined, is used as a receptacle of slaves and drunkards of the town; that as many as three drunken Irishmen were there at one time, whose filth passed down into the dungeon upon the bed of the accused and that he had been much annoyed, to which he had, as he was compelled to submit."

(The dungeon of the jail referred to was the same in which Beauchamp and his wife were confined prior to his execution. There were no windows or regular door to the room. The entrance was through the top with a trap door. A ladder was let down and when the prisoner went down, the ladder was withdrawn and there was no possible chance for him to escape. When the trap door was fastened, neither light nor air could enter from any source.)

The proof for the Commonwealth was in substance as follows: M. R. Wigginton stated that he saw Richardson and Waring standing near together on the stairs at the Mansion House. He heard Richardson exclaim, "What, what," and he saw Waring deliberately draw out a small pistol and cock it at Richardson, he got between them and got Waring off to his room, where he (Waring) got a large pistol and primed it and returned to the stairs where he again met with Richardson and got into an altercation with him and shot him, and that as far as witness knew or saw, Richardson was not armed.

Samuel English said that he was present and saw Waring shoot Richardson down, at a time when he was telling Waring to put up his pistol and when, as far as witness knew or saw, Richardson was unarmed and was making no warlike demonstration.

N. H. Hall testified that he heard Waring say in Lexington, that on a certain occasion in Frankfort, when there was a brawl between John Laffon and Richardson that he (Waring) went into his room and got a pistol and he would have shot Richardson had he not gone into the Dudley House.

Samuel M. Brown swore that Waring said to him he had been trying for two years to bring Richardson to the striking point that he might take satisfaction.

Felix G. Rupell testified that some two or three weeks before Waring killed Richardson, he heard Waring say that his first difficulty with Richardson was six or eight years before and that he told of various occasions from that time down to the time of speaking, when he had endeavored to provoke Richardson to fight, that he might squeeze a little blood out of him, but that he could not get him to fight.

Moses Morrow said that the Tuesday before Richardson was killed Waring told him he had a load in each barrel for Richardson and asked him if he thought such a man ought to have a load, and he said that if Richardson was to come in the room where he was, he would make him leave it like a damn dog; that he had several conversations with him in which he used menacing words towards Richardson and remarked generally that the day was not far distant when he would administer to him that justice he so much deserved.

Judge Robins testified that he heard Richardson say

after he was shot and just a few moments before he died, that he had avoided Waring for weeks and avoided going to places where Waring was.

Richardson detailed the meeting between him and Waring in substance as follows: He was coming up the stairs at the Mansion House and Waring met and assaulted him by drawing a small pistol and presenting it at him; that after they were separated Richardson went to Judge Robins' room and stayed a few moments and on his return while he was on the stairs Waring came out with another pistol and ordered him to leave the house and then shot him.

Richardson said that he was not armed and Judge Robins stated that he examined Richardson's clothes within fifteen minutes after the affair and that there was no arms on him at that time. A large number of witnesses testified on each side.

The defense proved by Samuel M. Brown that Richardson was a violent, rash, brave and dangerous man. Several witnesses testified that the deceased had threatened to shoot the defendant and by others, that Richardson said that he caused the attempted assassination of defendant in 1834, and that he was answerable for it.

John Laffon stated that Richardson was instrumental in getting up, by false charges or statements, the effort to assassinate defendant at the time stated. Another witness said that Richardson was apparently trying to draw a pistol at the time he was shot.

Reuben S. Landrom swore that Richardson sent a letter by him to Waring in which he threatened to shoot him, and that he also heard Richardson say that he caused the attempted assassination of Waring and that he was answerable for it.

Waring was tried at the March term, 1835, and again at the September term of the same year, and a third time he was tried at the September court, 1836, each of which trials resulted in a hung jury. He was tried for the fourth time in March, 1837, at which time the jury turned into court their verdict: "We, of the jury find the defendant not guilty as charged." The court thereupon ordered the defendant to be discharged from custody.

Samuel Q. Richardson was born in Lexington, Ky., in February, 1791. He was educated at Transylvania University, and he was regarded as one of the leading lawyers of the State. His son, Robert Carter Richardson, was also educated at Transylvania, read law with Judge George Robertson and became eminent at the bar. He represented Kenton county in the Kentucky Legislature and was Superintendent of Public Instruction for Kentucky. He was a writer of ability, well read, able and learned in the law.

John U. Waring came to Kentucky from Virginia. He was one of five children and was possessed of great wealth which he inherited from his parents. His father owned a line of steamships plying between Norfolk and Liverpool. John U., being the oldest child, inherited the most of his father's wealth. His brother, Francis G. Waring, was killed in a duel in 1819, and one of his sisters married Silas M. Noel, a pioneer Baptist preacher of considerable note. His wife was a Miss Helm, who lived in Woodford county. She was the niece of Samuel Q. Richardson. Waring was afterwards separated from his wife and this family trouble was the real beginning of the trouble between Waring and Richardson.

Waring followed as a business, the establishment of Virginia land grants in Kentucky. This necessarily led him into much litigation and Samuel Q. Richardson being an excellent lawyer was employed in a great many law suits against him. In that way the bitter feeling grew between them. Another source of trouble between the two men was some land deals in Ohio in which Richardson became involved and very much embarrassed financially, and in which Waring also had considerable interest. Richardson mortgaged everything he had, all of his household goods and an excellent law library and miscellaneous books to satisfy these demands, but this did not satisfy Waring. The greatest trouble however seemed to be the tale bearers, who were afraid of Waring and who evidently encouraged the trouble, in the hope that Richardson would kill him.

Edwin Upsher, of Virginia, who was related to Waring, brought suit against him to recover some property which he claimed. Richardson was employed as Upsher's attorney. The case was tried at Frankfort and during the trial there was an open rupture between them. After the trial and before Waring left the court room, two of the witnesses in the case made an assault upon, and severely beat him. This incident led to the charge made by Waring, that Richardson had caused the attempted assassination.

The name of John U. Waring appears for the first time on the criminal records of Franklin county in 1818. At every term of court after that for a quarter of a century he appeared as a defendant. He was before the court on peace warrants almost without number. He was charged with having shot Henry Crittenden, a close relative, and from the effect of which shooting Crittenden died several years later. He was a lawyer of more than ordinary ability and he owned large interests in real estate in Union, Franklin, Woodford and Fayette counties, Kentucky, and considerable real estate in the State of Ohio.

On Saturday, the 7th day of March, 1845, Waring was killed in Versailles, Ky. *The Frankfort Commonwealth* said of him: "Mr. Waring was himself a man of desperation and violence. He it was who slew the late Samuel Q. Richardson and he had been engaged in many a bloody encounter; indeed we can scarcely remember when he was not notoriously at deadly fued with reputable citizens and he was commonly regarded as an enemy of mankind, having made few friends and many bitter foes.''

A post mortem examination disclosed the fact that the bullet had passed through his head down his throat and had lodged in his lungs.

Waring's oldest daughter, Kate, was a beautiful and gifted woman. She was noted far and wide as the most accomplished and fascinating belle in the bluegrass region. She, at the time of her father's death was living with her mother near Versailles. She found that her father was expected to visit Versailles at the time stated and she wrote to her uncle and told him that her father was coming to Versailles to kill him and Shelton, who was running a tavern at that place, and as a result of the letter Waring was shot and died within an hour.

The evidence was strong that young Shelton, a boy only sixteen years old, was the person who killed him. It seems that no special effort was made to locate the assassin as it was generally considered that the country was well rid of such a bad character.

In the spring of 1845, *The Richmond Herald* described John U. Waring as a man of medium height with an eye that once beheld could never be forgotten; fierce, bold, determined and piercing in its glance, once seen you would remember it forever. He wore a long overcoat with sleeves like bags. Rumor had it that he carried pistols in these sleeves. He looked like a man among men, but not of them. He declared that he had brought saddle pockets along with him to fill with men's ears and he mentioned particularly Gov. Charles S. Morehead. Waring was well versed in the land laws of Kentucky, having caused infinite trouble to litigants without regard to justice.

The Wilkinson Trial.

On the 7th day of December, 1838, Judge Edward C. Wilkinson, Dr. Benjamin R. Wilkinson and John Murdaugh, arrived in the city of Louisville, from the State of Mississippi; they were on their way to Bardstown, Kentucky, where Judge Wilkinson expected to be married to Miss Eliza Crozier of that place.

The Mississipians came to Louisville several days prior to the date set for the marriage, in order to have some clothes made and to make other necessary arrangements for the approaching ceremony, which was to take place on the 18th of December. They stopped at the Galt House, at which place the killing occurred on the evening of December 15, 1838.

The Mississippians were regarded as aristocratic slave holders, while the two men who were killed were plain artisans.

Great excitement prevailed throughout the city, the newspapers took an active part in molding public sentiment which became so bitter against the accused that they petitioned the Kentucky Legislature to grant them a change of venue from Jefferson county to Mercer county. The act was passed January 24, 1839, and all three of the defendants were tried together at Harrodsburg. The trial was commenced on Monday, March 11, 1839. Hon John L. Bridges was the presiding Judge and the Hon. Frank Johnson was the Commonwealth's Attorney for the Fifth Judicial district, who drew the indictments.

The attorneys who represented the Commonwealth at the trial, were Edward J. Bullock, Prosecuting Attorney for the Mercer district, who was assisted by the celebrated and eccentric Ben Hardin. The defendants were represented by Judge John Rowan, Hon. Sargent S. Prentiss, of Mississippi; Col. Robertson, Samuel Davis, John B. Thompson, Charles M. Cunningham, James Taylor and C. M. Wickliffe.

There were two separate indictments, the first charged Judge Wilkinson with the murder of John Rothwell and it charged Dr. Wilkinson and John Murdaugh as principals in the first degree, as being present, aiding, abetting and assisting him in the murder.

The second indictment charged John Murdaugh with being guilty of the murder of Alexander H. Meeks and it charged Judge Wilkinson and Dr. Wilkinson as principals in the first degree, being present, aiding, assisting and abetting him. All three of the defendants were tried together on both indictments at the same time.

After reading the indictments, the clerk gave the prisoners in charge to the jury in this form: "Upon these indictments gentlemen, the prisoners at the bar have been arraigned and have pleaded 'not guilty,' and for their trial have thrown themselves upon God and their country, which country you are, you will therefore hear the evidence between the Commonwealth and the accused and a true verdict give according to the same, and if you find them guilty you will assess the punishment; if not, you will say so and no more." No further instructions were given to the jury, except such as were given by the council in the arguments of the case.

The main prosecuting witness was a man by the name of Redding. He testified in substance as follows: Sometime in December Dr. Wilkinson called at my shop to purchase a suit of clothes and he requested that they be ready on the following Saturday. He then agreed for an overcoat to be furnished the next week and also a pair of pantaloons. I had the clothes prepared and folded them on the counter to send to the Galt House on the appointed Saturday evening. My tailor shop is on the lower corner of

Third and Main streets, in the city of Louisville. There is but one square between my shop and the Galt House, but the shop is on the opposite side of Main street.

On Saturday afternoon the Doctor came to my shop about the clothes and I showed them to him. I asked him to try on the coat. He said " yes," and took off his old coat and tried on the new one, which he seemed to like very well. He merely remarked, as to the fit of the coat that it was a little loose, but he had been sick and had fallen away, and hoped soon to fill it up. He then took the things out of his old coat pockets and put them into the pockets of the new coat. He desired me to send the pantaloons and vest to the Galt House, and at the same time handed me a Mississippi one hundred dollar bank bill which, he requested, I would hold over for a week or two as he had information with regard to the arrangements of the banks below, that the discount in a few days would be considerably reduced. He then went away and in the course of an hour or so returned accompanied by two gentlemen. As I afterwards learned, his brother Judge Wilkinson and Mr. Murdaugh. When the Doctor came in the second time, he said he would have to throw the coat on my hands as it did not fit and his friends had told him it was badly made—not fashionable; it was the Judge who said most about its not being fashionable. I offered to get any alterations necessary, made. He said no that it was no coat at all. As soon as I found they were not disposed to take it, I said I would keep it. The Doctor then took out some money and said he would pay for the pantaloons and vest, which had been sent to the Galt House. The Judge said, " No, do not pay for them, perhaps they will not fit—they may be like the coat." I thought he and Murdaugh had more to say against the clothes than the Doctor, who, I saw would be pleased enough, only for them. He said the law was, that if a coat did not fit, it should be taken back. When the

Judge interfered so much, I said it took more than one to judge a coat, and that I thought he had already said more than he ought.

The Judge, who had been sitting near the stove, then jumped up and said that he did not come there to be insulted. I remarked that I did not intend to insult him. He snatched up the iron poker, at the stove, and rushed at me with it, attempting to strike me, but I received the blows on my arms. Seeing that no one in the store was interfering, and hearing something about a Bowie knife, I thought to get them to the street, where some one would be passing, and I seized the Judge and jerked him to the side door, near the corner going into Third street. As I got to the door, I think I slipped and fell and the Judge fell with me. I thought the whole three were on top of me, and I struggled till I got the Judge under me, and I raised to keep off the Doctor or pull him down, when he tried to stab me, with his knife, but was prevented by some one. The knife was like this handed me; I think it is the same knife.

The Judge still held on to the poker. I should have stated that when the Doctor drew his knife on me, a voice quite near, which I thought was Murdaugh's, cried out, "Kill the damned rascal." It was then that some one ran up and held the Doctor's arm. I threw them off and got out on the pavement. Murdaugh was on the pavement with his knife drawn. I picked up a brickbat and told them, I would whip the whole three of them if they would lay aside their weapons. Seeing no interference, I returned into the shop and the Doctor followed me, with his drawn knife in his hand demanding his hundred dollar bill. In the scuffle I had lost my pocketbook, in which it was; but some one, who had picked it up, handed it to me and I gave the Doctor his bill. They then went away with the knives drawn and the Judge carried off the poker. Several persons came into the shop after they had gone, and some advised me to get them taken up. I did not at first want to do it, but after a little time, was persuaded to go to the Mayor's office, accompanied by Bill Johnson; but before this I went to Mr. Fulton's store and got a small dirk knife from Mr. Noel, which I put in my watch pocket. As we went to the Mayor's office we called at Hymen's coffee house to inquire for the Marshal or one of the police officers. Not meeting any of them we proceeded to the Mayor's office. I told the circumstances to Mr. Pollard, the clerk of the Police Court, and told him I wanted a warrant. He asked me for their names, which I could not give. I told him, that I would go to the Galt House for the names, and bring them to the office. We then started to Market street and over towards Rothwell's corner, I saw Rothwell, my brother-in-law, and told him what had happened; he went along with me up Market street; we could not find the Marshal or the police officer, so we proceeded on to the Galt House. We went into the barroom and I asked the bar keeper for the register and the names of the Mississippi gentlemen, which he gave me. I then got to talking to Mr. McGrath who was inside the counter, and told him how I had been treated at my own store. In a short time Judge Wilkinson came in and took a glass of water. I was leaning on the counter, and said to him, "I think you are the gentlemen that struck me with a poker in my own house to-day?" He observed that he was; and then said, "I will not quarrel or fight with a man of your profession, but, if you lay a hand on me I'll kill you." As he said this he put his hand behind him, as I thought, in his coat pocket, for a weapon. I then called him a coward for coming to my house, with two others, to assault me; and I offered, if he and they would lay aside their weapons, and come into the street or into a room I would whip the whole three of them. He then walked backwards and forwards across the room and I kept telling him what I thought of him.

In a short time he passed out of the barroom. He was gone but a little while when he and the Doctor and Murdaugh came in. I saw the Doctor and the Judge behind, and Murdaugh came towards me, a little below where I stood at the counter. I remarked to him, as he came up, that he was the man who had drawn his knife on me in my own shop. He said he had understood that I had said that he had drawn a Bowie knife on me, and if I said so I was a damned liar, or any one else that said it, told a damned lie. As he was saying this, he threw up his hand with a drawn knife in it. I heard some one remark, that he was the man, for he had seen him, but the fight then began so suddenly, and the crowd rushed so closely together about Murdaugh, and the others, that they were hurried past me, and I could not see what was doing. I knew that Meeks was killed, but I did not see him killed. Mr. Rothwell came up when he heard the damned lie given, and pushed me back with his arms which caused me to be outside the scuffle. A little while after that I saw Judge Wilkinson with a large Bowie knife in his hand,—he came hurrying past me. The knife he had was probably eight or ten inches long in the blade and two inches wide, heavy and sharped at the point like other knives of that name. He was apparently stabbing at several persons. By that time Holmes had Dr. Wilkinson down in the left hand corner of the room—the left hand as you faced the fire.

The Judge went towards the door. Meeks was lying in the opposite corner between the counter and dining room either dead or dying. I did not know him.

The crowd in the left hand corner, by this time was retreating into the passage and making towards the stairs. I gathered up a chair, and followed them, and was in the effort of striking with the chair, but fearing that I might hit the wrong person I did not make the blow. I got towards the foot of the stairs, where I heard Mr. Oldham say, as if in answer to some one on the stairs, that he'd give the damned rascal a pistol, and a pistol was fired, but I did not know whether by him or from above.

On cross-examination it was developed that the first fight occurred about one hour before the killing and that the witness had employed Judge Hardin to prosecute the defendants and for which he was to receive one thousand dollars. It was also disclosed that Rothwell, Meeks, Monohan, Johnson, Holmes, Wallace, Marshall, Halbert, Oldham, Sloan, Reaugh, Oliver and Redding were present and participated in the attack on the Mississippians.

Mr. Pope testified that he was boarding at the Galt House, and saw the fight; after locating the parties and giving the statements which were testified to by Redding, said: "Some one caught Murdaugh's hand and the fight commenced; blows were struck at Murdaugh and the crowd closed up as they passed around towards the dining room door. Immediately after this my attention was attracted to the other corner of the room, near the folding doors into the passage, and I saw Judge Wilkinson standing in the doorway with a Bowie knife in his hand. Rothwell was standing a few feet from the door in a line towards the fireplace. The Judge looked a moment and then stabbed Rothwell under the shoulder. Rothwell was stooped a little, not as if fighting, but leaning over some one down on the floor. Almost instantly a fight commenced with raised chairs and the crowd moved out of the room into the passage. I saw the knife enter Rothwell's back."

Mr. Redman said: "I was at the Galt House that evening on my way to my supper. I live on Market between Brook and Floyd streets and passing the Galt House on my way home, I heard loud talking inside, which induced me to enter. When I went in Mr. Redding was abusing Judge

Wilkinson, who remarked that he did not want to have anything to do with a man of his profession, and if he laid hands on him he would kill him. He then walked up and down the room with his hand in his pocket. Mr. Everett called him to the counter and catching his arm told him he had better go to his room. He went out and in ten or fifteen minutes he returned accompanied by Mr. Murdaugh, the only one I noticed coming in with him. Redding said to Mr. Murdaugh, 'you are one of the gentlemen who drew a knife on me.' Murdaugh said, 'You are a damned liar.' Meeks said, 'You are, I saw you myself.' Murdaugh replied, 'You are a liar,' and made a pass at him with his knife, at the same instant that Meeks struck him with his whip. Some one caught Murdaugh's right hand and he changed the knife into his left hand and the second thrust he cut Meeks in the belly. Meeks staggered backward and finally fell towards the counter. As I was making my way out of the room I saw Holmes in the left hand corner of the room, scuffling with the Doctor. The Doctor had a knife in his hand. At the time, Rothwell was leaning over Holmes begging him to get off. Holmes said: 'Let me hit him one more blow.' Judge Wilkinson was at the door and made a thrust at Rothwell and stabbed him over the hip, when Rothwell straightened up and exclaimed, 'Oh, I am cut,' and the Judge retreated out of the door."

The Commonwealth introduced seventeen witnesses, nearly all of whom were present and saw the fight at the Galt House.

The defendants were not permitted to testify in the case. The evidence for the defense was in substance: that Redding and his friends had gathered at the Galt House, with the expressed intention "to give the Mississippians hell."

Mr. Pearson said: "When Judge Wilkinson returned to the barroom there must have been fifty men in the room, which induced me to go to the Judge and ask him to leave the room. He made a step or two with me, to retire, when about twenty men were crowding in and we heard some angry words, and the affray began. The Judge turned, and seeing this said, 'Sir, I can not leave the room and my friends till I see how this affair with these men ends.'"

The following facts were brought out by the defense: There were only two ways to enter the dining room at the Galt House; the main entrance, and the one generally used by the public, was through the barroom; there was also a side door which was used by only a few people who were well acquainted or connected with the hotel.

Judge Wilkinson received a wound about three inches deep and extending from near the shoulder blade, towards the spine. Murdaugh was bruised and cut about the head in several places. Dr. Wilkinson's face and head were greatly bruised. His face was very much discolored and his eyes were swollen until they were nearly closed. Johnson said that he thought Redding's friends ought to go to the Galt House and flog them. He said to Redding: "Jack, just say the word and I'll go for my friend Bill Holmes and we'll give them hell." Several witnesses said that they were invited to go with the crowd to the Galt House to punish the Mississippians.

Meeks said that he was going to the Galt House, "that he was bound to have a fight, that night, and by G—d he'd have it."

Halbert said, some time before the fight commenced, "we are going to have a hell of a fight here to-night." Rothwell had Dr. Wilkinson down and was beating him at the time Judge Wilkinson cut him.

Before the Mississippians came in, Rothwell asked Redding if they were there, and Redding said, "no." Rothwell then said, "come, let us go upstairs and bring them down and give them hell." Murdaugh was struck with a chair, Judge Wilkinson also had a chair thrown at him and some one said, " Shoot the damned rascal," and immediately thereafter a pistol was fired.

Sergeant S. Prentiss testified in the case. He said: " I have been acquainted with Judge Wilkinson, intimately in Mississippi, for six or seven years. My profession has brought me into intercourse with him as a practicing lawyer. I believe there is no man in the State of Mississippi, whose character stands higher than that of Judge Wilkinson, particularly to a marked extent for a modest and retiring disposition. I know this to be his character as a Legislator and public man; as a Circuit Judge, a distinguished member of the Legislature; a Commissioner, appointed by the State to go to New York on State business, and a public man. I know that no man ever stood higher in the estimation of the south." He also said the reputation of Dr. Wilkinson and Mr. Murdaugh were good. Other witnesses testified to the same facts.

The court did not instruct the jury as to the law in the case. In the arguments of counsel the law was either stated or read as counsel thought best.

There were, perhaps a thousand people who crowded into the court room to hear the arguments in the case; at least two hundred of whom were handsome well dressed ladies.

Judge Rowan suggested that on account of the immense crowd, the hearing of the arguments might be adjourned to the adjacent church, but Judge Bridges refused to proceed with the trial at any place except that designated by law.

Mr. Edward J. Bullock, Commonwealth's Attorney, opened the argument. A considerable portion of his time was used in reading to the jury the law which he thought had bearing on the case. Col. Robertson followed for the defense. He also read a great deal of law and he applied it to the facts proven in the case in a very skillful way.

The argument of Sergeant S. Prentiss, for the defense, and Benjamin Hardin for the prosecution, were the leading features of the trial. These two arguments have caused the Wilkinson trial to be designatel the greatest criminal trial in the history of the State. Sergeant S. Prentiss made the finest argument and most eloquent appeal to the jury that was ever heard in a court of justice in Kentucky. During its delivery he was frequently interrupted by applause from the vast assembly of people who had crowded in the court room; and when he closed his argument he was greeted with loud cheers and prolonged applause.

(The speech of Mr. Prentiss is given in full at the end of this chapter.)

The Hon. Benjamin Hardin commenced his argument to the jury by unrolling the cloth which was wrapped around the knives and caused them to fall on the table. And holding the bloody cloth in his hand he said: "My countrymen: these are the instruments of death used by the Mississippi aristocrats in slaughtering your fellow Kentuckians."

For five hours the logic and eloquence of the eccentric Hardin held the attention of the jury and the large assembly of people. Rarely, if ever, has such another argument been made. The wonderful argument of Prentiss seemed to have brought out the best that was in the able advocate who opposed him. This joint debate, as it were, to decide the question of life, or death, of the three Mississippians, is worth many times the cost of securing it, so we print in full at the end of this chapter the speeches of Mr. Prentiss and Mr. Hardin.

The arguments of Col. Robertson, John B. Thompson, Judge Rowan and Mr. Bullock were well delivered and were worthy of the men who made them but they were regarded as of small importance when compared to the other two.

The jury remained in consultation exactly fifteen minutes and upon returning to the court, gave the following verdict: "In the case of Edward C. Wilkinson and others for the murder of John Rothwell, We, the jury find the within named defendants and each of them not guilty of the offense charged against them in the indictment.

"ROBERT ALEXANDER, one of the jury."

The same verdict was rendered on the indictment for the murder of Alexander H. Meeks.

Judge Wilkinson married Miss Crozier of Bardstown, in January following the killing; this was before the trial.

The Wilkinson trial was before Boyle county was established. The people of Harrodsburg were opposed to giving any part of Mercer to form a new county and they were especially opposed to the idea of giving up Danville, which was at that time in Mercer.

Dr. Graham, owner of Graham Springs, and other prominent citizens of Harrodsburg, took an active interest in manufacturing sentiment and assisting the Mississippians in every way they could. Mr. Hardin felt that he had not been treated with proper courtesy by these gentlemen and that Mr. Prentiss had gotten too much credit. When he got on his old gray horse, ready to start for his home, he shook his finger at these gentlemen, who were in front of the hotel, and said, "I will make my sons-in-law (two of whom had been elected to the Legislature), cut off the best portion of your county and separate you fellows from the town of Danville forever."

The following Legislature established Boyle county and made Danville the county seat.

SPEECH OF THE HON. SERGEANT S. PRENTISS.

I rise to address you with mingled feelings of regret and pleasure. I regret the occasion, which has caused me thus accidentally and unexpectedly to appear before you, and has compelled you to abandon, for the time, the peaceful and quiet vocations of private life for the purpose of performing the most important and solemn duty which, in the relations of civilized society, devolves upon the citizen.

I regret to behold a valued and cherished friend passing through one of the most terrible ordeals ever invented to try human feelings or test the human character; an ordeal through which, I do not doubt, he will pass triumphantly and honorably, without leaving one blot or stain upon the fair fame that has been so long his rightful portion, but through which he can not pass unscathed in his sensibilities and feelings. The lightning scar will remain upon his heart, and public justice herself can not, even though by acclamation through your mouths she proclaims his innocence, ever heal the wounds inflicted by this fierce and unrelenting prosecution, urged on, as it has been, by the demons of revenge and avarice. Most of all do I regret the public excitement which has prevailed in relation to these defendants, the uncharitable prejudgment which has forestalled the action of law, the inhospitable prejudice aroused against them because they are strangers, and the attempt which has been, and is still making, to mingle with the pure stream of justice, the foul, bitter, and turbid torrent of private vengeance. But I am also gratified; gratified that the persecution under which my friends have labored, is about to cease; that their characters as well as the cause of public justice will soon be vindicated; that the murky cloud which has envoloped them will be dissipated, and the voice of slander and prejudice sink into silence before the clear, stern, truthful response of this solemn tribunal.

The defendants are particularly fortunate in being tried before such a tribunal. The bearing and character of His Honor who presides with so much dignity, give ample assurance that the law will be correctly and impartially laid down; and, I trust I may be permitted to remark that I have never seen a jury in whose hands I would sooner entrust the cause of my client, while, at the same time, I am satisfied you will do full justice to the Commonwealth.

I came before you an utter stranger, and yet I feel not as a stranger toward you. I have watched during the course of the examination the various emotions which the evidence was so well calculated to arouse in your bosoms, both as men and as Kentuckians; and when I beheld the flush of honorable shame upon your cheeks, the sparkle of indignation in your eye, or the curl of scorn upon your lips as the foul conspiracy was developed, I felt that years could not make us better acquainted. I saw upon your faces the mystic sign which constitutes the bond of union among honest and honorable men, and I knew that I was about to address those whose feelings would respond to my own. I rejoiced that my clients were, in the fullest sense of the term, to be tried by a *jury of their peers.*

Gentlemen of the jury, this is a case of no ordinary character and possesses no ordinary interest. Three of the most respectable citizens of the State of Mississippi stand before you indicted for the crime of murder, the highest offense known to the law of the land. The crime is charged to have been committed not in your own county, but in the city of Louisville, and there the indictment was found. The defendants during the past winter, applied to the Legislature for a change of venue and elected your county as the place at which they would prefer to have the question of their innocence or guilt investigated.

This course, at first blush, may be calculated to raise in your minds some unfavorable impressions. You may naturally inquire why it was taken; why they did not await their trial in the county in which the offense was charged to have been committed; in fine, why they came here? I feel it my duty before entering into the merits of this case, to answer these questions and to obviate such impressions as I have alluded to, which, without explanation, might very naturally exist.

In doing so it will be necessary to advert briefly to the history of the case.

My clients have come before you for justice. They have fled to you even as to the horns of the altar, for protection. It is not unknown to you that upon the occurrence of the events, the character of which you are about to try, great tumult and excitement prevailed in the city of Louisville. Passion and prejudice poured poison into the public ear. Popular feeling was aroused into madness. It was with the utmost difficulty that the strong arm of the constituted authorities wrenched the victims from the hands of an infuriated mob. Even the thick walls of the prison hardly afforded protection to the accused. Crouched and shivering upon the cold floor of their gloomy dungeon, they listened to the footsteps of the gathering crowds, and ever and anon, the winter wind that played melancholy music through the rusty gates was drowned by the fierce howling of the human wolves who prowled and bayed around their place of refuge greedy and thirsting for blood. Every breeze that swept over the city bore away slander and falsehood upon its wings. Even the public press, though I doubt not unwittingly, joined in the work of injustice. The misrepresentations of the prosecutor and his friends became the public history of the transaction, and from one end of the Union to the other these defendants were held up to public gaze and public execration as foul, unmanly murderers, and that, too, before any judicial investigation whatever had occurred, or any opportunity been afforded them for saying a single word in their defense.

I recollect well when I received the first information of the affair. It was in some respectable newspaper, which professed to give a full account of the transaction, and set forth with horrible minuteness a column of disgusting particulars. Instantly, openly and unhesitatingly, I pronounced the paragraph false, and trampled it under my heels. When rumor seemed to endorse and sustain the assertions of public prints, I laughed her to scorn. I had known Judge Wilkinson long and well. I knew him to be incapable of the acts attributed to him, or of the crime with which he was charged. Not an instant did I falter or waiver in my belief. I hurled back the charge as readily as if it had been made against myself. What! A man whom I had known for years as the very soul of honor and integrity, to be guilty, suddenly and without provocation, of a base and cowardly assassination! One whose whole course of life had been governed and shaped by the highest moral principle; whose feelings were familiar to me; whose breast ever had a window in it for my inspection, and yet had never exhibited a cowardly thought or a dishonorable sentiment; that such a one, and at such an era in his life, too, should have leaped at a single bound the wide gulf which separates vice from virtue, and have plunged at once into the depths of crime and infamy! Why, it was too monstrous for credence. It was too gross for credulity itself. Had I believed it, I should have lost all confidence in my kind. I would no longer have trusted myself in society where so slender a barrier divided good from evil. I should have become a man-hater, and, Timon-like, gone forth into the desert, that I might rail with freedom against my race. You may judge of my gratification in finding the real state of facts in the case responsive to my own opinion.

I am told, gentlemen, that during this popular excitement there were some whose standing and character might have authorized the expectation of a different course of conduct, who seemed to think it not amiss to exert their talents and influence in aggravating instead of assuaging the violent passions of the multitude. I am told that when the examination took place before the magistrate every bad passion.

every ungenerous prejudice, was appealed to. The argument was addressed, not to the Court, but to the populace.

It was said that the unfortunate individuals who fell in the affray were *mechanics,* while the defendants were *Mississippians—aristocrat slave holders*—who looked upon a poor man as no better than a negro. They were called *gentlemen* in derision and contempt. Every instance of violence which has occurred in Mississippi for years past was brought up and arrayed with malignant pleasure, and these defendants made answerable for all the crimes which, however much to be regretted, are so common in a new and rapidly populating country. It was this course of conduct and this state of feeling which induced the change of venue. I have made these remarks because I fear that a similar spirit still actuates that portion of this prosecution which is conducted, not by the State, but by private individuals.

I am not aware that the Commonwealth of Kentucky is incapable of vindicating her violated laws, or unwilling to prosecute the perpetrators of crime. The District Attorney has given ample proof that she is provided with officers fully capable of asserting her rights and protecting her citizens, and with the exception of one or two remarks, which fell from him inadvertently, I accord to his observations my most unqualified approbation. He has done equal justice to the State and the defendants; he has acquitted himself ably, honorably, and impartially. But, gentlemen, though the State is satisfied the Prosecutor is not. Your laws have spoken through their constituted agent; now private vengeance and vindictive malice will claim to be heard. One of the ablest lawyers of your country, or of any country, has been employed to conduct the *private part* of this prosecution; employed, not by the Commonwealth, but by the real murderer; him whose forehead I intend, before I am done, to brand with the mark of Cain—that in after life all may know and all may shun him. The money of the Prosecutor has purchased the talent of the advocate, and the contract is, that *blood* shall be exchanged for *gold.* The learned and distinguished gentleman to whom I allude, and who sits before me, may well excite the apprehension of the most innocent. If rumor speak truth he has character sufficient, even though without ability, and ability sufficient, even without character, to crush the victims of his purchased wrath.

I said that with the exception of one or two remarks, I was pleased with the manly and honorable course of the Commonwealth's Attorney. These remarks seemed to be more in the spirit of his colleague than in accordance with his own feelings.

I was sorry to hear him mention so pointedly, and dwell so long upon the fact that the defendants were *Mississippians,* as if that constituted an ingredient in their crime or furnished proof of their guilt. If to be a Mississippian is an offense in my clients, I can not defend them; I am myself *perticeps criminis.* We are all guilty. With malice aforethought, we have left our own bright and beautiful homes, and sought that land, the name of which seems to arouse in the minds of the opposing counsel only images of horror. Truly the learned gentlemen are mistaken in us; we are no cannibals nor savages. I would that they would visit us and disabuse their minds of these unkind prejudices. They would find in that far country thousands of their own Kentuckians who have cast their lot by the monarch stream, in the enjoyment of whose rich gifts, though they forget not, they hardly regret the bright river upon whose banks they strayed in childhood. No State has contributed more of her sons to Mississippi than Kentucky, nor do they suffer by being transplanted to that genial soil. Their native State may well be proud of them as they are of her.

But I do injustice to you and to myself by dwelling upon

this matter. Here in the heart of Kentucky my clients have sought and obtained an unprejudiced, impartial jury. You hold in your hands the balance of justice; and I ask and expect that you will not permit the prosecution to cast extraneous and improper weights into the scale against the lives of the defendants. You constitute the mirror, whose office it is to reflect, in your verdict, the law and the evidence which have been submitted to you. Let no foul breath dim its pure surface and cause it to render back a broken and distorted image. Through you now flows the stream of public justice; let it not become turbid by the trampling of unholy feet. Let not the learned counsel who conducts the private part of this prosecution act the necromancer with you, as he did with the populace in the city of Louisville, when he raised a tempest which his own wizard hand could not have controlled. Well may he exclaim in reference to that act, like the foul spirit of Manfred:

> "I am the rider of the wind,
> The stirrer of the storm;
> The hurricane I left behind
> Is yet with lightning warm."

Aye, so it is still "with lightning warm." But you, gentlemen, will perform the humane office of a conductor, and convey this electric fluid safely to the earth.

You will excuse these prefatory observations; they are instigated by no doubt of you, but by a sense of duty of the defendants. I wish to obviate in advance, the attempts which I know will be made to excite against them improper and ungenerous prejudices. You have seen in the examination of one of the witnesses, Mr. Graham, this very day, a specimen of the kind of feeling which has existed elsewhere, and which I so earnestly deprecate. So enraged was he because the defendants had obtained an impartial jury, that he wished the whole Legislature in that place not to be mentioned to ears polite, and that he might be the fireman; and all on account of the law changing the venue. Now, though I doubt much whether this worthy gentleman will be gratified in his benevolent wishes in relation to the final destiny of the Senate and House of Representatives of this good Commonwealth, yet I can not believe that his desires in regard to himself will be accomplished, and his ambitious aspirations fully realized in the ultimate enjoyment of that singular office which he so warmly covets.

Gentlemen of the jury—I ask for these defendants no sympathy, nor do they wish it. I ask for them only justice—such justice alone as you would demand if you occupied their situation and they yours. They scorn to solicit that from your pity which they challenge from your sense of right. I should ill perform toward them the double duty which I have assumed, both of friend and advocate, did I treat their participation in this unfortunate transaction otherwise than candidly and frankly; did I attempt to avoid responsibility by exciting commiseration. I know that sooner than permit deception and concealment in relation to their conduct, they would bare their necks to the loathsome fingers of the hangman, for to them the infamous cord has less of terror than falsehood and self-degradation.

That these defendants took away the lives of the two individuals whose deaths are charged in the indictment, they do not deny. But they assert that they did not so voluntarily or maliciously; that they committed the act from stern and imperative necessity; from the promptings of the common instincts of nature; by virtue of the broad and universal law of self-defense; and they deny that they have violated thereby the ordinances of either God or man. They admit the act, and justify it.

The ground of their defense is simple, and I will state it so that it can not be misapprehended. They assert, and I shall attempt from the evidence submitted to convince you that a conspiracy was formed by Mr. Redding, the prosecutor, and various other persons, among whom were the deceased, to inflict personal violence upon them; that the conspirators, by preconcerted agreement, assembled at the Galt House, in the city of Louisville, and attempted to accomplish their object; and that, in the necessary, proper and legal defense of their lives and persons from such attempt, the defendants caused the deaths of two of the conspirators. After discussing this proposition, I shall submit another, which is, that even though a conspiracy on the part of the deceased and their companions to inflict personal violence and bodily injury upon the defendants, did not exist, yet the defendants had *reasonable* ground to suppose the existence of such a conspiracy, and to apprehend great bodily harm therefrom; and that upon such reasonable apprehension they were justified in their action, upon the principle of self-defense, equally as if such conspiracy had in point of fact existed.

The law applicable to these two propositions is simple, being, in fact, nothing more than a transcript from the law of nature. The principles governing and regulating the right of self-defense are substantially the same in the jurisprudence of all countries—at least all civilized ones. These principles have been read to you from the books by my learned and excellent friend Col. Robertson, and require no repetition.

That a man has a right to defend himself from great bodily harm, and to resist a conspiracy to inflict upon him personal violence if there is reasonable danger, even to the death of the assailant, will not, I presume, be disputed. That *reasonable, well-grounded* apprehension, arising from the actions of others of immediate violence and injury, is a good and legal excuse for defensive action, proportionate to the apparent impending violence and sufficient to prevent it, I take to be equally indisputable. By these plain rules and upon these simple principles, let us proceed to test the guilt or innocence of the defendants.

First, then, as to the existence of the conspiracy. Before examining the direct evidence to this point, you will naturally inquire, was there any cause for this alleged conspiracy? Motive always precedes action. Was there any motive for it? If we establish the existence of the seed, we shall feel less hesitation in being convinced of the production of the plant. Was there, then, any motive on the part of Mr. Redding and his friends for forming a combination to inflict personal violence upon the defendants? In answering this question it will be necessary to take notice of the evidence which has been given in relation to events that transpired at the shop of Mr. Redding at a period anterior to the transaction at the Galt House, and which, except for the clue they afford to the motive, and consequently to the subsequent action of the parties, would have no bearing upon the case before you. You will take heed to remember that whatever of impropriety you may consider as attaching to the conduct of Judge Wilkinson and his friends during this part of the affair, must not be permitted to weigh in your verdict, inasmuch as that conduct is the subject of another indictment which is still pending in this court.

Judge Wilkinson visited Louisville for the purpose of making the preparations necessary for the celebration of his nuptials. The other two defendants had also their preparations to make, inasmuch as they were to act as his friends upon this interesting occasion. Dr. Wilkinson, a brother of the Judge, had ordered a suit of clothes of Mr. Redding, who follows the very respectable occupation of tailor, occasionally relieved and interspersed by the more agreeable pursuits of a coffee-house keeper. On the day but one preceding that fixed for the marriage ceremonies, the Doctor, in company with his brother and friend, Murdaugh, proceeded to the shop of Mr. Redding for the purpose of obtaining the wedding garments. Upon trying on the coat it was found ill-made and of a most ungraceful fit. It hung loosely about his shoulders, and excited by its awkward construction the criticism and animadversion of his friends. Even the artificer did not presume to defend the work of his own hands, but simply contended that he could re-organize the garment and compel it, by his amending skill, into fair and just proportions. From the evidence I presume no one will doubt that it was a shocking bad coat. Now, though under ordinary circumstances, the aptitude of a garment is not a matter of very vital importance in the economy of life, and ought not to become the subject of controversy, yet all will admit that there are occasions upon which a gentleman may pardonably indulge a somewhat fastidious taste in relation to this matter. Doctor Wilkinson will certainly be excused, considering the attitude in which he stood for desiring a well made and fashionable coat.

I confess I am not a very good judge in concerns of this sort. I have had no experience on the subject, and my investigations in relation to it have been exceedingly limited. Under favor, however, and with due deference to the better judgment of the learned counsel on the other side, I give it as my decided opinion that a gentleman who is about to participate in a marriage ceremony is justified in refusing to wear a coat, which, by its loose construction and superabundant material, indicates, as in the case before us, a manifest want of good husbandry.

Suffice it to say, Doctor Wilkinson and his friends did object to the garment, and Mr. Redding, after some altercation, consented to retain it. The pantaloons, which constituted a part of the suit, had been sent to the hotel, and the Doctor was in the act of paying for them, out of a $100 bill, which he had previously deposited with Redding, when the Judge remarked that he had better not pay for the pantaloons until he had first tried them on, as they might be found to fit no better than the coat. Mr. Redding, according to his own evidence, responded, that " they had said too much already about the matter," to which the Judge, he says, replied, that he did not come there to be insulted, and immediately seized the poker and struck him; upon which the Doctor and Mr. Murdaugh also fell on him, with their knives drawn. Redding then seized his shears, but did not succeed in cabbaging therewith any part of his assailants. He was successful, however, in dragging the Judge into the street, where, after a slight scuffle, which resulted in no personal injury to any of the parties, they were separated. After the separation, Redding offered, if they would lay down their knives, to fight them all. This kind proposition the defendants declined; but the Doctor returned into the shop, obtained his $100 note, and then the defendants retired from the place.

Such in substance is Mr. Redding's own account of the transaction at his shop. The witness Weaver also proves the altercation which occurred in relation to the fit of the coat and the scuffle which ensued in consequence. He, however, avers that Redding, in a very insulting manner told the Judge that he " was more meddlesome than the other," and that he " was too d—d meddlesome," or words to that effect; which insulting language so excited the Judge that he seized the poker and commenced the assault.

The other witness, Craig, Redding's journeyman, testifies in substance the same as Redding, as to what passed in the shop; corroborates his account of the altercation about the coat; and says he considered Doctor Wilkinson, not as assisting in the affray, but as attempting to separate the parties. Some of the witnesses think that the Doctor attempted, in the street, to stab Redding, as he was getting the advantage of his brother. The evidence on this point, as well as in regard to the conduct of Murdaugh, is somewhat contradictory. In the view, however, which I have taken of the case, the discrepancy is of little importance.

It is clearly proven, take the evidence in any way, that Mr. Redding used insulting language towards Judge Wilkinson, on account of the Judge's expression of an opinion in relation to the fit of his brother's coat. What was the exact language used, it is difficult to ascertain.

There were six persons in the room when the quarrel ensued—on the one side, the prosecutor (Redding), his foreman (Craig), and the boy (Weaver); on the other, the three defendants.

All the evidence on this point has been derived from the first party, and ought, consequently, to be taken with many grains of allowance. The prosecutor has given you his version of the affair, but his cunning has prevented the defendants from giving you theirs. Doctor Wilkinson, who was discharged by the examining magistrate, has been included in the indictment, one would judge, for the very purpose of precluding his testimony. No one can doubt that the conduct of Judge Wilkinson, however reprehensible, resulted from the abusive language and insulting demeanor of Mr. Redding. The happy facility with which he indulged, on a subsequent occasion, in the use of opprobrious epithets, gives good reason to suppose that his remarks on the present were not very guarded. The expression deposed to by Weaver is, I presume, but a sample. "You are too d—d meddlesome," was the observation, accompanied, no doubt, by the overbearing and bullying manner which illustrated his conduct afterwards, and which smacked more of his spiritual pursuit, as the Ganymede of a coffee-house, than of his gentle calling as a knight of the shears and thimble. He certainly did, on this occasion, "sink the tailor;" for tailors are proverbially polite and gentlemanly in their deportment.

I do not wish to be considered as justifying Judge Wilkinson or his friends in taking notice of the petulant and insolent conduct of Redding. I think they would have better consulted their character and feelings by treating him with contempt. I will go further, and candidly admit that I consider their course reprehensible; that it resulted from passion and sudden excitement, and not from deliberate determination. They were themselves convinced of this in a moment, and left the ground, ashamed, as they still are, of their participation in the matter—Judge Wilkinson rebuking and leading away his young and more ardent friend, Murdaugh, who seemed to indicate some disposition to accept the boastful challenge of Mr. Redding, that "he could, if they would lay down their knives, whip them all three." From all the evidence it is perfectly clear that, in the altercation, no personal injury resulted to any of the parties; that the defendants retired voluntarily from the quarrel, while Mr. Redding retained the field, and with boastful taunts and insulting outcries, invited a renewal of the fight. The Mississippians were manifestly satisfied. Not so Mr. Redding; he was "full of wrath and cabbage," boiling over with violence, and breathing defiance and vengeance against the retreating foe. He, doubtless, retired to his coffee-house and attempted to soothe his wounded feelings with some of the delightful beverages which it was occasionally his profitable province to dispense to others. Here his friends gathered around him; he recounted to them his manifold grievances; he grew warm in the recital; the two white-handled pocket-knives which had been drawn but not used in the affray, danced before his distempered imagination in the shape of trenchant and death-dealing blades. These little instruments of ordinary and general use, became, at once, Bowie knives, "in buckram." He believed, no doubt, and made his friends believe, that he was an injured man, and that some satisfaction was due to his insulted honor. I have presented this part of the case to you simply for the purpose of enabling you to judge of the subsequent action of the parties and to indicate on which side a desire for vengeance, and a combination to obtain it were most likely to originate. Upon the conclusion of the first affray which party would you have suspected of a disposition to renew it? Where could lie the motive on the part of Judge Wilkinson and his friends for additional violence? But who that is acquainted with the workings of human nature, or the indications of human feeling, will hesitate a moment in believing that revenge lurked in the bosom of Redding, and sought only a safe opportunity for development? His conduct indicated a state of mind precisely fitted for the formation of a conspiracy.

Having laid the foundation, I will now proceed to the erection of the superstructure. I will show, first by the direct and then by the circumstantial proofs, the existence of this foul and cowardly conspiracy. I will, however, here remark, that I doubt not the misrepresentations and falsehoods of Mr. Redding, in relation to the transaction, induced several of the persons implicated to join the combination, who, with a correct knowledge of the facts, would never have participated in the affair.

First, then, as to the direct and positive evidence. Mr. Jackson says, that immediately after the first affray he was passing Mr. Redding's, when his attention was attracted by loud talking in the store, which induced him to enter, where he found Redding, Johnson and Meeks. Johnson was expressing his opinion as to the course which should be pursued towards the Mississippians for their conduct, and said they "ought to go to the Galt House and flog them." "Jack," said he to Mr. Redding, "just say the word, and I'll go for Bill Holmes, and we'll give them hell;" at the same time boasting, in his own peculiar phraseolgy, "that he was as much manhood as was ever wrapped up in so much hide." Upon some hesitation being evinced at this proposition, Meeks said, " Let's go anyhow, and we'll have a spree."

Mr. Jackson further deposes, that some time after he was stopped by Johnson, on the street, who told him he was going after Holmes; that Jack Redding was a good man, and that he, Jackson, ought to go with them to the Galt House and see him righted. Jackson declined, alleging as an excuse his religious character, and his desire to abstain from fighting; whereupon Johnson exclaimed, in his ardent zeal for enlisting recruits, that " church, hell or heaven ought to be laid aside to right a friend." Jackson said he understood it distinctly, that it was a fight to which he was invited.

Mr. Jackson's testimony is entitled to credit. He did not participate in the affair; and he can have no inducement to speak falsely, for all his prejudices must naturally be enlisted on the side of the prosecution. His character is sustained by unexceptionable testimony, and has been impugned by no one except the Salamander gentleman, whose ambition seems to be, to pursue in the next world that occupation which in this is principally monopolized by the descendants of Ham.

The next direct evidence of the conspiracy is from Mr. Deering, whose character and testimony are both unimpeachable. He says he was passing down Market street, on the evening of the affray, when he saw, near the market-house, Johnson, in company with Holmes and others, and that they were discussing the subject of the quarrel between the Mississippians and Redding. This proves that Johnson was carrying into effect his proposition at Redding's store, viz.: " to go and get Bill Holmes and give them hell." He had already found Bill Holmes, and, we shall presently see, made all his arrangements for " giving them hell."

Mr. Deering says that soon after he met Mr. Johnson

again, who inquired for Mr. Turner, the City Marshal. Mr. Deering told him he would be too late with his officers, for the Mississippians would be gone; to which Mr. Johnson responded, "*there were enough gone there—that if they came down, their hides would not hold shucks.*" What did this mean, if it did not indicate that the conspiracy had already been formed, and a portion of the conspirators assembled at the Galt House, for the purpose of preventing the game from escaping, and holding it at bay, until the arrival of the rest of the hunters. They had gone, it seems, too, in sufficient numbers to authorize the classical boast of Mr. Johnson, "that if they (meaning the Mississippians) came down, their hides wouldn't hold shucks."

There is one more witness, whose testimony is positive to the point. It is Mr. Harris. He swears, clearly and unequivocally, that Johnson met him on the evening of the affray, told him that the Mississippians had insulted Mr. Redding, and directly solicited him to go with Redding's friends to the Galt House and see him righted. Mr. Harris says he refused to go, whereupon Johnson exclaimed, "Are you a friend of Redding's?" thereby showing how strong was the feeling when even a mere refusal to participate in the violence was considered as proof that the man refusing was no friend of Redding.

Such, gentlemen, is the positive proof of the conspiracy. It consists of the evidence of three disinterested and honest witnesses, two of whom were directly and strongly solicited to participate in the matter. The testimony of each of these witnesses corroborates that of the other two. The facts sworn to have a natural order and connection. There is a verisimilitude about the whole story, which would not belong to either portion by itself. The testimony is entitled to much more weight than if it had been the recital of a single witness; for if you believe one of the witnesses you must give credit to all. One of them swears that he heard Johnson, in Redding's shop, propose to Redding and his friends that he should get " Bill Holmes " and " give them hell." The next witness saw Johnson on the street immediately after, in company with " Bill Holmes," who seems to have been the Achilles of these Myrmidons; explaining to him how his dear Patroclus, Redding, had been insulted by the hectoring Mississippians, and urging him to vengeance. Again the same witness met Johnson, and was informed by him that a portion of his banditti had already taken possession of the passes of the Galt House, and that if the Mississippians appeared, " their hides wouldn't hold shucks." The third witness swears to a positive solicitation from Johnson, that he should join in the foray, and to the expression of strong indignation by this slayer of cattle upon his refusal to do so.

Johnson was the " Malise " of the party, " the messenger of blood and brand " sent forth to summon the clansmen true. Too well did he perform his duty. He collected his friends and conducted them like beasts to the slaughter; while he himself found the " manhood," which, according to his boast, distended his hide, rapidly descending to his heels. But enough, for the present, of this vaporing worthy; I shall pay my respects to him hereafter.

I will now proceed, in pursuance of the plan I had prescribed, to show the existence of the conspiracy, by the circumstantial evidence, which is, if possible, more irrefragable than the direct testimony; but yet most beautifully illustrates and confirms it. I will exhibit to you a chain of facts, linked together by a natural and necessary connection, which I defy even the strong arm of the opposing counsel to break. I will weave a cable upon whose unyielding strength the defense may safely rely to ride out the storm of this furious prosecution.

Mr. Redding went to the Galt House after the affair at his shop for the purpose, as he avows, of obtaining the names of the Mississippians that he might procure process against them from the civil authorities. On his way, as he confesses, he armed himself with a deadly weapon, which, however, I am bound in justice to say, he never had the courage to use. A number of individuals accompanied and followed him, whose manner and strange appearance excited universal attention even in the barroom of the most frequented hotel in the western country. Their strange faces and strange actions excited general apprehension. Nearly every witness to the unfortunate catastrophe, has deposed that he was struck with the " strange faces " congregated in the barroom. The learned counsel on the other side has attempted to prove in the examination, and will, no doubt, insist in the argument, that that room is daily crowded with strangers from every part of the country; that the excellence of the fare and the urbanity of its proprietors, invite to the Galt House a large portion of the traveling public, and that consequently it is nowise remarkable that strange faces should be observed in the barroom. Though I admit the gentleman's premises, I deny his conclusion. That strangers should frequent the Galt House is not wonderful; they do it every day, and for that very reason strange faces, under ordinary circumstances, arouse neither remark nor attention. That the " strange faces " of Mr. Redding's friends should have excited remark and scrutiny, not only from the inmates of the house but from strangers themselves, is truly wonderful, and can be accounted for only by admitting that there was something very peculiar in their conduct and appearance.

They went there prepared for pre-concerted action. Having a common object and a well-arranged plan, a glance or a motion sufficed to convey intelligence from one to the other. Telltale consciousness spoke from each countenance. Their looks, unlike the mysterious brotherhood, gave up to the observer the very secret they wished thereby to conceal. There is a strange and subtle influence, a kind of mental sense by which we acquire intimation of men's intentions, even before they have ripened into word or action. It seems, on such occasions, as if information was conveyed to the mind by a sort of natural magnetism, without the intervention of the senses.

Thus, in this case, all the bystanders were impressed at once with the conviction that violence was intended by the strange men who had attracted their attention. These men, it is proven, were the friends and intimate companions of Redding. Most of them, though living in the city of Louisville, were not in the habit of going to the Galt House, and yet, by a singular coincidence, had all assembled there on this occasion. They were remarkably stout men, constituting the very elite of the thews and muscle of Louisville, and many of them noted for their prowess in the vulgar broils of the city. Why had they thus congregated on this occasion. Why their strange and suspicious demeanor? I will show you why. It will not be necessary to await the actual fight to become fully conversant with their purpose. It found vent in various shapes, but chiefly bubbled out in the unguarded remarks and almost involuntary expression of the more garrulous of the party.

I shall be compelled, even at the risk of being tedious, to glance at the evidence of a number of the witnesses in showing you the circumstances at the Galt House, which conclusively indicates the existence of the conspiracy.

Mr. Everett, one of the proprietors of the Galt House, says he was admonished by his bar keeper that a difficulty was about to arise, and he had better persuade Judge Wilkinson out of the barroom. Accordingly, he went in and took the Judge away, and gives as a reason that he was alarmed at the strange faces in the barroom, and apprehended difficulty; alarmed, not because the faces were those of strangers, but because of something in their appearance which indicated concert and threatened violence.

Mr. Trabue was waiting in the room for supper, and says he heard someone remark, " if the Mississippians had not gone upstairs, they would have been badly treated;" in connection with which remark, Redding was pointed out to him. This it seems was after the Judge had retired at the solicitation of Mr. Everett. Now who were to have treated the Mississippians badly, except Mr. Redding and his friends? Who else had any pretense for so doing? Can you doubt for a moment that the remark had a reference to Mr. Redding's party. It was probably made by one of them; but whether by one of them, or a stranger, it equally indicated their violent determinations. Mr. Trabue also proves that after Judge Wilkinson retired, Mr. Redding also retired; and when the Judge returned into the barroom, Redding presently entered; followed, to use the language of Mr. Trabue " by a right smart crowd " of his friends. Now why did Redding thus go out, and return with his gang at his heels? Why were his movements thus regulated by the motions of the Judge?—Wherefore was it that every one expected a difficulty?

Mr. Redding, according to his own story, went to the Galt House simply for the purpose of obtaining the names of the gentlemen who had insulted him.

He had accomplished his ostensible object. He had obtained the names, and more than that, had gratified his base appetite by abusing one of the gentlemen in the most indecent and disgusting manner. No rowdy who ever visited his coffee house could have excelled him in this, to the vulgar mind, sweet mode of vengeance. He had even driven the Judge from the room by the overwhelming torrent of his billingsgate epithets. To use an expression suited to his comprehension and feelings, he remained " cock of the walk." Yet he was not satisfied. He retired, and watched the return of the Judge, and then emboldened by his previous impunity followed with his cutthroat band to complete the work of vengeance.

But to proceed with the circumstantial evidence. Mr. Montgomery states that he was with Mr. Trabue at the Galt House when Redding came in after the names, and, also, when he came back just before the conflict; heard him use very rough language, and, also, heard Halbert remark that there would be "rough work with the Mississippians." Now this fully corroborates the testimony of Mr. Trabue on the same point, who heard the remark, but did not recollect who made it. This Marshall Halbert is the man who boasted, after the affair was over, that he had knocked down one of the Mississippians with a chair while his back was towards him, and recounted many other feats of daring to the astonishment of the listeners. I should judge him to be of the blood of honest Jack Falstaff, whose killing, as everybody knows, was always by word of mouth, and whose deeds of desperate valor were so unfortunate as to find neither historian nor believer except himself. At all events Halbert, according to his own confession, was one of the conspirators, and I have no doubt performed his part in the affray as well as he knew how, and with much greater humanity than he pretends. In addition to the above remark of Halbert's, Mr. Montgomery states that he heard several persons say, at a time when the defendants were not in the room, that they would beat the Mississippians well.

General Chambers, who lives opposite the Galt House, and is in the daily habit of visiting it, says he went into the barroom just before the affray, that he observed persons whom he was not in the habit of seeing there, and that from their appearance and demeanor, his suspicions were immediately aroused.

I attach great weight to the testimony of Gen. Chambers.

His character for intelligence and observation needs no comment from me; and the fact that his suspicions were aroused, must convince everyone that cause for alarm existed.

The next testimony to which I shall refer is that of Mr. Oliver. He says that he was acquainted with Mr. Meeks, and was taking a social glass with him on the evening of the affray, when Meeks started off, saying he must go to the Galt House (which was on the opposite side of the street), that he was bound to have a fight that night, and "by G—d he would have one." You will recollect that Meeks was one of the persons who collected around Redding immediately after the affair at the shop, and seconded Johnson's proposition to get Bill Holmes and "give them h—l," by saying "they would go anyhow, and have a spree." Can you doubt for a moment, that the observation made by this unfortunate man to Mr. Oliver, as just recited, had relation to the previous arrangement with Johnson and others at Redding's shop? The remark of Meeks seems to me, taken in connection with his previous and subsequent conduct, almost conclusive of itself as to the existence of a conspiracy. I had almost forgotten to observe Mr. Oliver's statement that Meeks, before he started, tied a knot in the small end of a cowhide which he carried, manifestly to prevent it from slipping out of his hand in the conflict which he so eagerly courted. His knife, by a sort of pious fraud, had been taken from him by Mr. Oliver, otherwise the result might have been very different. The prudent caution of Mr. Oliver in disarming him of this weapon, proves how strong must have been in the indications of his violent disposition.

Mr. Reaugh says he was at the Galt House on the evening of the affray, and saw Redding in conversation with Rothwell and Halbert—he also saw Holmes and Johnson. Something in the demeanor of the party induced him to ask

Johnson what was the matter. Johnson replied by relating the affair of the shop. Upon which Reaugh observed "if the Mississippians fall into the hands of these men, they will fare rather rough." "Yes," replied the worthy butcher, "they would skin them quicker than I could skin a sheep." Mr. Reaugh states that he made the remark to Johnson because of the remarkable size and strength of the men to whom he alluded; the strange manner in which they had assembled, and the fact that he knew them to be friends of Redding, and that Redding had been in a quarrel with the Mississippians.

Mr. Miller states that being a member of the grand jury, and having heard of the affray at Redding's, he went into a tin shop to enquire about the matter, when Mr. Halbert came in and boasted much of what he intended to do. Witness then went to the Galt House for supper, when he heard Redding abusing Judge Wilkinson, and challenging him for a fight. Witness advised Halbert to take Redding away, observing that he, witness, was on the grand jury, had the names, and would have all the matter attended to. Someone, he thinks Johnson, then remarked that "if he didn't leave the room, he'd see the finest sort of beefsteak served up." Presently he heard the exclamation, near the counter, "there they are, all three of them," and the crowd immediately closed in upon the persons so indicated.

Mr. Waggry, also, heard, the remark about the "steaks," and then heard someone exclaim "we'll have a hell of a fight here just now." He also heard Mr. Miller advise Halbert to take Redding away.

Mr. Brown swears that he heard Mr. Miller tell Mr. Redding he was not taking the proper course; he should have the matter before the grand jury; whereupon someone said "hush you Billy Miller, if it comes to handy-cuffs the boys will settle it." The witness then became so apprehensive of a fight that he left the room.

Though Miller is not positive as to the person who made use of the expression about " serving up beefsteak," yet no one, I take it, will hesitate as to his identity. Who but Johnson could speak in such rich and technical language? Who but Johnson could boast of " having as much manhood as was ever wrapped in the same extent of hide "? While, at the same time, he had so arranged it, that the " hides " of the Mississippians " would not hold shucks." Who but this unmitigated savage would talk of " skinning " a gentleman " quicker than I could skin a sheep "? Why, he rubs his hands, licks his lips, and talks of serving up Christians in the shape of " steaks," with as little compunction as you or I would exhibit in eating a radish. The cannibal! He should go, at once, to New Zealand and open his shambles there. His character would suit that country, and I doubt not he would obtain great custom, and find ample demand for his human " steaks." Why, gentlemen, I should be afraid to buy meat out of his stall. He talks as if he supplied it by burking. I should expect some day to swallow an unbaptized infant in the disguise of a reeking pig, or to eat a fellow citizen, *incog.*, in a " steak." Such a fellow should be looked to. But again. What meant the expression deposed to by Reaugh, " There they are, all three of them, now "? It was the signal for the conspirators to close in. It clearly proves a pre-concerted plan. No names were mentioned, and without a previous understanding, the expression would have been nonsense. Most of the party did not know the Mississippians, hence it was necessary that some one should give intimation when they entered the room. The expression, " There they are," was the signal for the onset. What meant the expression sworn to by Waggry, " We'll have a hell of a fight here just now "?

What conclusion do you draw from the response made to Miller, when he advised Redding to bring the matter before the grand jury, " Hush you, Billy Miller, and if it comes to handicuffs the boys will settle it "? If what comes to handicuffs? And who were the boys? Why, if the quarrel with the Mississippians comes to handicuffs. And as for the " boys," there was not a man present who did not know who they were.

Redding was one of the " boys," and a very bad boy, too. Billy Holmes was another. Marshall Halbert was a perfect " broth of a boy," and if his own story is entitled to credit, he must have been twins, for he acted the part of at least two in the fight. Bill Johnson was as much of a boy as ever was " wrapped up in the same amount of hide," though his extraordinary modesty has induced him to deny the soft impeachment. The unfortunate Meeks and Rothwell were two of the " boys "; and last, though not least, comes Harry Oldham, the " Jack Horner " of the party. He " sat in the corner " till the fight was nearly over, when he " put in his thumb " and " pulled out," not " a plum," but a pistol, and ever since has been exclaiming, " What a brave ' boy ' am I."

Yes, gentlemen of the jury, these were the " boys " whose strange appearance aroused the suspicions and excited the apprehensions of all.

Permit me, now, to call your attention to the testimony of Mr. Donoghue. It is clear and conclusive. He swears that on the evening of the affray, and just before it occurred, being in the barroom of the Galt House, he heard Rothwell ask Redding " if they were there "; upon being answered in the negative, he exclaimed " come, let us go upstairs and bring them down, and give them hell." Rothwell, was the brother-in-law of Redding, had been informed by Redding of his grievances, and had accompanied him to the Galt House. Whom did he mean, when he asked if " they were there "? The Mississippians undoubtedly. Whom did he propose to drag from their rooms, and chastize? Of course the same persons for whom he has just enquired. Rothwell asked "if they were there," when the defendants came in, someone cried out "there they are, all three of them." These two expressions manifested from persons who understood each other, and were engaged in pursuit of a common object.

If these remarks had not relation to some previous concerted plan of action, they would be unmeaning and foolish: but granting the existence of the conspiracy I have supposed, and every word is pregnant with meaning; full of force, weight and effect.

Mr. Raily deposes to the caution given by Miller to Redding; also to the fact that Redding left the room when Judge Wilkinson had retired, and came back again immediately after the Judge had returned. He also saw Oldham after the affair was over, putting a pistol into his pocket, and wiping, with his handkerchief, the blood from a double-edged dirk.

Mr. Pearson says he went to the Galt House just before supper, on the evening of the affray. As he stood behind the bar, one Capt. Rogers observed that there would be a fight. Presently, witness met Marshall Halbert, and told him he ought to stop it, meaning the fight. Halbert said "no, let it go on." This was before Redding had commenced abusing Judge Wilkinson, and proves that the idea of a fight did not originate from that circumstance. The Judge came, and Redding abused him. He went out, and Redding followed. He returned, and presently so did Redding with a crowd at his heels. Seeing the crowd, and apprehending violence, Mr. Pearson was in the act of leading the Judge out of the room, when the crowd rushed upon Murdaugh; the affray commenced, and the Judge stopped, refusing to leave the room until he saw his friend out of the difficulty. Need I ask you if he was right in so doing. Mr. Banks says he saw Redding just after the first affray and asked him if he was hurt. He said no, but that he would have satisfaction and that he could whip them all three. Dr. Graham says that after Judge Wilkinson had left the barroom the first time he heard someone observe, " the d—d coward has run."

Does not Mr. Oldham's testimony prove the conspiracy? I do not mean directly, but circumstantially. He says he was not present at the fight in the barroom, and knew nothing of the affair, nor of the defendants. He says he was standing in the passage when the door opened, and he received a cut from Dr. Wilkinson, whom he knocked down for his pains. After fighting in the crowd awhile, he saw Murdaugh retreating upstairs, and asking for a pistol, whereupon he was reminded of his own pistol, which he immediately drew and discharged at the young gentlemen, giving him not the weapon, but its contents, to-wit, a bullet, split in three pieces. This worthy gentleman, who is certainly

" as mild a mannered man
As ever scuttled ship or cut a throat,"

swears positively that he did not know either of the defendants; that he belonged to neither party in the affray, and that he fought, to use his own descriptive and unrivalled phraseology, entirely " upon his own hook."

Surely Mr. Henry Oldham must be the knight-errant of the age, the Don Quixote of the west, the paragon of modern chivalry. He fights, not from base desire of vengeance, nor from sordid love of gold—not even from patriotism or friendship; but from a higher and loftier sentiment—from his pure ardent, disinterested, unsophisticated love of glorious strife. Like Job's war-horse, he " smelleth the battle afar off," and to the sound of the trumpet he saith, " Ha! ha! " To him

" There's something of pride in the perilous hour,
What'er be the shape in which death may lower,
For fame is there to tell who bleeds,
And honor's eye on daring deeds."

You have heard, gentlemen, of the bright, warm isles which gem the oriental seas, and are kissed by the fiery sun of the tropics, where the clove, the cinnamon and the nutmeg grow; where the torrid atmosphere is oppressed with a delicious, but fierce and intoxicating influence. There the spirit of man partakes of the same spicy qualities which distinguish the productions of the soil. Even as the rinds of their fruits split open with nature's rich excess, so do the human passions burst forth with an overwhelming violence and prodigality unknown till now in our cold, ungentle clime. There, in the islands of Java, Sumatra, the Malaccas, the other of the same latitude, cases similar to that of Mr. Henry Oldham are of frequent occurrence. In those countries it is called "running amuck." And individual becomes so full of fight that he can no longer contain it. Accordingly, he arms himself with a species of dagger, very similar to that from which Mr. Oldham wiped the blood with his pocket handkerchief, and rushing into the public streets, wounds and slays indiscriminately among the crowd. It is true that this gallant exploit always results in the death of the person performing it, the people of the country entertaining a foolish notion that it is too dangerous and expensive a mode of cultivating national bravery. But in the present instance I trust this rule will be relaxed. Mr. Oldham is the only specimen we possess of this peculiar habit of the spice-islands, and he should be preserved as a curiosity.

But, alas! the age of chivalry has gone by, and in the performance of my duty I fear I shall have to exhibit some little defects in the character of Mr. Oldham, calculated in this censorious day to detract from his general merits.

It is with great pain I feel constrained to say (for he is a sort of favorite of mine), that telling the truth is not one of his knightly accomplishments, and that his heroic conduct in the affray at the Galt House was nothing more nor less, according to his own story, than a downright cowardly attempt at assassination.

First, as to his veracity. He says that he was cut in the passage by Dr. Wilkinson, to whose identity he swears positively; yet it is proven by half a dozen unimpeachable witnesses that the Doctor was, at that time, *hors du combat,* beaten to a mummy—almost lifeless and perfectly limber—while his knife had fallen from his relaxed and nerveless grasp upon the floor of the barroom, where it was afterwards picked up.

Yet Oldham swears, manfully, that it was the Doctor who cut him, though, when asked if his face was not bloody, he replied that the passage was too dark to enable him to distinguish faces. If he could not see whether the face of the person who cut him was bruised or bloody, how dare he swear it was Dr. Wilkinson, whom he admits he had never seen before?

Yet, though his vision was so dull in regard to this matter, it was almost supernaturally keen upon another. He swears that he was cut by a dirk knife, "*with a white handle.*" Now in this dusky passage, where he could not see his assailant's face, how could he distinguish so accurately the character of the weapon, and more especially of the handle. The handle of such a knife as either of those exhibited would be entirely concealed in the grasp of the holder. But Mr. Oldham could see through the hand and swear to the color of the handle, even when he could not distinguish the color of the assailant's face.

The prosecution seems to be afflicted with a monomania on the subject of white-handled knives. The white handles cause them greater terror, and excite more of their observation, than the blades. One would be almost led to suppose, from the evidence, that the defendants held by the blades and fought with the handles. The white handles flash before their eyes like the bright inscription upon the dim steel of a Turkish cimeter. I hope, though with many misgivings, that none of them will ever die of a " white handle."

But, to return to my subject, why in the name of all that is human or humane, did Oldham shoot at Murdaugh, whom he acknowledges he did not know, of whose connection with Dr. Wilkinson he was unacquainted, and who had not attempted to do him the slightest injury? According to his own account of the matter, he acted the part of a base and cowardly assassin. If he tells the truth, he is an assassinating villain. If he does not, he is a perjured villain. I leave him choice of these two horns of the dilemma, though I doubt not the latter is the one upon which he is destined to hang. I can not believe in the existence of such a monster as he would make himself out to be, and have offered his conduct to you as evidence of the existence of a conspiracy, and of his participation in it. It is better that he should have the excuse of having fought in Redding's quarrel than no excuse at all.

Gentlemen of the jury, I have now performed that portion of my task which embraced the circumstantial evidence. Out of the mouths of fifteen different witnesses, most of them gentlemen of high character and undoubted veracity, I have exhibited to you an almost countless variety of circumstances, the occurrence of which, or any great portion of them, is absolutely incompatible with any other hypothesis than that of the existence of the conspiracy, which I proposed at the outset to prove. Upon that hypothesis all these circumstances are easily explicable, and in perfect accordance with the ordinary principles of human action. I have combined the scattered strands of evidence. I have finished the cable which I promised, and now challenge the opposing counsel to try their strength upon it. They may pick it into oakum, but I defy them to break it.

There is one other argument in favor of the view that I have taken of the origin of this unfortunate affray, which may be properly introduced at this time, and with which I shall close this branch of the subject.

It arises out of the respective characters and positions in life of the two parties, and is, in my opinion, entitled to great weight. Who, judging of character and situation, was most likely to have sought and provoked the unfortunate conflict—Judge Wilkinson or Mr. Redding? The conduct of the Judge, under the opprobrious epithets heaped upon him by Redding in the barroom, sufficiently indicates that, though he had previously given way to sudden passion, he was now cool, collected, and forbearing. His mind had recovered its balance, and he behaved on this occasion, as well as subsequently, with philosophical calmness. I doubt, gentlemen, whether any of you would have permitted Mr. Redding to have indulged, with impunity, in such unmeasured abuse. But the situation of the Judge was peculiar, and every inducement which could operate upon a gentleman warned him against participation in broils and battles. With buoyant feelings and pulse-quickening anticipations he had come more than a thousand miles, upon a pilgrimage to the shrine of beauty, not of blood—upon an errand of love, not of strife. He came to transplant one of Kentucky's fairest flowers to the warm gardens of the sunny South, there to bloom in beauty and in brightness. The marriage feast was spread; the bridal wreath was woven, and many bounding hearts and sparkling eyes chided the lagging hours. The thoughts of the bridegroom dwelt not upon the ignoble controversy which, for an unguarded moment had occupied his attention, but upon the bright and glorious future, whose rapturous visions were about to become enchanting realities. Under such circumstances Judge Wilkinson could not have desired the conflict. Had the fires of hell blazed in his bosom, they must have been quenched for a while. The very fiend of discord would have been ashamed, fresh from a voluntary, vulgar, bloody quarrel, and reeking with its unsightly memorials, to have sought the gay wedding banquet.

You can not believe he coveted or courted the unfortunate affray, without, at the same time, considering him destitute, not only of all sentiment of delicacy and refinement, but every characteristic of a man. Does his previous character warrant such a conclusion? He has, as has been shown to you in evidence, ever entertained the character of an honorable and upright gentleman. I see, by the sneer upon the lip of the adverse counsel that the term grates harshly upon his sensibilities. But, I repeat it, Judge Wilkinson has ever entertained the character of a gentleman, a character directly at war with the supposition that his conduct on this occasion resulted otherwise than from necessity. I mean by " a gentleman " not the broadcloth but the man; one who is above doing a mean, cowardly, or a dishonest action, whatever may be the temptation; one who forms his own standard of right and will not swerve from it; who regards the opinions of the world much, but his own self-respect more. Such men are confined to no particular class of society, though, I fear, they do not abound in any. I will save the learned counsel the trouble of translating his sneer into language, by admitting that they are to be found as readily among mechanics as elsewhere.

Such a man I believe Judge Wilkinson to be. Such has ever been his character, and he is entitled to the benefit of it on this occasion. It ought to have, and I know it will have very great weight with you. Good character always has been, and ever should be, a wall of strength around its possessor, and a seven-fold shield to him who bears it.

This is one of the advantages virtue has over vice—honorable over dishonorable conduct—an advantage which it is the very highest interest of society to cherish and enforce. In proportion to the excellence of a man's character is, and ever ought to be, the violence of the presumption that he has been guilty of no crime. I appeal, then, to Judge Wilkinson's character, to prove that he could not have desired this unfortunate controversy; that it is impossible he should have been guilty under the circumstances which then surrounded him, of the crime of wilful and malicious murder. What, on the other hand, was the condition of the conspirators. Redding had been going about from street to street, like Peter the Hermit, preaching up a crusade against the Mississippians. Johnson, like Tecumseh—but no, I will not assimilate him to that noble warrior—like an Indian runner, was threading each path in the city, inciting his tribe to dig up the tomahawk, and drive it, not into the scalps, but the "steaks" of the foe. But I will not pursue this point at greater length.

I proposed, after arguing the position that there actually was a conspiracy to chastise the defendants, and inflict upon them great bodily harm, to show, in the next place, that the defendants had good reason to believe such a conspiracy existed, whether in point of fact it did or not. Most of the arguments bearing upon this proposition have been already advanced in support of the other. These I will not repeat. There are one or two others worthy of notice. What could Judge Wilkinson have supposed from the conduct of Redding, but that he sought and provoked a difficulty? What else could he conclude from the unmitigated abuse which was heaped upon him, from the very sluices of vulgarity? That the Judge apprehended violence is evident from the warning which he gave. He told Redding that he might say what he pleased, but not to lay his hands upon him; if he did, he would kill him. He could not be supposed to know that Redding came only for the names. When Meeks stepped up to Murdaugh and struck him with his clubbed whip, while the crowd closed in around, what could Murdaugh reasonably expect but violence and bodily harm, resulting from preconcerted arrangement? Without going at length into an argument on this point, I take it for granted, no one will deny that the defendants had ample grounds for apprehending the existence, on the part of Mr. Redding and his friends, of a conspiracy, to commit upon them personal violence.

Let us now look a moment at the conduct of the defendants, at the Galt House, and see whether it transcended the bounds of right, reason or prudence. When Murdaugh and the Doctor entered the room, the exclamation was made, by someone, loud enough for all to hear, " There they are—all three of them, now "; upon which according to nearly all the witnesses, Mr. Redding made the remark to Murdaugh, " You are the man that drew the bowie knife on me." You will recollect Redding had just crossed Judge Wilkinson's path, and placed himself with his back against the counter, manifestly with the object of bringing on the fight. Murdaugh, indignant at being publicly charged with having drawn a bowie knife upon an unarmed man, replied, " that any one who said he had drawn a bowie knife told a d—d lie; " whereupon instantly steps up Meeks, with his knotted cowhide, exclaiming, " You are the d—d little rascal that did it," at the same time inflicting upon him a very severe blow. By the by, this assertion of Meeks proves that he had been at Redding's after the first affray, and heard a full account of it. It is urged against the Judge, that when Mr. Everett led him to his room, he asked for pistols. I think an argument may be drawn from this circumstance in his favor. His requisition for arms proves that he considered himself and his friends in great personal danger. He manifestly required them not for offense, but for defense. Had he intended an attack, he would not have gone down to the barroom without first obtaining the weapons he desired. Men do not voluntarily attempt the lives of others without being well prepared.

It is evident that Judge Wilkinson and his friends thought only of the protection of their own persons; for they went downstairs provided only with the ordinary weapons which they were accustomed to bear. Murdaugh and the Doctor had a pocket knife each; the same they had previously carried. They had added nothing to their armor, either offensive or defensive. The Judge, apprehensive of difficulty, had taken his bowie knife, which, probably, he had not previously worn. When, at the solicitation of Mr. Everett, he retired, he doubtless informed his friends of what had just transpired in the barroom, and expressed his fears of violence. This accounts for the readiness with which Murdaugh met the assault of the two powerful men who simultaneously rushed upon him.

The evidence is conclusive that Meeks commenced the attack, upon Murdaugh, by two rapid, violent blows of a cowhide; accompanied by a heavy blow from a stick or cane from the hands of Rothwell. At the same time he seized the hand of Murdaugh, in which, prepared for defense, was an open knife; but Murdaugh, with coolness and celerity, changed the weapon to his left hand, and used it according to the dictates both of law and common sense. The very first blow had driven him to the wall. The crowd closed around him: he could not retreat, and was justified, according to the strictest and most technical principles of even English jurisprudence, to take the life of the assailant. No man but a fool or a coward could have acted otherwise than he did. Was he not, according to the rule read by the District Attorney, in imminent danger of his life or of great bodily harm? Let the unhealed wound upon his head respond. Let his hat, which has been exhibited to you, answer the question. Upon this you may perceive two incisions, which must have been caused by a sharp, cutting instrument. No obtuse weapon was capable of the effect. The blows were manifestly sufficient to have caused death, but for the intervention of the elastic material, upon which their principal force was expended. The part, then, taken by Murdaugh in the affray was clearly defensive and justifiable. It is not protended that Doctor Wilkinson took any other part in the affray than attempting to escape from its violence, unless you notice the evidence of Oldham, that he cut him as he fled from the room. He was beaten, first by Rothwell, then by Holmes, and if you take their own statements, by those two worthies, Halbert and Oldham. He was crushed almost to atoms. He had not a chance even for self-defence. Rothwell had left Murdaugh, after striking him one blow, in charge of Meeks, and fell upon the Doctor. While beating the Doctor, he was stabbed by the Judge, near the dining-room door. The Doctor fled around the room, still followed by Rothwell, who was again struck by the Judge, when upon the opposite side. The two blows paralyzed his powers; when Holmes stepped in and so completely prostrated the Doctor, that he was compelled to hold him up with one hand while he beat him with the other.

Neither offensive word nor action, upon this occasion, on the part of Doctor Wilkinson, is proven or pretended. It is perfectly clear that he was beaten by Redding's friends, simply because he was of the Mississippi party. I consider it highly disgraceful to the grand jury who found the bill, that he was included in it.

In reference to the part taken by Judge Wilkinson. It is proven beyond contradiction, by Mr. Pearson, a gentleman of undoubted veracity, that the Judge, at his solicitation, was in the act of leaving the room, as the affray commenced; when, witnessing the attack upon Murdaugh, he stopped, refusing to leave until he saw the result of the controversy, in which his friend was engaged. Standing in the corner of the room, he did not at first take part in the conflict; perceiving, doubtless, that Murdaugh was making good his own defense. Presently, however, he cast his eyes around and saw his brother trodden under foot, entirely powerless, and apparently either dead or in immediate danger from the fierce blows of Rothwell, who, as you have heard, was a man of tremendous physical power, and armed with a bludgeon, some say, a sword cane. Then it was he thought it necessary to act; and advancing through the crowd to the spot, he wounded the assailant, who was crushing out his brother's life. Gen. Chambers swears positively that Rothwell was beating, with a stick, and with great severity, someone whom the other witnesses identify as the Doctor, at the time he was stabbed near the dining room door. This produced a slight diversion in the Doctor's favor, who availed himself of it, by retreating, in a stooping posture, towards the passage door. Rothwell, however, pursued and beat him down, but was arrested in his violence by another blow from Judge Wilkinson, which, together with the puncture in his throat, received in all probability from a chance thrust of the sword cane in the hands of one of his own party, disabled him and caused his death. About this time Holmes was completing Rothwell's unfinished work, and the Doctor, hunted entirely around the room, fell, utterly exhausted, at the feet of his relentless pursuers. It is wonderful that he had strength enough to escape with Murdaugh and the Judge.

Such, briefly, were the parts enacted by these defendants, respectively, in this unfortunate affray—the result of which, none regret more than themselves. Considering the proof of the conspiracy, and the knowledge, or even the reasonable apprehension on the part of the defendants, of its existence, as affording them ample justification for their participation in the matter, I have not thought it necessary to go into a minute analysis of the evidence on this branch of the subject, nor to attempt to reconcile those slight discrepancies which will always occur in the testimony of the most veracious witnesses, in giving an account of a transaction viewed from different positions and at different periods of time.

The law of self-defense has always had, and ought to have, a more liberal construction in this country than in England. Men claim more of personal independence here; of course they have more to defend. They claim more freedom and license in their actions towards each other, consquently there is greater reason for apprehending personal attack from an enemy. In this country men retain in their own hands a larger portion of their personal rights than in any other; and one will be authorized to presume an intention to exercise and enforce them, upon grounds that, in other countries, would not excite the slightest suspicion. It is the apprehension of impending harm, and not its actual existence, which constitutes the justification for defensive action. If mine enemy point at me an unloaded pistol or a wooden gun, in a manner calculated to excite in my mind apprehensions of immediate, great bodily harm, I am justifiable in taking his life, though it turn out afterwards that I was in no actual danger.

So, on the other hand, if I take the life of another without being aware of any intended violence on his part, it will constitute no excuse for me to prove that he intended an attack upon me.

The apprehension must be reasonable, and its reasonableness may depend upon a variety of circumstances—of time, place and manner, as well as of character. The same appearance of danger would authorize greater apprehension, and of course readier defensive action, at night than in the daytime. An attack upon one in his own house would indicate greater violence and excuse stronger opposing action, than an attack in the street.

Indications of violence from an individual of known desperate and dangerous character will justify defensive and preventive action, which would be inexcusable toward a notorious coward. A stranger may reasonably indulge from the appearance or threats of a mob, apprehensions that would be unpardonable in a citizen surrounded by his friends and neighbors.

Bearing these observations in mind, let us look at the situation of the defendants. They were attacked at their hotel, which, for the time being, was their house. They were strangers, and a fierce mob had gathered around them, indicating, both by word and deed, the most violent intentions. They were three small, weak men, without friends—for even the proprietor of the house, who should have protected them, had become alarmed and left them to their fate. Their enemies were, comparatively, giants—dangerous in appearance and desperate in action. Was there not ample ground for the most fearful apprehensions?

But the District Attorney says they are not entitled to the benefit of the law of self-defense, because they came down to supper, and thus placed themselves, voluntarily, within reach of the danger. According to his view of the case, they should have remained in their chamber, in a state of siege, without the right to sally forth even for provisions, while the enemy, cutting off their supplies, would doubtless, soon have starved them into surrender. But it seems there was a private entrance to the supper table, and they should have skulked in through that. No one but a craven coward, unworthy of the privileges of a man, would have followed such a course. The ordinary entrance to supper was through the barroom. They had a right to pass this way. No law forbade it. Every principle of independence and self-respect prompted it. And through that barroom I would have gone, as they did, though the floor had been fresh sown with the fabled dragon's teeth and bristling with its crop of armed men.

I care not whether the assailing party had deadly weapons or not, though I will by and by show they had, and used them, too. But the true question is, whether the defendants had not good reason for believing them armed and every way prepared for a desperate conflict. I have shown already that Dr. Wilkinson and Murdaugh did not transcend the most technical principle laid down by the Commonwealth's Attorney; not even that which requires a man to run to the wall before he can be permitted to defend himself—a principle, which, in practice, is exploded in England, and never did obtain in this country at all. But, says the learned attorney, Judge Wilkinson interfered, and took part, before he was himself attacked; he had no right to anticipate the attack upon himself; he had no right to defend his friend; he had no right to protect his brother's life. Now, I differ from the worthy counsel on all these points; I think he had a right to prevent, by anticipating it, violence upon his person; he had a right to defend his friend, and it was his sacred duty to defend his brother's life. Judge Wilkinson was the most obnoxious of the party; his friends were already overpowered; he could not expect to escape; and in a moment the whole force of the bandit gang would have been turned upon him.

The principles of self-defense, which pervade all animated nature, and act toward life the same part that is performed by the external mechanism of the eye toward the delicate sense of vision, affording it, on the approach of danger, at the same time, warning and protection, do not require that action shall be withheld till it can be of no avail. When the rattlesnake gives warnings of his fatal purpose, the wary traveler waits not for the poisonous blow, but plants upon his head his armed heel, and crushes out, at once, "his venom and his strength." When the hunter hears the rustling in the jungle, and beholds the large green eyes of the spotted tiger glaring upon him, he waits not for the deadly spring, but sends at once through the brain of his crouching enemy the swift and leaden death.

If war were declared against your country by an insulting foe, would you wait till your sleeping cities were wakened by the terrible music of the bursting bomb? till your green fields were trampled by the hoofs of the invader and made red with the blood of your brethren? No! you would send forth fleets and armies—you would unloose upon the broad ocean your keen falcons—and the thunder of your guns would arouse stern echoes along the hostile coast. Yet this would be but national defense, and authorized by the same great principle of self-protection, which implies no less to individuals than to nations.

But Judge Wilkinson had no right to interfere in defense of his brother; so says the Commonwealth's Attorney. Go, gentlemen, and ask your mothers and sisters whether that be law. I refer you to no musty tombs, but to the living volumes of nature. What! a man not permitted to defend his brother against conspirators? against assassins who are crushing out the very life of their bruised and powerless victim? Why! he who would shape his conduct by such a principle does not deserve to have a brother or a friend. To fight for self is but the result of an honest instinct, which we have in common with the brutes. To defend those who are dear to us, is the highest exercise of the principle of self-defense. It nourishes all the noblest social qualities, and constitutes the germ of patriotism itself.

Why is the step of the Kentuckian free as that of the bounding deer; firm, manly and confident as that of the McGregor when his foot was on the heather of his native hills, and his eye on the peak of Ben Lomond? It is because he feels independent and proud; independent in the knowledge of his rights, and proud in the generous consciousness of ability and courage to defend them, not only in his own person, but in the persons of those who are dear to him.

It was not the blood that would desert a brother or a friend which swelled the hearts of your fathers in the "olden time," when, in defense of those they loved, they sought the red savage through all the fastnesses of his native forest. It was not such blood that was poured out, free as a gushing torrent upon the dark banks of the melancholy Raisin, when all Kentucky mourned her warrior sires. They were as bold and true as ever fought beneath a plume. The Roncesvalles pass, when fell before the opposing lance the harnessed chivalry of Spain, looked not upon a braver or a better band.

Kentucky has no law which percludes a man from defending himself, his brother, or his friend. Better for Judge Wilkinson had he never been born, than that he should have failed in his duty on this occasion. Had he acted otherwise than he did, he would have been ruined in his own estimation, and blasted in the opinion of the world. And young Murdaugh, too; he has a mother, who is looking even now from her window, anxiously watching for her son's return—but better, both for her and him, that he should have been borne a bloody corpse to her arms, than that he should have carried to her, unavenged the degrading marks of the accursed whip.

But there was danger, as well as degradation. Their lives were in imminent hazard. Look at the cuts in Murdaugh's hat and upon his head, the stab received by the Judge, and the wounds inflicted upon the Doctor. Besides the overwhelming superiority in number and strength, the conspirators had very greatly the advantage in weapons. We have proven the exhibition and use, by them, of knives, dirks, a sword-cane and a pistol, without counting the bludgeons, which, in the hands of such men, are weapons little less deadly than the others.

Need I dwell longer on this point? Need I say that the defendants are no murderers? that they acted in self-defense, and took life from necessity, not from malice?

But there is a murderer—and strange to say, his name appears upon the indictment, not as a criminal, but as a prosecutor. His garments are wet with the blood of those upon whose deaths you hold this solemn inquest. Yonder he sits, allaying for a moment the hunger of that fierce vulture, conscience, by casting before it the food of pretended regret, and false, but apparent eagerness for justice. He hopes to appease the manes of his slaughtered victims—victims to his falsehood and treachery—by sacrificing upon their graves a hectacomb of innocent men. By base misrepresentations of the conduct of the defendants, he induced his imprudent friends to attempt a vindication of his pretended wrongs, by violence and bloodshed. His clansmen gathered at his call, and followed him for vengeance; but when the fight began, and the keen weapons clashed in the sharp conflict—where was this wordy warrior? Aye, "Where was Roderick then?" No "blast upon his bugle horn" encouraged his companions as they were laying down their lives in his quarrel; no gleam of his dagger indicated a desire to avenge their fall—with treacherous cowardice he left them to their fate, and all his vaunted courage ended in ignominious flight. Sad and gloomy is the path that lies before him. You will in a few monents dash, untasted, from his lips the sweet cup of revenge; to quaff whose intoxicating contents he has paid a price that would have purchased the goblet of the Egyptian queen. I behold gathering around him, thick and fast, dark and corroding cares. That face, which looks so ruddy, and even now is flushed with shame and conscious guilt, will from this day grow pale, until the craven blood shall refuse to visit his haggard cheek. In his broken and distorted sleep, his dreams will be more fearful than those of the "false, perjured Clarence"; and around his waking pillow, in the deep hour of night, will flit the ghost of Rothwell and Meeks, shrieking their curses in his shrinking ear. Upon his head rests not only all the blood shed in this unfortunate strife, but also the soul-killing crime of perjury; for, surely as he lives, did the words of craft and falsehood fall from his lips, ere they were hardly loosened from the Holy volume. But I dismiss him, and do consign him to the furies—trusting, in all charity, that the terrible punishment he must suffer from the scorpion-lash of a guilty conscience will be considered in his last account.

Johnson and Oldham, too, are murderers at heart. But I shall make to them no appeal. There is no cord in their bosoms which can render back music to the touch of feeling. They have both perjured themselves. The former cut up the truth as coolly as if he had been carving meat in his own stall. The latter, on the contrary, was no longer the bold and hot-blooded knight, but the shrinking, pale-faced witness. Cowering beneath your stern and indignant gaze, mark you not how "his coward lip did from its color fly," and how his quailing eye sought from floor to rafter protection from each honest glance?

It seems to me that the finger of Providence is visible in the protection of the defendants. Had this affair occurred at Mr. Redding's coffee house, instead of at the Galt House, nothing could have saved them. Their lives would have been sworn away, without remorse, by Redding and his gang. All that saved them from sacrifice was the accidental presence of gentlemen, whose testimony can not be doubted, and who have given an honest and true account of the transaction.

Gentlemen of the jury, I shall detain you no longer. It was, in fact, a matter of supererogation for me to address you at all, after the lucid and powerful exposition of the case which has been given by my respected friend, Colonel Robertson. It was doubly so, when it is considered that I am to be succeeded by a gentleman (Mr. Rowan), who, better, perhaps, than any other man living, can give you, in his profound learning and experience, a just interpretation of the laws of your State; and in his own person a noble illustration of that proud and generous character which is a part of the birthright of a Kentuckian.

It is true, I had hoped, when the evidence was closed, that the Commonwealth's Attorney might have found it in accordance with his duty and his feelings to have entered at once, a *nolle prosequi.* Could the genius of "Old Kentucky" have spoken, such would have been her mandate. Blushing with shame at the inhospitable conduct of a portion of her sons she would have hastened to make reparation. Gentlemen, let her sentiments be spoken by you. Let your verdict take character from the noble State which you in part represent. Without leaving your box, announce to the world that here the defence of one's own person is no crime, and the protection of a brother's life is the subect of approbation, rather than of punishment.

Gentlemen of the jury, I return you my most profound and sincere thanks for the kindness with which you have listened to me, a stranger, pleading the cause of strangers. Your generous and indulgent treatment I shall ever remember with the most grateful emotions. In full confidence that you, by your sense of humanity and justice, will supply the many defects in my feeble advocacy, I now resign into your hands the fate of my clients. As you shall do unto them, so under like circumstances may it be done unto you.

SPEECH OF HON. BENJAMIN HARDIN.

I little expected when I engaged in this cause in Louisville last winter, that I should ever have to address *you* on the subject. Although I have been fifty years practicing at the Kentucky bar, this is the first time I have ever had to address a jury in this place, and I can not help feeling that I am as much a stranger here as any gentleman who has addressed you. I shall, however, in speaking to you, apply myself to an exposition of the facts and of the law bearing upon them, and whatever may be your feelings, you will, I am sure, keep in mind that you are bound to exercise your reason, and that you owe a duty of no ordinary responsibility to yourselves, your characters, and your country. That duty is a sacred trust reposed in you which you can not weigh lightly without injury to yourselves as well as wrong to others. Nor must you surrender up your reason to your passions and allow yourselves to be carried away by the shouts of applause from a fashionable audience, as if you were in a theater where a Junius Brutus Booth and a Miss Ellen Tree exhibited the practiced arts of controlling the feeling, and successfully eliciting the noisy plaudits of excitement. This is not a theater—this trail is not a farce—nor are you seated on those benches for amusement. This, gentlemen, is a solemn court of justice—a solemn tribunal in which your Judge, presiding with becoming dignity, represents, the majesty of the law, and in which you are expected to deliberate with becoming gravity upon circumstances of awful import. The appalling death of two fellow-creatures is the occasion of your being here assembled, and the guilt or innocence of those at whose hands they fell, is the object of your solemn investigation.

Even though I knew I should have to address a jury of strangers, and an assemblage to whom I am personally unknown, I little anticipated that I should have to make a speech to any other audience than that usually to be found in our halls of justice. But my friend Colonel Robertson, whose youth and warmth in that way, urge him to precedence, has taken me by surprise, and placed before me a gallery of beauty and fashion, which might well deprive me of my presence of mind, if I were not fortified with less of the ardor of youth in my veins than himself, and were I not less practiced in those graces of person and manners which he can so successfully play off to woo and win their fascinating smiles.

By law, and in conformity with the original institutions upon which all law is founded, this trial was to have taken place where the occasion of it occurred—in the county of Jefferson. The Legislature, in its wisdom, has thought fit to change the venue from Jefferson to Mercer county; but why, I am unable to say. For, even Colonel Robertson, the very able counsel for the defense, has admitted that, although for a time great excitment existed in Louisville, yet, after the investigation at the examining court, that excitment was altogether allayed. In this country experience has always taught us that when a change of venue is sought, the object is not to obtain justice, but to evade it. The object is to thwart and embarrass the prosecution, and multiply the chances of eluding the responsibility of the law. How is this effected? Is it not by removal to some place esteemed favorable to the accused, by removal so distant from the scene of action, that the expense and inconvenience render it probable but few of the witnesses can attend; by removal to where witnesses of character dubious, if not infamous were known, may find credit because they are known? Here we are some seventy or eighty miles from the stage on which this tragedy was acted, yet we are asked why we did not bring the stick and cowhide, and Bill Holmes the pilot, as if we would be afraid to produce them were they within our reach. I would ask the opposite side, in my turn, why gentlemen have brought us eighty miles from the scene where we could have elicited the truth in every particular?

I listened yesterday with great pleasure to Colonel Robertson, whose speech was very good, and evinced as much of the fire of youth as the flowers of rhetoric; but I can not say it was much calculated to convince the understanding that the "worse can be made to appear the better cause." I also listened with great pleasure to Mr. Prentiss, who addressed you yesterday, and in part to-day, and I must say that, although there were in his speech some things which I could not approve, and many deductions which I could not admit, yet, on the whole, it was an oratorical effort which I could not help admiring. I am even disposed to go farther, and say that I am utterly astonished that such forensic powers, and so ably wielded, did not prove less abortive—but I must attribute the feebleness of the effect, more to the weakness of the cause, than to the want of genius in the advocate. However, Mr. Prentiss really astonished me with one proposition he laid down with respect to the common law of this country, that every man is to judge for himself where the point of danger lies, that entitles him to disable another, or to kill him, lest he might, in turn, by possibility, become the killed; so that, in fact, if it were so, the point of danger never could be defined by law, because what brave man would consider no danger at all, a timid man would consider the point of danger bristling with a thousand deaths. Was there ever such a monstrous doctrine recognized by the laws of any community!

Mr. Prentiss. I only urged that what might be considered by a man, from apparent circumstances, the point of danger, where resistance was necessary for his own preservation, would in the law be grounds for justifiable homicide.

Mr. Hardin. I will come to that in due time. The dilemma can not be removed, that the same point, according to this doctrine, is, and is not, the point for the resistance contemplated by the law. No, gentlemen; the law recognizes no such absurdities. The law was laid down yesterday correctly by the District Attorney, that when the killing of a man has taken place, it is a murder in the eyes of the law, and must be pronounced by the law to be a murder, till the contrary is shown. What then becomes of this new doctrine, unknown to the law, that the slayer and not the law, is to judge and presume the justification? The law itself says, all killing of one man by another is murder. The slayer, according to Mr. Prentiss, says, "Oh, no, I killed my man because I fancied he would kill me—it is not murder, it is justifiable homicide!" Yet, the law again says, if a Sheriff, who hangs a man by lawful authority and in doing so commits only a justifiable homicide, should, even for the best of motives, instead of hanging the man, as bound to do, chop his head off with a sword, though death must necessarily follow either way, yet is he guilty of murder and liable to the punishment, for the killing contrary to the prescribed mode of his duty.

These three gentlemen now arraigned before you, are residents of the State of Mississippi, and they came to Kentucky early in December, for what, is of no import that I can see, although it is made to cut a conspicuous figure here as a favor conferred on Kentucky—a contemplated marriage at Bardstown. They arrived at the Galt House. Where Judge Wilkinson had his clothes made up, if he had any prepared for the occasion, is not shown. Where Mr. Murdaugh had his made, if any, is not shown. But it is shown that Dr. Wilkinson was to have clothes made at Mr. Redding's. They were made with great punctuality, and the Doctor came to Redding's store at the appointed time. He tried on the new coat and seemed well pleased with it. So satisfied was he with the coat that he wore it on the spot, and left a $100 bank bill on account of payment, requesting Mr. Redding would hold over the bank bill, which was of a Mississippi bank bill, till some expected change for the better would take place in the rates of discount. Dr. Wilkinson then went away, wearing the coat, and desiring the other things to be sent to the Galt House. As I now come to where it will be necessary for me to mention the names of witnesses, I beg it to be understood that I do not mean to avail myself of the example set by the opposite side. I will not shelter myself behind my professional duty, to vilify an unfortunate witness, disarmed of his self-defense—unfortunate, because of his inability to make any reply in the same public court in which he is maligned. Younger gentlemen at the bar than I am, may indulge in the practice, and, perhaps, the rashness of youth and inexperience may excuse what wisdom and manliness could not justify. No character, however spotless—no reputation, however unstained before— can escape the sullying hand wantonly raised to tarnish it, where there is no immediate opportunity of wiping away that which corrodes while it damps the lustre.

When Dr. Wilkinson returned to Redding's store, accompanied by his brother and Mr. Murdaugh, some objection was made to the collar of the coat. It was no serious objection, we may suppose, for we hear from Mr. Prentiss himself, " the expectancy and rose of the fair State," that he, perhaps, would not have been quite so fastidious. Perhaps, some young fellow, like my friend, Colonel Robertson, " the glass of fashion, and the mould of form," might have been a little squeamish; but, for myself, every one knows I am not particular. I never should have knocked down a tailor with an iron poker because there was a shade of fashion lacking in the collar of my brother's coat. The whole thing, I admit, is a matter of taste, the poker included.

But there was, however, some objection to the fashion of the coat—and that objection was thought grave enough to enlist the triple wisdom of a dignified Judge of the land, an eminent doctor of a distant State, and a sage member of the Mississippi bar. Yes, with this formidable array of judicial wisdom, pharmaceutic skill and legal research, these three gentlemen came to a little store in Louisville, to fight a poor tailor! And all about an unfashionable twist in the collar of a coat.

To be sure they came from the Eldorado of the South, with their thousands of bales of cotton condensed into their pockets. They were perfect magnets of attraction, for the secret of their loadstone lay wrapt up in their Mississippi bank notes. Hotel keepers were bowing to them on all hands, tradesmen and storekeepers honored the pavement they trod, and as to tailors, I am ready to believe they became perfectly fascinated with them. Nay, I even make no doubt that the keepers of watering establishments and medical springs, submitted to the soft impeachment, and became devoted to their interests. It is the necessary consequence of the influence of cotton bales.

Here was this hard working tailor, ever on the watch for good customers, bowing to them as assiduously, if not more assiduously, tahn the hotel keepers, or spring doctors—taking back his coat, I have no doubt, with tears in his eyes; but is it reasonable to suppose that, fascinated as he was, by the ability of such customers to pay, he would be so blind to his own interests as to give unprovoked quarrel to such customers? However backward he may have been from prudence and circumstances, it seems there was no want of readiness to carry matters with a high hand on the part of those with whom he was dealing.

Judge Wilkinson is sitting on a stool at the stove, and when he sees his brother about to pay for the pantaloons and vest he interferes without being called upon to do so, and opposes the payment of these things, upon which the tailor very naturally asks him what business he has to interfere. The Judge, without telling him that he was the Doctor's brother, which Redding did not know, and that as such he had a right to advise him, jumps up, snatches an iron poker, with which a man could be knocked down as readily as with a crowbar, and for the small provocation of a tailor saying, "You make yourself a little too busy in the matter," ignorant that he was addressing a dignified Judge, the Judge aims a deadly blow at his head, which, if not fortunately warded off, might have involved consequences to which I must not advert. What does this prove? If it proves nothing else, does it not show plainly that Judge Wilkinson is not quite as mild and forbearing in his disposition as his friend, Mr. Prentiss, would have you to believe. Did Judge Wilkinson's conduct show that it was his belief men's passions should be subject to the control of law, if not of reason? that he was in principle a respecter of the law in this instance?

I know it will be argued that there is a wider latitude given to the restraints of law in the Southern than in the Northern States, and a false assumption is built upon this circumstance, that the free use of personal liberty to avenge private quarrels gives greater bravery to a people. But I have read, I have witnessed, and I believe that the people of New England, a section of this great republic, where you can get no man to fight duels, and where every man throws himself under the protection of law for the redress of his private wrongs, when they have been called into the field for the protection of their country, have shown the brightest examples in modern history of personal bravery and national valor. Show me where men have been more prompt to rush upon the bayonets of their country's invaders than the heroes of New England. Sir, courage and bravery belong to the respecters of the law which protects every man's rights in a civilized community. Climate, in a country of such vast extent as this, may have its influence on men, as it is known to have on the inferior race of animals. You may meet the lion, distinguished for his courage and his power, in the Barbary States, where conscious of his strength, you may pass him unmolested, if you are not the aggressor. As you descend to the more southerly latitudes, you meet the leopard and the panther, with whom treachery and ferocity are the substitutes for courage; and when you pass the equator you meet the hyena, the emblem of uncompromising cruelty, and without a redeeming quality. Men may in like manner be affected by climate; and he who on the iron-bound coast of the frozen North, or on the arid rocks of New Plymouth, would illustrate every noble virtue of his nature, not less distinguished for his piety than his patriotism, for his endurance than his courage, and for his generosity than his bravery, when transplanted to the enervating regions of the South may become different and degenerated, trusting more to his interest than his patriotism, to advantage than to courage, and to conceal weapons than to bravery.

But to resume my review of evidence. Judge Wilkinson, so remarkable for his mildness and forbearance, as a sample of these qualities, aims a blow, as I have said before, at the tailor's head, which probably would have killed him had he not warded off the blow with his arm in a manner to give great offense to Mr. Prentiss, who can not see the propriety of a tailor grappling with a Judge to prevent a repetition of blows that might break his head. The little tailor, however, did grapple with the Judge, and, dragging him to the side door, he falls with his adversary out on the pavement. The tailor, though small, being strong and active, turned the Judge under, and as he did so Murdaugh hallooed out, "Kill the damned rascal," a command which the Doctor was about to obey, and when he was within a couple of inches of plunging his dirk into the tailor's heart, Mr. Redmond caught the Doctor's arm. But for that interference it would have been the last of Redding's career. Mr. Murdaugh had hallooed out to the Doctor, "Kill the damned rascal!" and in the next breath, "Part them! Part them!" This is easily accounted for. When he saw that Redding, by Redmond's interference, had gained the advantage, he perceived that the tables were turned, and fearful of the consequences became as impatient to have them parted as he had before been anxious to have the tailor killed. Well, they are parted; and when they get up, Dr. Wilkinson still has his knife drawn; Mr. Murdaugh has his knife drawn, and the Judge has his favorite weapon the poker. The little tailor's courage, notwithstanding this formidable array, is up, and he steps forth, a David before Goliath, and offers to fight the whole three of them if they will lay aside their weapons. This, I think, however, was a mere *brag* with the *poker-players,* for I do not believe he could have done it. Five witnesses swear that both Dr. Wilkinson and Mr. Murdaugh had out their knives. Several concur that Dr. Wilkinson re-entered the store with his knife drawn, demanding his $100 bank bill. All agree that he got it, and many agree that when he and his companions left for the Galt House, two went away exhibiting their knives, and one rejoicing in the poker. The knives, to be sure, have been identified as *white-handled knives.* Mr. Prentiss, in that able speech which you have all heard and admired, and which, it must be admitted, like a West India tornado, swept through this house carrying everything before it, even to the reason of many who heard it, seemed to think that we had some particular fancy for the handles of the knives, because they were white handles. He thought we dwelt uncommonly on the whiteness of the handles, till like spectres they were continually flitting before our visions. With all this poetical or forensic coloring we have nothing to do; we only identified them, and the gentleman has failed to contradict us by proving that they were black, green or red.

We have now, gentlemen, traced a small portion of this affair at the tailor's shop. In what occurred there immediately after what has been mentioned, we find the following facts established: Mr. Redding swears that he was advised to enforce the law against these gentlemen. The principal officer of police, the city marshal, is usually to be found about the Mayor's office or jail, from the peculiar nature of his duties. Mr. Redding proves that he and Johnson went toward the Mayor's office and looked for the marshal at Hyman's and Vacaro's coffee houses. Not finding him there, they went on to the Mayor's office. They applied at the Mayor's office to Mr. Pollard, clerk of the City Court, and told him that one of the gentlemen was named Wilkinson, and that the names of the others they did not know. They were told by Mr. Pollard that they should have the names; or, if they wished, they might have a blank warrant to be filled up with the names when ascertained. This Redding declined upon being told that if he could meet the marshal he could arrest the parties without a warrant. Redding and Johnson proceeded to the jail in search of the marshal. Not finding him there, Redding returns by Market street, at the corner of which he met Rothwell, near his residence. As he tells Rothwell, his brother-in-law, the nature of the affair, Rothwell goes along with him. And here I must remark, that to come down to Market street from the jail is the shortest way, though my friend, Colonel Robertson, thinks that a man may go around by Jefferson street a few hundred yards out of his road by way of a short cut. But Redding being but a plain man not given to sophisticated deductions, believes the nearest road is the shortest cut and took the shortest cut by Market street, where he met Rothwell, as I have said, and told him what had occurred. He did not ask his brother-in-law to go with him, but his brother-in-law did think proper to accompany him. There was no Bill Holmes—no Marshall Halbert—no Billy Johnson—no one but Rothwell accompanying Redding. Mr. Graham swears that there was no one with Redding but Rothwell, when he met them near the Galt House. Where was this terrible array of giants and Patagonians of which we have heard so much? Why, nowhere to be sure; the gentlemen have only drawn largely on their imagination. As Sheridan once said of Dundas, they are indebted to their imaginations for their facts, though I will not go so far as to say of my sprightly friend Colonel Robertson, or my brilliant friend Mr. Prentiss, that either is indebted to his memory for his wit.

Jackson swears, indeed, that he heard propositions made of going to the Galt House to give the Mississippians a beating; yet Graham swears Jackson would always lie a little. This Jackson, whom we have shown to be unworthy of credit, swears to that being a fact which is contradicted by Redding, by Johnson, and by Craig, whose credibility is unimpeached and unimpeachable. But it seems Mr. Prentiss takes peculiar exceptions to Bill Johnson, because he uses strange figures of speech and low and outlandish tropes and metaphors. Well, the gentleman ought not to blame poor Johnson for imitating his betters in the arts and graces of oratory. I suppose he has been reading the newspapers in which the reported speeches of the most eminent members of Congress are recorded, and he finds one distinguished gentleman charges a party with being like a greasy packs of cards, all spotted and marked and shuffled together. Another young aspirant compares the Secretary of the Treasury, a dignitary old enough to be his father, to a she-bear, running through cane-breaks and dropping her cubs at every step; and yet Johnson is blamed for his figures, if he ever used them, of "hides full of shucks," and "skinning of sheep." I thought Mr. Prentiss, who so lately returned from Congress, would have admired Bill Johnson for being so apt a scholar, like that classic personage, Zip Coon, in picking up the new and approved styles of tropes and metaphors now so fashionable in the places which he himself has made resound with the aptness of his illustrations.

Gentlemen, I had got to this place in the affair at the Galt House, where Redding and Rothwell were seen unaccompanied by any one entering that hotel. Mr. Redding says when he went into the barroom he looked over the register and called for the names. Scarcely had he got them when Judge Wilkinson entered and stepped up to the counter to take a drink of water. Redding addressed him thus: "Sir, I believe you are the gentleman who struck me with the poker in my own house, this evening." If Judge Wilkinson was sorry for his imprudence, why did he not then say it was in a hasty moment and upon reflection, he felt that he was wrong? Could Redding have resisted the ingenuousness of such an answer to his inquiry? Could he have harbored for a moment longer any irritation for an acknowledged injury? But what did Judge Wilkinson say or do? Why, he heaped insult upon injury by an aristocratic allusion to the tailor's profession. "I will not," he replied, "fight or quarrel *with a man of your profession!*" Now, although I agree with Mr. Prentiss that there is nothing disgraceful in a profession, and I think the poet has expressed himself with scarcely less felicity than Mr. Prentiss on the subject:

> **"Honor and shame from no conditions rise;**
> **Act well your part, there all the honor lies."**

And as Burns says,

> **" The heart's ai the part, ai**
> **That's right or wrang; "**

yet, we can not help imbibing with our literature, and our sentiments many trifling prejudices from the mother country where aristocratic pretensions have too successfully attached disgraceful notions to certain pursuits of industry, and among these, the profession most sneered at by the would-be wits of the last century, is that of a tailor. And although a man of that profession here may justly feel that he is as respectable, and follows as respectable a calling as any other man, yet when he thinks those old sneers are leveled at him as an insult, he naturally resents it with the indignation of an honest and industrious and free citizen, not bound by a servility unknown to us, to succumb to him who dares to utter it.

There is, I fear, a principle growing up amongst us inimical to our republican institutions—a principle of classification favorable to aristocratic distinctions. We have our bankers, lawyers, and doctors, arrogating one rank in our society; the statesmen, heads of departments and officials, another. Our mechanics and those who toil by the sweat of their brow to produce our riches, are cast into the shade; and knowing, as they do, that such an attempt, however noiselessly it is made, still exists palpably, is it any wonder they should be sensitive to every whisper that is breathed to mark the invidious distinctions? An apparent unimportant word may wound deeper than rough language. Call a man a knave, and he may forget it; but call him a fool, and he never forgives you. Call a young lady a coquette, and she may pardon you; but tell her she is ugly, and she will never abide you the longest day she lives. Tell a tailor he is a botch, and he may not even get angry with you; but sneer at him about his *goose* and his *profession,* and you insult him, though the words in themselves are harmless. It is the allusion to prejudices that have existed which carries the poison of insult in its barb. Sir, we must not disguise the fact that there is a line of demarkation drawn by the proud and arrogant between themselves and those who live by the sweat of their brow; between the comparatively idle, who live but to consume, and the industrious, who work but to produce, between the drones of the hive and the laboring bees. And to which, pray, is the country in its strength, prosperity and wealth, indebted for its teeming productiveness? To which for her energy, enterprise, protection, genuine patriotism and celerity in national or municipal times of danger? Go to Louisville when a portion of the city is enveloped in flames, and you will see a thousand mechanics rushing into the devouring element for the protection of property, while the lawyer and the Judge, and the haughty aristocrat walk about as spectators with their hands in their pockets. The mechanics compose the moving power and the labor-working machine upon whose industry we all feed and fatten. Their labors are the wealth of the country, and when we cease to honor and cherish them, we poison the springs of our own invigorating prosperity, and cut off the sources of our own enjoyments. Do we treat them with gratitude when we taunt them with epithets, which they esteem derogatory or insulting? Are we to treat them thus in the halycon days of peace, and when the thunder cloud of war gathers around our course, with a monstrous pusillanimity, fling ourselves into their arms as our only hope and rescue? Has not the history of our country shown, and will it not show again, that when the storm of invasion ravages our coasts, our safety is to be found alone in the strong sinew and ready arm of our laboring population? Where, then, are your bowie-knife-and-pistol gentry, your duelists and your despisers of the man who lives by the sweat of his brow? Sir, they will be found cowering and lurking where they may snuff the battle afar off, and hide their once lofty heads in ignoble safety. But I will not consume your time with recitals which may be found in every page of our history. I shall return to the evidence in the case before you.

Mr. Everett is told by Mr. Sneed that there is likely to be some difficulty. Mr. Everett goes into the bar and by some indications to the Judge, meets him in the passage and takes him to his room where they find Dr. Wilkinson and Mr. Murdaugh. Judge Wilkinson relates to them what has happened. The Judge having made this relation, asks Everett to provide him with pistols. Why? For what did he want them? Was any one attacking them there or likely to do it? They were safe in their room. They could only want pistols for the purpose of descending and making the attack themselves. But Everett is asked to provide pistols. He said he would try, and with that avowed purpose, left them. He had not been gone fifteen minutes, in the opinion of some—in the opinion of others scarcely ten, when Judge Wilkinson, with this lower-country toothpick (taking up the bowie knife), not trusting this time to the more merciful weapon with which he had been practicing, the tailor's poker; with this lower-country toothpick he started down prepared to use it. Did he know Rothwell? Did he know any but Redding? No man had accosted him but Redding. Why, then, did he come down with this terrible implement of murder? Why, sir, just exactly for this reason, that he had been mortified at the result of what happened at Redding's store. The Judge of the land had been turned over by a tailor. He had been bearded and abused by a tailor, and he provided himself with his bowie knife and went down to have another deal with that tailor.

Mr. Prentiss seems to think the Judge had a right to go down to his supper. Why, so he had; but he had a right to wait for the bell to ring. He had no right to eat his supper before it was served up—no right to take his bowie knife down to the kitchen and terrify the cooks to allow him to devour the supper while it was cooking. And had the supper been ready, there were table knives wherewith to carve his meat, and he had no right to carve it with a bowie knife. But the supper was hardly cooking when he went down. The bell had to be rung over the private passage upstairs before it was rung below, and when rung below the folding doors had to be thrown open. But the bell had rung nowhere and Judge Wilkinson, Dr. Wilkinson and Mr Murdaugh came down before any bells were rung; therefore it was not to supper they had come down. Which table had Judge Wilkinson been in the habit of going to? the large table or the ladies' table? There is no proof that he and his companions boarded at the large table; and it is known that many gentlemen as familiar with the house as they had been, prefer the private or ladies' table. We have every reason to believe that was the table at which they boarded. The entrance to the room where that table is kept is not through the barroom. One entrance to the large dining room, is, indeed, through the waiting room, and there is a bar in that waiting room, at which many gentlemen who are not pleaders, become suitors, make motions, and put in their pleas. I sometimes make my appearance at that bar, but I am not summoned by the attachment of the bottles. I go to hear the politics of the day—for, although I have long since quit the field, I can not be cured of the curiosity to know what wrangling is going on among the little juntas in every village as well as among the mighty ones of Congress.

When these three gentlemen got into the barroom, Mr. Redding was at the counter; Mr. McGrath was inside of it; Mr. Reaugh was at the fire. Some say Mr. Redding came in immediately after the Judge. You must expect that out of twenty witnesses no two will agree in all the facts; but in a transaction like this, where several fights were going on—

where in every corner a man was bleeding, or dying or suffering—that no two men could see everything or anything alike, is to be expected. But, gentlemen, by collecting all the evidence together, contrasting, comparing, and justifying one by another, we can arrive at the facts of the case clearly and beyond the probability of doubt. We can arrive at them with as much certainty as we can at any other set of facts. And from this manner of collating the facts, I am enabled to present them to you without fear of contradiction.

One of these facts is that Judge Wilkinson walked across the barroom, some twenty-five feet, when he came in. Mr. Trabue, a man whose evidence is to be depended upon, seems assured that when Judge Wilkinson came in, he walked three or four times across the room, and then stood awhile with his eye fixed upon Mr. Redding, his foot advanced, and his right hand behind in his coat pocket, and, I make no doubt, with his hand grasping the handle of this very bowie knife. At that moment Mr. Murdaugh went up to Redding. I will not say, with one of their own witnesses, that in going up to him, he rattled like a viper; but as he went up he addressed Redding, saying, "I understand that you say I drew a bowie knife on you in your shop this evening? If you say so you are a damned rascal, or liar!" And as he said so, he opened his knife and elevated it, as one said, or held it down, according to another. Yes, he accosted Redding in the most insulting terms and threw open his knife at the same time. Is there any witness who has said Redding accosted *him* in an angry manner? One person said of the knife—"Lord, how it gleamed in the candlelight!"

The most warlike nation the world ever saw, was Sparta. When the Spartans prepared for battle, they polished their arms to glisten in the sun. They washed their clothes clean, combed their long black hair, and sang the song of battle.

I have no doubt Mr. Murdaugh, if in the ranks, would have done the same. I make no doubt he would be the last to run. I make no doubt he would have been amongst the foremost to make his gleaming blade glisten in the sun. The highest evidence of a man's dexterity and intent to use his weapons, is the high polish he gives them, and the high state of preservation in which he keeps them for use. Of Murdaugh's dexterity in the use of his knife in the work of death, we have unfortunately too much proof; of his disposition to use it, we have the evidence of the high order in which he kept it for use, even to that state of Spartan polish, which made it gleam in the candlelight, as the sword of the Spartan would glisten in the sun.

We are told Meeks was determined for a fight; yet Oliver, whose friendship for these gentlemen seems of the most ardent and disinterested kind, gives up to Meeks his knife, after having so easily obtained possession of it on the small pretense of picking his nails. He had been invited by Oliver to drink at a "saloon" opposite the Galt House. They dignify these establishments now-a-days by the high-sounding title of "saloons"; but when you enter one of them you find it the vilest groggery in the world. These dignified groggeries exist to a shameful extent in Louisville, and why? Because the politicians of Louisville are too busy with their unimportant bickerings, or too truckling to put them down. They are the strongholds of the voting interests of Louisville; and the truckling politicians, who are ready to sacrifice every principle for the triumph of party, court the coffee house keepers, and bend in supplication for their election to the inmates of the groggeries. Even the municipal government is either influenced by paltry mercenary motives in its avidity for the revenue of licenses, or it has not the nerve or public spirit to grapple with the monster. Talk of our constitution being the greatest, the purest, and the most efficient on the face of the earth!

Yet, here is an evidence of its working in a duplicate government. The most destructive of vices, because the parent of most, is licensed, encouraged, fostered, pandered to, by politicians, and through their truckling by the very local government itself, as if the misery and debasement of the community were more the end and aim of their rule than the encouragement of virtue, industry, sobriety and rational enjoyment.

We learn that Meeks was unknown to many; a slender, small, and weakly man, with a bit of cowhide, the lash of which some one says was knotted. From what we learn of this cowhide, I verily believe it would take at least five hundred knocks of it to kill a man—and I doubt if he could be well killed, after all, even with five hundred knocks of it. Meeks, unfortunately for himself, stepped up to Murdaugh, and said, " Yes, you are the d—d little rascal who did it." In reply to this, the very first lunge Murdaugh made at him severed a vital artery and caused his instant death. I am not physician, and know not technically what effect the cutting of that artery may have; but I believe it to be as deadly as if the brains were blown out, or the heart pierced. A man stabbed through the heart no longer lives or breathes, but he may stand a minute. Meeks fell, and in attempting to resume his feet, as he leaned on a chair, pitched forward upon his face, and when examined, he was dead.

When did Rothwell strike Murdaugh? Not till Meeks was killed. Then, it is proven, Rothwell struck with a cane, and Murdaugh was beaten back, and at that instant the tide of battle rolled on to the right corner as you face the fire, and then Rothwell was seen losing his grip of the cane in his right hand, and he was seen endeavoring to resume his grasp of it. General Chambers thinks it was Dr. Wilkinson whom Rothwell was beating at in the right-hand corner, but every one else says it was Murdaugh, and it is of course evident the General is mistaken. Every one of the witnesses swears that Rothwell was engaged with Murdaugh in the right-hand corner, while Holmes was engaged with Dr. Wilkinson in the left-hand corner. Let us now consider the wounds received by Rothwell. Dr. McDowell says the puncture in Rothwell's chest might be made with this knife carried by Murdaugh. The skin by its elasticity might yield without having an orifice as large as the blade, afterward apparent.

Who gave Rothwell that wound? Why, Murdaugh, and nobody else. This accounts for Rothwell losing the grip of his stick or cane. The moment this knife penetrated his chest on the right side, that moment his arm became paralyzed, and he could not hold his cane. He caught at it, but he did not use it after. Just then, Judge Wilkinson came up behind with his bowie knife in his hand, and General Chambers says he saw him make a lunge at Rothwell and stab him in the back. If two men are engaged in a fight, one with a dirk knife like this, and the other with a stick, in the name of God let another with such a bowie knife as this stand off; but if he must interfere on behalf of him who has the deadly weapon, and against him who has not a deadly weapon, let him do the work of death, front to front—let him stab in the breast and not in the back. But, to come up behind and to stab *him* in the back, who is already overmatched by his opponent in point of weapons, evinces a disposition which I shall not trust myself to dwell upon or to portray. Ossian, speaking of Cairbar's treachery, says:

> **"Cairbar shrinks before Oscar's sword! he creeps in darkness behind a stone—he lifts the spear in secret—he pierces my Oscar's side!"**

By this time Dr. Wilkinson was down in the left-hand corner and Holmes over him. The fact is, Holmes was the only man that knocked the Doctor up against Trabue, though Halbert boasted of having done it. It was only a boast in Halbert, for I believe he goes over his foughten-fields more at the fireside than on the battle-ground. In the language of Dryden, speaking of Alexander:

"The King grew vain;
Fought all his battles o'er again,
And thrice he routed all his foes, and thrice he slew the slain."

March 16.

Gentlemen of the jury, I would endeavor to resume the few remarks on the evidence which I offered yesterday, as near the precise place where I left off as possible, if I did not know that in the present case such particularity is not so requisite as in the case cited by John Randolph, who once told a man that was so precise that he could, if interrupted and called off in the middle of his dinner by the sound of a horn, on resuming his seat some hours after upon resounding the horn, take up his dinner exactly at the identical bite where he had left off. I am not quite so particular, and shall probably recapitulate some of the evidence I have already gone over.

Yesterday evening I endeavored to give you the law and the facts of the case as nearly as possible, as far as I went. I shall now repeat that you are not to take as facts all that may be sworn in a cause. Although witnesses may be men of undoubted integrity and veracity, yet all they state are not facts. They are fallible beings, and likely to misconceive and misinterpret facts without any intention of doing so. We are to ascertain the facts from the mass of evidence, and judge of each witness's competency by contrasting his evidence with that of others, and when it agrees with all or the majority of witnesses, we may safely infer he is right. I endeavored yesterday to examine the facts that occurred at the tailor's shop, for the purpose of showing the ill blood fomented in these gentlemen's hearts against Redding. I then showed that they acted in concert, and provided themselves with what weapons they could, not being able to get all they wanted; and how, upon a small occasion, they were prepared to use these weapons. Indeed, there seems to be no witness as to what occurred when Judge Wilkinson remained in consultation with his companions in his bedroom.

If Judge Wilkinson, Dr. Wilkinson and Mr. Murdaugh were known to be frequenters of the bar before meal times, why has it not been proven by one of their witnesses? That not being proven, I have a right to assume that it could not be done, because it was not the fact.

Next I have to ask, why these gentlemen came into the barroom provided with arms? Could it be with any other design than to run Redding out of the room? Were they going into a room where they commonly resorted? It is evident they were not. Did they go there on their way to supper. It is evident they did not, for supper was not near being ready.

What disposition for eating supper merely, does it show in Judge Wilkinson to pace the room three or four times and then fix the eye of destruction on Redding while his purpose kindles and he grasps his bowie knife behind in his pocket? What more eagerness for supper does Murdaugh exhibit in going straight up to Redding, rattling like a viper and insulting him with being a liar? Sir, I care not if a man go into any crowd and before an angry word is used to him, he goes up to as meek a man as Job himself, and says to him, "You are a damned liar or rascal," and flings open his blade to inflict mortal injury, as his words indicate, if the person so accosted strike his insulter, it is not surely any great wonder. And yet Redding did not strike a blow. Mr. Murdaugh may say, "I kept within what I thought was the safe side of the law—I approached with my drawn knife—insulted the person to draw on the attack from him, that I might have some excuse for using my knife in the manner in which I came to use it at any rate.'' If any man come up and call you a damned liar, or rascal, and spring open his knife in the attitude of striking, should you strike or slay such an assailant, would you not be excusable? But Col. Robertson attributes to an act of this kind nothing but a manifestation of innocence and high spirit. The Colonel is really a gallant man, and judges of others by the fire and chivalry raging in his own breast. You must not laugh, gentlemen, for if you could look upon the volcanic mountain, though you would see its head capped with snow, you would find its bosom like *his,* rumbling with fire, smoke, and brimstone. In former times, the highest honor known to a Roman soldier was to have saved a man in battle, but here it is argued that if a young aspirant to fame pinks and kills his man, he is to be sent home to his parents in honor, crowned with the chaplets of victory. Nay, it is believed, if Bonaparte in his youthful prime, in his Italian campaigns, had had Murdaugh by his side he would have confided to his ready and unerring arm the *execution* of many a hardy adventure. Col. Robertson may say what he pleases, but I say it was Murdaugh commenced the assault, and that all fighting done by him was in the wrong. All fighting done on his account was in the wrong, because he had commenced in the wrong.

Well, gentlemen, as I remarked to you yesterday, when I stopped, for I am now returned once more to that point, Murdaugh had given the first provocation, had killed his man, had stabbed another to the death, when Judge Wilkinson stepped up and gave Rothwell a stab in the back, while engaged with and probably receiving the stab in his chest from Murdaugh. Yes, gentlemen, a third man comes up and lunges this beautiful little weapon into Rothwell's side, and starts back! Sir, if men are engaged with deadly weapons, part them if you can; but do not come up behind them and lunge a bowie knife into the vitals of one, and then come into a public court and demand of a jury not only to acquit you but to do it with shouts of, "Glory, glory, go, go!" And yet, gentlemen, this is the polite invitation given to you by Mr. Prentiss, to acquit such a man with acclamation. When engaged with a man who has only a cane no bigger than his thumb, his opponent gives that man a deadly stab in the chest which paralyzes his arm—a third person, Judge Wilkinson for instance, comes up *behind* and stabs the paralyzed man *in the back*, it is, no doubt, high time for you to be called upon to mark your approval of the deed by shouts of acclamation. Mr. Prentiss by way of winning your favor with complimentary allusions, thinks Kentucky should no longer be called the "bloody ground," because the river Raisin has carried off the palm in feasts of human butchery. But I think the Mississippi gentlemen, of Vicksburg, have bidden fair of late to obtain for that part of Louisiana opposite their city, the palm of being the "dark and bloody ground." I suppose in the far-famed Menifee duel with rifles, if some one had stepped up and lunged a bowie knife into the vitals of one of the combatants, the shouts of acclamation that would have arisen in that quarter of the world would have resounded to the uttermost ends of the earth.

Dr. Wilkinson, by this time, became engaged with Holmes. Holmes is a stout and large man; but his size has been greatly exaggerated. Like the Patagonians, the first discoverers thought them ten feet in height; the next voyagers only eight, and the next but six. I recollect reading of Captain Smith, that when he first explored the interior of this country, on his return he represented the inhabitants as all Goliaths, six cubits and a span in height. Yet, subsequently, more matter-of-fact men found they were only miserable and cowering Indians of ordinary dimensions. In this manner appearances are magnified.

We are asked why Holmes is not here? We echo to the

other side, "Why Holmes is not here?" Our answer is, because he was not to be had, being a pilot down the river and not within the control of the State's Attorney or any process issuing from him.

Sir, among other appeals made to you for acquitting them, you are told, as a set-off, that there is no State in the Union on which you are more dependent than that of Mississippi. They take their cotton South and receive either through shipping agents, or drafts direct, their money for it from the merchants of Great Britain. True, Kentucky gets some of these dollars from the Mississippians for what they think better than their money, or produce, or they would not buy it. We, in the rounds of trade, pay these dollars, or what represents them, to the Liverpool merchants for merchandise that we think better than the money. The Liverpool merchants in the next turn of the wheel, pay the same dollars back to the Mississippians for their raw cotton, and the Mississippians are nothing loth to take our produce again for the same dollars. And after several twists of this kind, when we get them back and recognize one of them as an old acquaintance, we may say, "How do you do, friend dollar, I am very glad to see the face of an old acquaintance; step into my pocket and warm yourself; I always give shelter to a traveling friend." We are proverbially a hospitable people, and never refuse a night's lodging to a dollar, or its liberty to travel further next day upon leaving us an equivalent for what we lent it. But to be serious, are we not all dependent on each? I know this, and can not admit that we owe more to Mississippi than Mississippi owes to Kentucky; and why there should in this case be made any parade about our indebtedness to that State, not founded in reality, is for you, gentlemen, to weigh.

To resume the facts of this case; what does Judge Wilkinson do? He stabs Holmes in the arm; but he is not indicted for that. He stabs Rothwell when he is engaged with Murdaugh in the right-hand corner; and again, when in the left-hand corner, standing over Holmes, and trying to get him off his own brother. Rothwell had been disabled by two stabs.—Judge Wilkinson, standing at the dining room door, when Rothwell was saying nothing, except in mercy trying to persuade Holmes to spare Doctor Wilkinson, comes across the room to the opposite door, finds Rothwell's back turned to him, and then makes the last, the second thrust of his bowie knife into his victim's back. Robert Pope says, I saw Rothwell's back to Judge Wilkinson, when the Judge stabbed him—up to the very handle. I ask you, gentlemen, I speak to you not in language other than the broad and naked truth—is there any witness denies this? Every one who knows Robert Pope, knows that he would not state what de did not know to be the fact. We know that each and all of these wounds contributed to Rothwell's death. The last stab is given by Judge Wilkinson to Rothwell; Doctor Wilkinson and Murdaugh retreat out into the passage, and fight their way to the foot of the stairs. I care not what was done there, it was done after the offence previously committed. Suppose Oldham had shot one of them, and not missed as he did; suppose Murdaugh had been knocked down; and suppose Judge Wilkinson received blows in the passage, does it lighten the offence previously committed? I care not what took place, when a man has killed another. When making his escape, I care not not how many guns are fired at him, how many rocks thrown, because it alters not his previous offence.

If there is any evidence that anyone in the barroom laid a hand on Judge Wilkinson, who has proved it? Is it not plain, that any bruises or injuries he did receive, were received in the passage.

Mr. Prentiss said he was willing to stack arms with the Kentuckians. What arms had they? They had a cowhide whip! We hear of a cane, which he thinks may be conjured into a sword cane. Mr. Holmes, indeed, had his fists, but he could not stack them.

We are told that Oldham had arms by a witness who viewed the scene from the outside of a window, like one of the venerable birds perched on a dry limb eyeing the slaughter with a prospective instinct—one of those remarkable birds, renowned alike for their gravity and great stillness. We have heard a good deal said, and well said, if true, about Oldham. That he was unsteady—that he cast his eye to his counsel for relief. Yet we really saw nothing in his conduct to warrant his being called perjurer, scoundrel, coward and rascal; and here I must remark that this very talented young gentleman, Mr. Prentiss, in using such epithets to a witness without even a shadow of justness in the application, warranted me in saying that though I admired some passages in his speech, yet others I should feel bound to denounce as unworthy alike of his profession and of his character.

No man in this State can boast a prouder ancestry than that very Oldham, whom it has been attempted to brand as odious and infamous. They have been among the earliest settlers and most esteemed of our citizens—trusted with command in our army, and venerated on the judicial bench. And has a man sprung from such honored stock no pride in upholding his name—no feeling to rouse his indignation when epithets, as gross as they are groundless, are poured out to tarnish his reputation for the paltry purpose of influencing a jury to discredit his testimony, and to warp their judgments from the straightforward path of truth and justice?

What proof has Mr. Prentiss to sustain the course he has taken? Sir, there is not a shade of proof. The gentleman is indebted to the fertility of his fancy, and his best friends must regret that he has not, in this instance, cultivated that productive soil for some more praiseworthy object than an ignoble and disgraceful crop of baneful, destructive and loathsome weeds. Does the gentleman think he is one of the angels appointed to pour out the vials of wrath? Has he not indulged in pouring out gratuitously his vials of wrath on Mr. Redding, who could not escape? Redding is stigmatized as a murderer, to be haunted by the ghosts of the slain at his nightly couch. Yet what was his offense? He raised his arm to ward off the blow of an iron poker aimed at him by Judge Wilkinson. He had profaned a Judge's person on this trifling provocation by seizing him, dragging him to the door, and turning him under! "Oh! you scoundrel," would Mr. Prentiss exclaim, "why did you do that?" He had retorted upon Judge Wilkinson when taunted by him about his profession; and, worse than all, he did not, when the killing was going on, stay in some convenient place to be killed. "Why did you not, you coward, rascal, murderer, perjurer, and so forth, *turn your back* to be stabbed *with safety?* Why did you not stand up with your face to the breeze when the sirocco swept along, carrying death on its pinions? Why did you fall on your face, and let the pestilential blast pass over you? Why did you not breath till it was gone You, and your friends, have offended us by your want of submission, and now you aggravate your offense by coming here to testify against us."

Really, it is astonishing they are yet alive! But it will be more astonishing, perhaps, when it is told that they will return to Louisville, and there stand, in point of reputation, just as they stood before these slanders were concocted, digested, and spewed upon them. It will turn out that they are yet unpolluted and unscathed. The same protecting Providence which carried the Israelites through the Red Sea will protect even these persecuted and wronged few.

Gentlemen, I have endeavored to trace facts as far as I

have gone, with minuteness, and having presented these facts to you, it is for you to determine whether they do not establish these conclusions. When the fight occurred in the barroom, it was brought on by these gentlemen intentionally: if they brought it on, did they fight in their own defence, or because they had drawn the conflict on themselves: could Meeks have inflicted death with a cowhide, or Rothwell with a walking stick, so as to render the killing of them necessary or justifiable according to the true spirit of the law?

But here there is a proposition of law advanced by Mr. Prentiss, which I must combat. He says the law recognises that the point of resistance unto death, begins where a man himself believes the point of danger ought to be fixed. Then we have no law at all—we may burn up our law books—this revokes all that they contain on the subject of homicide. There are two men engaged in a quarrel; one as brave as Caesar—the other as timid as a hare; one kills the other, when the quarrel arrived at a certain point. The brave man, if he were a Marshal Ney in courage, is to be hanged, because he had no fear of his life when he killed his adversary. If the timid man is the survivor, he is to be acquitted with acclamation, because of his cowardice, which made him imagine danger where there was none.—Thus cowardice and rashness are to be rewarded and cherished and bravery and forbearance punished with an ignominious death. Is it possible, you, an intelligent jury, can be imposed upon by such sophistry? Is there so low an estimate of your understandings as to suppose it?

I knew what I should have to combat the moment I saw the hack driving into town with a head peeping out of the window, which head I knew belonged to the shoulders of a certain gentleman from Mississippi. When I was in Vicksburg, I asked a gentleman how it was that Mr. Prentiss defended so successfully so many notorious murderers, who really merited the gallows? "Oh," said he, "he has hit upon a principle which he calls law, that charms every jury to which it is addressed." I asked the gentleman to repeat the magic words to me. He did so. It was the very principle I have been combating. It is possible that as the gentleman afflicted with the chronic principle, which he belches up with so much advantage to himself and relief to others, is now in the neighborhood of Medical Springs, esteemed so potent by Mississippians, he may resuscitate by a few drinks of the charming water, a sophism which I have shown to be no longer tenable by any one who values what is healthy and sound, above that which is merely delusive. Sir, the principle of self-defense does not warrant a man in killing under the name of self-defense, if he is himself in fault by being the aggressor.

Is the principle of self-defense among nations to be carried into effect as justly applicable to the right of self-defense among individuals? In national controversy, the law of nations, an imaginary code of mutual convenience, is referred to, according to the custom of the country, but in a conflict between individuals, there is a defined law, which must be the redresser. A nation with right and justice on her side, may be conquered by another nation in the wrong, and can not sue for or obtain redress from the wrongdoer; but an individual, in a community, may be wronged by another, and can obtain redress, because he has the law common to both, and a superior power to appeal to. Therefore, there can be no dependent analogy between the laws of nations, and the laws of individual communities. There was some crude idea thrown out yesterday that the laws of Great Britain ought not to be enforced here. We are not to be told at this day that we have any other common law than that derived from the common law of England. The very principles of our statutory laws are dictated by the genius of English common and statutory law, with the exception of such local differences as require local application of principles. If the gentleman could take from us the right to apply the law of England where it would be in point for us, we could by reciprocity, deprive them of any they might most rely upon.

I shall now advert to the perculiar necessity enforced upon us of becoming a law-abiding people, if we preserve any regard for our present form of government and constitution. In empires, monarchies, and kingly governments, armies are formed to keep the people in order; but in a republic, what could preserve the social compact, but the law? The moment you dissolve or dispense with the law, that moment you dissolve all national constitution. Every government, and most especially a republican government, is bound to protect each citizen in his property, reputation and life. How can a republican government do it, but by and through the law rigidly and justly administered? Whenever you dispense with the law, you allow men to arm themselves, and to become their own avengers, independent of, and above all law. When they are not permitted to do so, but to return home as innocent men, what is the effect? Every man will arm himself, and like the turbulent and licensed armed mobs at the fall of the Roman Republic, brutal violance will reign instead of law; all government will be dissolved, and anarchy and confusion will pave the way to usurpation and tyranny. You must venerate the law, if you would not see such a state of things. If you do not, A and B will arm themselves, like the Turk, up to the throat, and kill whom they please out of mere wantonness and sport.

If you go into the Northern States, it is a rare thing if you can find a man in ten thousand with a deadly weapon on his person. Go into other States that shall be nameless, and you will hear of them as often as of corn-shuckings in an Indian Summer. Go further South—to Arkansas or Mississippi, for instance, and though you would be a peaceable man, shuddering at the name of a " toothpick " in the North, in these States you may arm yourself to the teeth, and track your steps in blood with impunity. Why is this, but from the relaxation of the laws that are elsewhere enforced and obeyed.

I was down the river lately, and it was pointed out to me where the *Black Hawk* had blown up and killed her scores; to another place where the *General Brown* had blown up and killed her hundreds; to one spot on the shore where two gentlemen blew each other's brains out with rifles; to another, where the widow somebody's overseer was butchered; to another, where the keeper of a wood yard was shot for asking pay for his wood; to another, where an aged gentleman had his guts ripped out for protecting his slave from cruel treatment. " Great God! " cried I at last, " take me back to where there is more law though less money "—for I could not stand the horrid recital any longer—when every jutting point or retiring bend bore the landmark of assassination, and irresponsible murder.

Why does the law call for punishment? Surely it is not in vengeance for the past, but to deter others from the too frequent and free use of deadly weapons, whether in Kentucky, Louisiana, Mississippi or Arkansas. Is it to be left to the vitiated taste of the brutal few to give tone to the mind of a comunity in setting up the code of the bowie knife against the common law? It was but the other day that in the Legislature of Arkansas, a member on the floor was a little disorderly, and the speaker, to keep quietness, stepped down, brandishing his bowie knife, to silence the ardor of the unruly member, which he did, effectually; for, of all the ways in the world of putting down a young and aspiring politician, whose tongue will keep wagging in spite of his teeth, your bowie knife is, I admit, the most effectual. And the speaker, on this occasion, bent upon having silence, silenced the offender, not only then, but for all time to come. To be sure, he went through the form of a court of inquiry, but a life is only a small matter there, and he was acquitted according to the laws of that State.

Coming events cast their shadows before, and here we have one symptom of that downfall of our glorious Republic, which has been so often predicted, but which has been reserved for the present generation to consummate. The symptom is to be found in the flash of those deadly weapons carried about and used with such unerring fatality by our legislative sages and judicial dignitaries. As if the next should come from high places, too, we have a fatal symptom of our downfall furnished by the corruption of those in office, who share in or connive at the grossest defalcation—the widest system of public plunder, even in our monetary defalcations, ever known in any government.

Why should we deceive ourselves with the vain hope that our Republic will boast greater permanency than that of Rome, when we are fast falling into the very track, step by step which leads to the precipice over which she plunged headlong. That once magnificent mistress of the world marched up the hill of fame and glory with irresistible strides, till she reached the summit and looked around upon the hundred nations in her rule. But, at last, satiated with prosperity, she began to repose supinely upon her laurels, and she permitted herself gradually to relax that discipline and good order, which had been to her not only her shield and buckler, but her bond of union. The people were permitted to fight in twos and threes at first with impunity. They became accustomed to it, and then fought without interruption in gangs; by and by, mobs fought with mobs; and finally the whole people became arrayed against each other in regular armies, till they had to retire to the plains of Pharsalia, where the doom of the greatest republic the world has ever known was sealed forever.

Are we not relaxing the laws—which leads to anarchy, and from personal violence to popular usurpation? Are we not relaxing our financial vigilance,—which leads to corruption at the fountain head, and from private peculation to public defalcation? Is there no sympton in all this great crisis? I tell you again and again, when you can lay your hands on great delinquents, make *them* an example; when you can grasp great defaulters, punish them; then will you more easily check pernicious discords, and restore to its proper tension and tone the harmonizing power of your laws and your government. Whenever you see men wearing bowie knife and daggers—hunt them down as you would bears and their cubs, from whom you can expect nothing but injury. The whole State of Kentucky looks to you this day for justice, for this is an awful investigation concerning the loss of two of her citizens. Two of our fellow-citizens have been murdered, and these gentlemen are here to answer for it. Some of the best blood of the country has been spilled as if in the pen of slaughtered hogs; but because the relatives of one of these butchered men employ counsel to aid the prosecution in developing the truth and guarding against the delusions of sophistry from the greatest array of talent the country can boast, or that wealth unbounded can procure, to elude the punishment due to the offended laws, you are told to take but a one-sided view of the evidence, and to decide at any rate against the paid advocate. I have not asked these gentlemen what they are to be paid for eluding justice, because I did not consider that a sort of evidence which ought to influence your verdict.

Gentlemen, one question is, are we to tolerate this bowie knife system under the false pretense of self-defense? I say, let your verdict act like the ax laid to the root of the tree, and many a prayer will bless you for your timely check of its growth. Many a woman is made a mourning widow, many a child made a pitiable orphan, and many a father childless by the use of this accursed weapon. You have it in your power to prevent the recurrence of such scenes.

We have had an exhibition here in miniature of those Roman scenes which prepared the public mind for the downfall of that great people. There was a vast amphitheater where the Roman people could be crowded together, and in the presence of some hundred thousand persons of both sexes, a man would be brought into the arena, and a ferocious tiger turned in upon him. He might, or he might not, possess skill or courage to meet the formidable beast and evade the deadly spring; but if not so fortunate, when the tearing of his vitals was seen, and the craunching of his bones heard, the solitary shriek of the victim's wife, as it arose upon the air, would instantly be drowned by the acclamations and thunder of applause bestowed upon the ferocious beast, prolonged by its renewed efforts to suck the blood, tear the flesh, and grind the bones of its prey. As *we* have no amphitheater, a hall of justice is made to answer for a miniature arena; and as we can not have tigers, nor men who will submit to be their victims, we have forensic gladiators, and witnesses whose private feelings and characters may be wounded, lacerated, and tortured to the infinite delight and encouraging shouts and plaudits of a fashionable auditory, while the victim is helpless and gloomy in his unmerited prostration. Yes, it is all for the amusement of enlightened minds, and it is intended, perhaps, for the edification of the rising generation. But, I protest, I can not yet perceive that it is any more for the honor of the applauders, than it is necessary for the good of the country, that these gentlemen should be honored and glorified for their dexterity in the use of the bowie knife and dirk. In the time of public danger, or foreign invasion, is it these bowie knife gentry, these pistol men in private life, that mount the breach and face the danger? Are they the brother Jonathans that face John Bull and eye him and his scarlet coats with defiance? Where are they then? Why, like the gnats and mosquitoes, who glisten in the sunshine and the calm, but when the storm rages, and the thunder growls, and the lightning flashes, and the earth is rocked to its center, they are stowed away from the danger; though they are sure to emerge from their hiding place to annoy with their stings when the succeeding calm and sunshine invite them out once more. Brave men may be voluptuous and effeminate in private life, but in the hour of danger, they put on a new nature. But these fighters in time of peace, clothe themselves in the skin of the lamb in time of war. Sardanapalus, who sat all the while with his women and eunuchs in times of peace, spinning and knitting, and telling long stories no doubt, and sometimes wearing petticoats to make himself more effeminate, when conspired against by Belesis and Arsaces, gave up his voluptuousness, and at the head of his army gained three renowned battles; and though beaten and besieged at last in the city of Ninus, to disappoint his enemies, burned himself his eunuchs and his concubines, with his palace and all his treasures. Alexander the Great, who was kind, courteous, familiar, and confiding with his officers in private life, when leading the Macedonians, moved to battle like a pillar of fire, irresistible in his might. When the great Frederick led on his brave Prussians, they fought and fell and fought and fell, as long as any were left. And thus men imbibe the spirit of their chief. If led by a brave man, they are brave; but if led by a coward, they are poltroons, and if led by the bowie-knife-and-pistol gentry, I make no doubt they would be either assassins, or nothing better than mosquitoes, to be dispersed by the very first report of the cannon. Even at home, in our own rural districts, we see the influence of leading men on whole neighborhoods. Let a virtuous and enlightened man, whom all will look up to as a pattern, settle in your neighborhood, and every one will partake of his good influence. Why was it that Nelson in his death, did more for the glory of his country than ever he did in his life? Because he ascended to heaven in the arms of victory, like Elijah, who tasted not of death. Let us never dream of selecting for our leaders or our examples, those who have so little moral courage as to trust to bowie knives and pistols for the preservation of their manhood, instead of to their blameless conduct in peace and bravery in war.

Gentlemen, I beg of you in the name of Him who sits upon the cloud and rides upon the storm, mete out the measure of justice to these men, and vindicate the honor of Mercer county. But do not stigmatise your country by doing, as Mr. Prentiss would have you to do, by shouting "Glory! glory! go, ye righteous; go to your homes, in honor and in innocence." Whatever you may do, I shall content myself with the conviction that in my professional capacity, I, at least, have done my duty. I have been deputed by the widowed mother of the murdered Rothwell, and at the instance of his mourning sisters, to implore your justice. I have closed my mission. Between you and your country —between you and your God, I leave their cause.

The Trial of Matt F. Ward.

On the second day of November, 1853, William H. G. Butler, principal of the Louisville High School, and brother of Noble Butler the school book writer and educator, was shot and killed by Matt F. Ward, son of Robert J. Ward, Sr., who was at that time regarded as the wealthiest man in Kentucky.

The prominence of the two men who were engaged in the difficulty, the circumstances under which the killing occurred, and the prominence, in the legal profession, of the many lawyers who were employed to prosecute or defend, made it one of the celebrated trials in the history of the Commonwealth.

On account of the great excitement which prevailed in the city of Louisville, as a result of the tragedy, a change of venue was granted to the defendant, and the case was tried in the Hardin Circuit Court at the April term, 1854.

Alfred Allen, of Breckenridge county, was the Prosecuting Attorney for the district and he was assisted in the prosecution by R. B. Carpenter, of Covington; Sylvester Harris, of Elizabethtown, and T. W. Gibson, of Louisville.

There were eighteen lawyers employed to defend, the most prominent of whom were Hon. John J. Crittenden, of Frankfort; Gov. John L. Helm, of Hardin county; Hon. Thomas F. Marshall, of Woodford county; Hon. George A. Caldwell, Nat Wolfe and T. W. Riley, of Louisville; C. G. Wintersmith, J. W. Hays and R. B. Hays, of Elizabethtown.

The indictment charged, in the first count, that M. F. Ward and R. J. Ward, Jr., shot with malice aforethought, W. H. G. Butler, in the city of Louisville, on the second day of November, 1853, and which shooting caused his death on the third day of the said month. The second count charged Matt F. Ward with the shooting and R. J. Ward, Jr., with being accessory. The defendants were committed to the Hardin county jail without bail. On Tuesday, April 18, 1854, at half past eight o'clock in the morning the defendants were taken from the jail and conducted to the court house, attended by their relations who were deeply affected, some of whom were weeping audibly.

The defendant Matt F. Ward was suffering from the effects of rheumatism and he walked with a crutch.

Gov. Helm moved the court to grant the defendants a separate trial, which motion was sustained and the Commonwealth's Attorney thereupon elected to try Matt F. Ward first. Only a few of the men who had been summoned for jury service had made up their minds, consequently the jury was easily empaneled.

After the jury had been selected and sworn the Judge addressed them as follows: "Gentlemen: the defendant Matt F. Ward has been arraigned and has entered the plea of not guilty, throwing himself upon God and his country for trial. You are to try him according to your oaths, upon the indictment. If you find him guilty, you will say so and no more. If you find him not guilty, you will say so and no more. In case the killing shall be proved to have been done under the influence of passion, you can find the defendant guilty of manslaughter and will say so; should it be proved that the act was done in self-defense, it is not an act of voluntary homicide and you will find him not guilty."

The shooting occurred about ten o'clock in the morning at the High School building in the city of Louisville, in the presence of the whole school; twelve of the High School boys were introduced as witnesses for the prosecution; the facts which were testified to by them were in substance as follows:

On the day prior to the shooting, William Ward, the

youngest brother of Matt F. Ward, and who was a pupil in the High School, had some chestnuts during the class recitation and he and a classmate by the name of Al Fisher had a controversy about them. Prof. Butler spoke to them about the disturbance and told them not to make so much noise. Notwithstanding the reproof, William continued to talk to Fisher about the trouble. Prof. Butler spoke to them again and after the class was through he asked Al Fisher what they were talking about. Fisher told him it was in reference to some chestnuts and he admitted that he had eaten some during school hours when he knew that it was against the rules; and thereupon Prof. Butler gave him five or six licks on the legs with a leather strap. Fisher then told him that William Ward had also eaten some chestnuts, at the same time, but when William was asked about it he denied it. Several of the boys said that they saw him eating the nuts and the teacher then told William that he had evidently told a lie, and that he would have to be whipped for it, and he then gave him about the same number of licks with the strap that he had given Al Fisher.

Shortly after the whipping William Ward left the schoolroom and said that he was going to tell Matt and that Matt would give Butler hell. The next morning about half past nine o'clock a negro of Mr. R. J. Ward, Sr., called at the school building and left word for the books of the Ward's to be sent home. About ten o'clock Matt F. Ward, Robert J. Ward, Jr., and William Ward came into the schoolroom together, William took a seat and the other two remained standing. Matt inquired for Mr. Butler and when he came in, Matt said to him: "I have a little matter to settle with you; which is the most to blame, the little contemptible puppy who begged chestnuts and then lied about it, or the boy who let him have them." Mr. Butler requested Ward to go in to the private room and stated that he would explain the affair to him. Mr. Ward said, " No; here is the place to answer the question." Mr. Butler refused to answer without making an explanation. Mr. Ward then said, " Why did you call my brother William a liar ? " Mr. Butler said that he was not disposed to answer the question without an explanation. Mr. Ward said, " You are a d—d liar and a d—d scoundrel." Ward then made a motion as if to strike him. Butler moved back a short distance and then raised his right arm and moved towards Ward, and Ward thereupon drew his hand from his pocket, presented a pistol to Butler's breast and fired. Butler dropped immediately to the floor and exclaimed: " Oh, my wife and child! My God! I'm dead! " Matt then drew another pistol and Robert J. Ward, Jr., drew a knife. Mr. Sturgus, the assistant teacher, came out of his recitation room and Robert said, " Come on, I am ready for you." Mr. Sturgus retreated to his room and jumped out of a window. During the controversy between them, Mr. Ward spoke loud and Mr. Butler low. After the shooting, all the Wards left the schoolroom and the students carried Mr. Butler into Col. Harney's residence and sent for a doctor. Several doctors attended him, all of whom testified in the case.

Dr. D. D. Thompson said: " I saw Butler about twenty minutes after ten; I removed his coat, tore open his shirt and found the wound an inch and one-half above the left nipple; the surface all around was burnt. I asked what position he was in when he was shot. He said, ' Matt Ward called me a liar and struck me, I struck back and was immediately shot, I did not know who shot me.' Soon after this conversation I heard the air splurge through the wound. Butler asked what it was and I told him; he said he was a dead man."

The post-mortem examination disclosed the fact that the ball passed between the third and fourth rib, through the left lobe of the lungs and passed into the backbone and lodged there. The ball caused his death. He was a small man; he weighed about 135 or 140 pounds. His fingers on his right hand had been injured, they were about half closed and could not be straightened.

J. J. Gilmore testified that he was a gunsmith, his store was on Third street between Main and Market. "On the second of November, Matt F. Ward came to my store about nine o'clock in the morning and asked to look at a pistol. He examined one and asked the price. He said that if I would load it he would take it; I loaded it and handed it to him. He then asked me the price of the pair; I told him. He hesitated a moment and then said if I load the other, he would take them both. I did so and he paid for them and went away. He asked for self-cocking pistols. I loaded them both with powder and ball and put caps on them. They were good pistols, they would send a ball through an inch board two feet away. The bore was two hundred to the pound. I loaded them with buckshot; they were of the smallest bore I had."

The Commonwealth introduced twenty-one witnesses, a great many questions were asked without any apparent object in view and many statements were made which would not be competent under modern rules of criminal evidence.

The defense introduced over seventy witnesses, the most of whom were in reference to character. Among them was a cabinet officer, two members of Congress and a score of other men of great distinction, one of whom was George D. Prentice, who was a personal friend and a great admirer of Matt F. Ward.

The plea of the defendant was self-defense. He was physically weak and in feeble health, he was troubled with rheumatism and ordinarily walked with a crutch, he was thoroughly educated, being a graduate of Cambridge, his writings had attracted the notice of the literary world; his book styled the " Letters From Three Continents " was of more than ordinary merit, a copy of which was exhibited at the trial and several times referred to and quoted from, during the arguments to the jury.

It is doubtful if any man ever proved a better reputation for peace and good order. It was proved that he was, " mild," " amiable," " peaceable," " gentle," " kind," " tender," " affectionate," " universally respected," " well disposed," " quiet," " retired," " unexceptionably good," " courteous, generous, high-toned, beloved, pleasant, good tempered, lovely, a favorite, affable," " by his publications he was widely known as a literary character," " gentle as a woman," " never knew a more gentle and kind," " he was so to a fault," etc. Mrs. Robert J. Ward, mother of the defendant, testified about conversations had with the defendant; almost the entire part of her evidence was hearsay; very little of what she said would be admissable under the present rules of criminal evidence. Mrs. Ward created considerable excitement by fainting. She was carried from the court room.

The statement of Robert J. Ward, Jr., gave the theory upon which the defense was based. He said: " I arrived in Louisville, on the morning of this occurrence, we reached home about nine o'clock a. m." After telling a number of things which happened at his home, he said: " I was going to mother's room when I saw mother and Matt standing in the front door. Matt told me to get my hat; I got it and started; at the gate, Matt said he was going to ask an apology of Mr. Butler for whipping William. William said ' Butler is a stouter man than you, and Sturgus has a big stick.' Matt said he apprehended no difficulty, that Butler was a gentleman. He asked me not to interfere unless Butler and Sturgus both attacked him at once. We conversed on different subjects as we went along; we met

Lucy Stone in bloomer costume and he spoke of that. On entering the schoolroom Matt asked for Butler and in a short time he came in. Matt remarked, ' I wish to have a talk with you.' Butler said, ' Come into my private room.' Matt said, ' No, here is the place.' Mr. Butler nodded. Matt said, ' What are your ideas of justice? Which is the worst, the boy who begs chestnuts, and throws the shells on the floor and lies about it, or my brother who gave them to him? ' Mr. Butler said he would not be interrogated, putting his pencil in his pocket and buttoning up his coat. Matt repeated the question. Butler said, ' There is no such boy here.' Matt said, ' That settles that matter; you called my brother a liar and for that I must have an apology.' Butler said he had no apology to make. ' Is your mind made up? ' said Matt. Butler said it was; then said Matt, ' You must hear my opinion of you; you are a d—d scoundrel and coward.' Butler then struck Matt twice and pushed him back against the door; Matt drew his pistol and fired; Butler held his hand on him for a moment. As the pistol fired, Sturgus came into the room; I drew my knife and told him to stand back. We all three, Matt, William and myself went out to the gate; William said—

Mr. Carpenter, attorney for prosecution, said, " Stop Sir, stop."

The witness appeared as if he was going on and Mr. Carpenter repeated, "Stop."

Mr. Marshall said to witness, " Keep cool, don't be offended at the manner of the counsel, we will attend to that."

Mr. Carpenter: " Well, we will."

Mr. Marshall: " Yes! we will."

Mr. Carpenter: " Certainly, we will."

Mr. Marshall: " Damned if we don't."

The witness continued: " Matt was pushed back to a

glass partition in the door.'' On cross-examination the witness said, that he drew his knife when Sturgus came. "I did not go up the aisle in the schoolroom, I made no gestures towards the boys with the knife. As we entered the school house Matt's hands were by his side; after entering he held his hat in his left hand gesticulating with his right; we did not shut the door as we went in; Butler's manner was rather stiff, not as cordial as usual. Butler might have struck more than twice. Matt did not put his hand in his pocket till Butler seized him. I have carried weapons since I was fourteen years old; sometimes pistols; sometimes a knife.''

After all of the evidence had been introduced on both sides, the court did not instruct the jury in reference to the law governing the case, as the presiding Judge is required to do under the present law. The law was left for the lawyers, who argue the case, to read and comment upon and construe or misconstrue in a way to suit his side of the case.

The first argument was made for the prosecution by R. B. Carpenter. He read extensively from law books and his argument dealt more particularly with the legal phase of the case. Hon. Thomas F. Marshall, of Woodford county, made the first argument for the defense. He made what would be termed at the present day, a scattering speech, it was not worthy the name of argument. He gave only a few citations of law, he did not confine himself to either the law or the facts in the case.

The sixth and seventh day of the trial were used by Sylvester Harris and T. W. Gibson for the prosecution and Nat Wolf and Gov. John L. Helm for the defense. Mr. Gibson made the best argument which was made for the prosecution but he weakened it very materially by stating that he did not contend or believe that Ward went to the school building with the design of killing Butler. He weakened his argument further by stating that the defendant was a "damned villain and his act a damnable crime."

Hon. John J. Crittenden closed the case for the defense. His argument dealt almost exclusively with the facts in the case. They were so marshalled and so well presented, that the slightest occurrence, even Lucy Stone in her bloomer dress, was used with telling effect for the benefit of the defendant. He freely admitted the excellent character of the deceased and deplored the ill-fated circumstances that led to his death; at the same time he denied that there was any malice or wickedness on the part of the defendant which could make it a crime.

After an exhaustive speech to the jury, Mr. Crittenden concludes:

"In examining these facts, may not one judge of them more kindly, and hence ascribe better motives than another? The consideration of the facts and the causes that produced them, is the proper place for mercy to be applied. The law says the murderer shall be punished; but it is your province to ascertain what constitutes the murderer.

"You have a solemn duty to perform, and I want you to perform it. I want you to perform it like men—like honest men. I ask your sober judgment on the case, but it is right for that judgment to be tempered with mercy. It is according to the principles of law, one of whose maxims tells you 'it were better for one hundred guilty men to escape than for an innocent one to be punished.' Is not here your commission for mercy? It is alike your honest minds and your warm hearts that constitute you the glorious tribunal you are—that make this jury of peers one of the noblest institutions of our country and our age. But the gentlemen would make you a set of legal logicians—calculators, who are to come to your conclusion by the same steps a shop-keeper takes to ascertain the quantity of coffee he has sold by the pound. That may be a jury in name, but it is in nothing else.

"But I wish to call your attention to another fact that figures in this case. Mr. Carpenter, with more adroitness than Mr. Gibson, but with less scrupulousness, has attempted to create a prejudice against this prisoner, by speaking of his family as aristocratic—as believing themselves better than ordinary mortals. I suppose I feel no personal offense at this, for I have always belonged to that class usually called 'poor men.' But, in this country, no man can be above a freemen, and we are truthfully told that 'poor and content is rich enough.' * * *

"In conclusion, gentlemen, I beg leave to call your attention to an important consideration, bearing on the whole case, and affording a key, I think, to the heart of this young man. I allude to his general character and disposition through life. I need not recall your attention to what we have shown it; it is all perfect in your recollection. I have no occasion to exaggerate; he has shown, in the clearest and most conclusive manner, a character of which you or I, or any man living, might be proud. As in boyhood, so in manhood. His riper years only exhibited to the world the amiable and lovely and genial traits of the boy, more illustriously developed in the man.

"I am one of those who believe in blood, and in consistency of character. Show me a man that for twenty or thirty years has been kind and honest and faithful in all the relations of life, and it will require a great deal of evidence to induce me to believe him guilty in any instance of a gross and outragous wrong. You have seen the character of this man, from his earliest boyhood—so kind, so gentle, so amiable—ever the same, at school and at college, in the city or in the country, among friends or strangers, at home or in foreign lands. There was no affected superiority. You see how many mechanics and artisans have been his constant associates and friends. With health impaired, and with literary habits—never seen in drinking saloons or gaming houses—his associations with men of all classes—he has ever been the same mild, frank and unoffending gentleman, respecting the rights of others and only maintaining his own. This is the man you are called upon to convict. His act was an unfortunate one, but it was one he was compelled to do. And though he has been misrepresented and reviled and wronged, I trust it will be your happy privilege, by a verdict of acquittal, to vindicate his character in the eyes of all good men, and restore him to that family whose peace, happiness and honor are at stake on your verdict. Your decision must cover them with sorrow and shame, or restore them to happiness that shall send up to Heaven, on your behalf, the warmest gratitude of full and overflowing hearts.

" Gentlemen, my task is done; the decision of this case—the fate of this prisoner, is in your hands. Guilty or innocent—life or death—whether the captive shall joyfully go free, or be consigned to disgraceful and ignominious death—all depends on two words from you. Is there anything in this world more like Omnipotence, more like the power of the Eternal, than that you now possess?

" Yes, you are to decide; and as I leave the case with you, I implore you to consider it well and mercifully before you pronounce a verdict of guilty—a verdict which is to cut asunder all the tender cords that bind heart to heart, and to consign this young man, in the flower of his days and in the midst of his hopes, to shame and to death. Such a verdict must often come up in your recollections—must live forever in your minds.

" And in after days, when the wild voice of clamor that now fills the air, is hushed—when memory shall review this busy scene, should her accusing voice tell you you have dealt hardly with a brother's life—that you have sent him to death, when you have a doubt, whether it is not your duty to restore him to life. Oh, what a moment that must be—how like a cancer; will that remembrance prey upon your hearts!

" But if, on the other hand, having rendered a contrary verdict, you feel that there should have been a conviction, *that* sentiment will be easily satisfied. You will say: 'If I erred, it was on the side of mercy; thank God, I incurred no hazard by condemning a man I thought innocent!' How different the memory from that which may come in any calm moment, by day or by night, knocking at the door of your hearts, and reminding you that in a case where you were doubtful, by your verdict, you sent an innocent man to disgrace and to death.

" Oh, gentlemen, pronounce no such verdict, I beseech you, but on the most certain, clear and solid grounds. If you err, for your own sake, as well as his, keep on the side of humanity, and save him from so dishonorable a fate—preserve yourselves from so bitter a memory. It will not do then to plead to your conscience any subtle technicalties and nice logic—such cunning of the mind will never satisfy the heart of an honest man. The case must be one that speaks for itself—that requires no reasoning—that without argument appeals to the understanding and strikes conviction into the very heart. Unless it does this, you abuse yourselves—abuse your consciences, and irrevocably wrong your fellow man, by pronouncing him guilty. It is life—it is blood with which you are to deal; and beware that you peril not your own peace!

" I am no advocate, gentlemen, of any criminal licentiousness—I desire that society might be protected, that the laws of my country may be obeyed or enforced. Any other state of things I should deplore; but I have examined this case, I think, carefully and calmly; I see much to regret—much that I wish had never happened—but I see no evil intentions and motives—no wicked malignity, and, therefore, no murder—no felony.

"There is another consideration of which we should not be unmindful. We are all conscious of the infirmities of our nature—we are all subject to them. The law makes an allowance for such infirmities. The Author of our being has been pleased to fashion us out of great and mighty elements, which make us but a little lower than the angels; but he has mingled in our composition weakness and passions. Will He punish us for frailities which nature has stamped upon us, or for their necessary results? The distinction between these, and acts that proceed from a wicked and malignant heart, is founded on eternal justice; and in the words of the Psalmist, 'He knoweth our frame—He remembereth that we are dust.' Shall not the rule He has established be good enough for us to judge by?

"Gentlemen, the case is closed. Again I ask you to consider it well, before you pronounce a verdict which shall consign this prisoner to a grave of ignominy and dishonor. These are no idle words you have heard so often. This is your fellow citizen—a youth of promise—the rose of his family—the possessor of all kind and virtuous and manly qualities. It is the blood of a Kentuckian you are called upon to shed. The blood that flows in his veins has come down from those noble pioneers who laid the foundations for the greatness and glory of our State—it is the blood of a race who have never spared it, when demanded by their country's cause. It is his fate you are to decide. I excite no poor, unmanly sympathy—I appeal to no low, grovelling spirit. He is a man—you are men—and I only want that sympathy which man can give to man.

"I will not detain you longer. But you know, and it is right you should, the terrible suspense in which some of these hearts must beat, during your absence. It is proper for you to consider this, for in such a case all the feelings of the mind and heart should sit in council together. Your duty is yet to be done; perform it as you are ready to answer for it, here and hereafter. Perform it calmly and dispassionately, remembering that vengeance can give no satisfaction to any human being. But if you exercise it in this case, it will spread black midnight and despair over many aching hearts. May the God of all mercy be with you in your deliberations, assist you in the performance of your duty, and teach you to judge your fellow being as you hope to be judged hereafter.

"Counsel would have you tell the Judge of the quick and dead, when you stand at His tribunal, how manfully you performed your duty by sending your fellow man to the gallows! He apprehends that it will go a great way to insure your acquittal there and your entrance to the regions of eternal bliss, if you are able to state that you regarded no extenuating plea—took no cognizance of the passions and infirmities of our common nature—showed no mercy, but sternly pronounced his irrevocable doom. I understand that it would be more likely to send you in a contrary direction. I understand that a lack of all compassion during life will hardly be a recommendation there. I understand that your own plea will then be for mercy; none, we are taught, can find salvation without it—none can be saved on their own merits.

"I have somewhere heard or read a story from one of those transcendent German writers, which tells us that when the Almighty designed to create man, the various angels of his attributes came in their order before Him and spoke of his purpose. Truth said: 'Create him not, Father. He will deny the right—deny his obligations to Thee—and deny the sacred and inviolate truth—create him not.' Justice said: 'Create him not, Father. He will fill the world with injustice and wrong—he will desecrate Thy holy temple—do deeds of violence and blood, and in the very first generation he will wantonly slay his brother —therefore, create him not.' But gentle Mercy knelt by the throne and whispered: 'Create him, Father. I will be with him in all his wanderings—I will follow his wayward steps—and by the lessons he shall learn from the experience of his own errors, I will bring him back to Thee.' 'And thus teach, O man, mercy to thy fellow man, if thou wouldst bring him back to thee and to God.'"

* * * * * * *

At the conclusion of his argument, the large assembly of people commenced a vigorous applause, which was promptly checked by the court.

The prosecuting attorney, Mr. Alfred Allen, closed the argument for the Commonwealth. He said of Mr. Crittenden's argument that he thought one man could not in a lifetime make two such speeches as the one he had just heard.

When the arguments were closed the Judge said: "The usual practice in criminal cases in this district of reading and discussing the law before the jury by the counsel, having been adopted in this case, relieves the court of the necessity, and to some extent renders it improper to enter into a discussion of the various principles of law applicable either directly or indirectly to the facts proved in the case."

The court defined murder and manslaughter and then said: "Although you may believe from the evidence that the killing was not done maliciously, yet under the indictment in this case you may find the prisoner guilty of manslaughter—if the facts proved in the case will, in your opinion justify such a verdict."

The case was submitted to the jury about five o'clock p. m. on Wednesday and on Thursday morning about nine o'clock they returned into court a verdict of "not guilty as charged in the indictment."

The prisoner was discharged and a *nolle prosequi* entered in the case of Robert J. Ward, Jr.

The news of the verdict was received in Louisville with the greatest indignation. Every one seemed to think that a great injustice had been done to the people of the Commonwealth. A mass meeting was called. The people of Louisville were called to meet at the court house on Saturday evening, April 29, 1854, "at early gaslight." Pursuant to the call, a large assembly of people were gathered, at an early hour, in and around the court house, the number present was estimated to be from eight to ten thousand. On motion, Bland Ballard and six others were appointed to draft resolutions. These resolutions, eight in number, expressed in strong language the disapproval of the verdict; after they were read in the court house, they were taken out and read to the assembled thousands, who were not able to crowd into the court room. After this, other resolutions were moved and carried requesting the two Wards to leave the city, also inviting Nat Wolf to resign his seat in the State Senate, and follow them; and requesting John J. Crittenden to resign his seat in the United State Senate to which he had been recently elected.

After the adjournment of the regular meeting a large number of people remained in the court house yard where effigies of Matt F. Ward, the members of the Hardin county jury and a number of other persons were hung and burned; a large crowd of men and boys gathered in front of Robert J. Ward's residence and did considerable damage by throwing stones through his front door and windows and by breaking the glass in his conservatory. While this rioting was being engaged in, effigies of Matt F. and Robert J. Ward, Jr., were strung up in front of the door; they were afterwards set on fire and while burning they were thrown against the front door and thereby set it on fire. The fire alarm was given and several engines responded to the call, after overcoming considerable opposition on the part of the mob the flames were extinguished.

There was no other act of Mr. Crittenden's life which brought upon him so much bitter censure and abuse as his volunteering as counsel in this case.

The newspapers and public men in all sections of the country took sides in the controversy, some condemning and others excusing. On July 11th, the grand jury of Hardin county indicted, for perjury, four members of the Matt F. Ward jury.

The following communication was sent to Mr. Crittenden by members of the bar:

"Frankfort, September 12, 1854.

"To Hon. J. J. Crittenden:

"Dear Sir:—The undersigned, members of the bar practicing before the Court of Appeals, have witnessed with regret and mortification the newspaper attacks upon you for appearing as counsel on the trial of Matt F. Ward, and feeling that it is not less an act of justice to the profession to which they belong than to yourself, one of its most distinguished ornaments, beg leave without entering into details, to express to you their convictions that there has been nothing, either in the manner of your appearing or in the conduct of the case on your part inconsistent with the highest professional propriety, and that your entire conduct has met their full and cordial approbation.

"We have the honor to be, very respectfully,

"Your obedient servants."

Signed by:

Garrett Davis, Mason Brown, M. C. Johnson, Thomas P. Porter, B. Monroe, John M. Harlan, James Harlan, John Rodman, J. C. Breckinridge, J. M. Stevenson, C. S. Morehead, and twenty-two other prominent members of the bar.

The Execution of Sue Mundy.

During the civil war there was no other State in the Union so evenly divided in sentiment between the north and south as Kentucky. It was a border State between the two great warring sections of the country. At first, there was a declaration of neutrality, but it was evident that each side was making a strong effort to control the State and it became questionable whether or not Kentucky would secede. Section was divided against section, neighbor against neighbor and in many instances brother against brother and father against son. During the early part of the war strenuous efforts were made to prevent the State from going with the south and equally as strong effort was made to induce it to leave the Union.

The question of neutrality was soon abandoned and it became a question upon each side as to which could secure the largest number of volunteers.

During the four years of bloodshed many bloody battles were fought with Kentuckians against Kentuckians; this was especially so at the battle of Murfreesboro, where Kentucky had seventeen regiments of Confederates and fourteen regiments of Federals.

At Missionary Ridge the Federals had ten regiments and the Confederates seven.

When General Burbridge with his four thousand Kentuckians undertook to destroy the Salt Works at Saltville, Va., he was met by Kentuckians under General John S. Williams and driven back.

The contending armies at Clinch Mountain and Laurel Gap were composed almost exclusively of Kentuckians on both sides.

EXECUTION OF SUE MUNDY.

The bitterness which marked the closing days of this great internecine struggle was exhibited more in Kentucky than elsewhere.

The bloody rule of General Burbridge as commander in chief of the Kentucky forces, intended by him to prevent the guerilla warfare, only increased its horrors. His retaliatory method of executing two or three helpless prisoners for each murder committed by the guerrilla forces, was more revolting and more horrible than the crimes which he was trying to prevent. As a rule the guerrilla had some excuse, either real or imaginary; then too a great many crimes were charged against him for which he was not responsible; many evil disposed men took advantage of the conditions then existing and burnt his neighbor's home or assassinated him and charged it to the guerrilla.

When Col. R. J. Breckinridge was captured, near the close of the war, he had an order from General John C. Breckinridge, the Confederate Secretary of War, directing him to come to Kentucky and order all Confederate officers and soldiers out of the State upon the penalty of being handed over to the Federal Government to be treated as guerrillas, if they failed to obey the order.

During the closing days of 1864, and the first part of 1865, many roving bands of men were found in different sections of the State. They acknowledged neither civil nor military authority; they were a law unto themselves, and went from place to place, robbing, burning, killing and doing all kinds of lawless acts.

One of the most noted leaders of the guerrilla band was Marcellus Jerome Clark, who had assumed the name of Sue Mundy. For months prior to his capture, the newspapers were full of daring acts and desperate deeds, done by Sue Mundy and his guerrilla band in Shelby, Nelson, Jefferson, Spencer, Bullitt, Hardin, Breckinridge and other counties in that section of the State. On January 28, 1865, the Federal home guards went to Bloomfield in Nelson county and were engaged in plundering the stores, when sixty guerrillas under Sue Mundy and Billy Magruder dashed into the town and attacked them, and in the battle seventeen members of the home guards were killed. On January 29, there was a skirmish at Bardstown, between a detachment of Col. Buckley's Fifty-fourth Kentucky (Federal) and Sue Mundy's band, in which Mundy was repulsed. On March 3rd, there was a battle between eight home guards and Billy Magruder's band in Hancock county, One of Magruder's men named Jim Jones was killed and Magruder was desperately wounded and was carried away by his men. This wounding of Magruder brought about the capture of Sue Mundy. The capture of Mundy, Magruder and Medkiff and execution of Sue Mundy was given in one of the Louisville papers as follows:

These three outlaws, so notorious for the number and the barbarities of their murders, were captured on Sunday last at a short distance from the small town of Webster, about ten miles from Brandenburg. The post commandant of Louisville, Col. Dill, heard that Magruder was lying wounded in a tobacco barn on the place of Mr. Cox in the vicinity spoken of, being nursed by Sue Mundy and Medkiff. He immediately dispatched a detachment of fifty men of the 30th Wisconsin Volunteers down the river to make an effort to capture the outlaws. About sunrise, on Sunday morning the soldiers reached the barn, and quietly surrounded it and demanded the surrender of its inmates. No answer being given, they broke the door open, when Sue Mundy fired quickly and with true aim, a revolver in each hand, wounding four of the soldiers, one mortally. He refused to surrender unless he should be treated as a prisoner of war till the party should reach Louisville. Medkiff was also taken and with his companion, was strongly ironed and brought to Louisville. Magruder was brought up also and in such a weak condition that it was thought he would not live till the next day. The trial of the outlaws was immediately ordered by a military commission, General Whitaker presiding. Positive testimony was offered as to several murders Sue Mundy had committed, and also as to his throwing a train of cars from the track and robbing the passengers. He was found guilty of murder and sentenced to be hung. General Palmer approved the finding and sentence and named the 15th day of March, 1865, at 4 o'clock p. m. as the time for execution.

Sue Mundy was an assumed name, the person being a young man by the name of Jerome Clark, son of ex-Governor Clark of Kentucky. The condemned man was ignorant of his fate until the morning of the day on which he was to be executed. The Rev. Mr. Talbott of the St. John's Episcopal church, was his spiritual advisor. When he asked Mundy if he knew what would be done with him, he said, that he thought he would be executed, as the court martial had refused to have him introduce witnesses. The minister then asked him if he had any idea when his execution would take place. He replied, "In a few weeks." The minister then told him that the execution would take place within a few hours and that the order was for him to be hung in the place of shot.

He displayed a great deal of nerve. He was very calm and collected. He declared that he was not guilty of the many outrages with which he was charged and that the newspapers had done him a great injustice. He positively declared that he was not present at all, when the negro soldiers were killed near Simpsonville. He said that he held a captains commission from Col. Jack Allen and that he was a Confederate soldier.

When he realized his condition, that he had only a few hours longer to live, he knelt with his minister in prayer and requested him to pray with him. After instructions and confessions of faith in the church, he requested to be baptized. This ordinance was administered an hour before his execution, after he had declared that he had no malice against any one and loved everybody. He then requested Mr. Talbott to write letters to his sister, aunt, cousin and a young lady of this State, having a lock of his hair cut off and placed in each letter.

He requested that his body should be sent to his aunt in Franklin, Simpson county, Kentucky, and that he be buried by the side of his father and mother, in his uniform, or if that would not be permitted, at least bury him with his jacket.

Sue Mundy was nearly six feet tall, straight and remarkably well built, and would weigh about one hundred and sixty pounds. His complexion was fair; he had long dark hair which touched his shoulders, he had a beautifully shaped mouth, and in short was a handsome man. His whole demeanor was firm, polite, quiet and unassuming; he bore the air of a man of culture and gentlemanly refinement. He said he would have been twenty-one years of age in the following August and would die before he reached his manhood, and yet, had been a man to his country. He wore a black velvet cap, a black or dark blue jacket with one row of Kentucky State buttons, a pair of dark cassimere pants and a pair of old boots, cut down in imitation of a pair of shoes.

Notwithstanding the result of the trial was kept secret, a very large crowd gathered at the place of execution on Broadway, near Eighteenth street. The gallows was a hastily constructed affair; the material was the same which was used in the scaffolding on which Nathan Marks, the guerrilla, was hung some months before and was built exactly like it. The platform or trap door was supported by a prop—a rope attached to the lower end. A rough wooden coffin was brought and placed under the scaffold half an hour before the execution.

The condemned man was conveyed from the military prison in a carriage accompanied by his Spiritual adviser, under a strong guard; they arrived at the place of execution about a quarter of four o'clock, preceded by martial music. It required several minutes to form the troops in proper order; the prisoner, in the meantime, remaining in the carriage, his lips moving as if in prayer, a white handkerchief up to his eyes and his head leaning against the side of the carriage.

Captain George Swope, of the Fifth Indiana Cavalry, and provost marshal had charge of the execution. The condemned man was conducted to the gallows in company with the minister. Both of them knelt and offered up a prayer, after which Captain Swope read the charges and specifications to the prisoner. He seemed to pay little attention to this. His eyes were half closed and his lips continually in motion, evidently offering up his petition to God. "Lord have mercy upon my poor soul," seemed from his lips to have been his prayer.

He was asked if he had anything to say, to make it known. He directed his remarks to his spiritual advisor in a very low voice, he said: "I am a regular Confederate soldier, and have served in the Confederate army for four years. I fought under General Buckner at Fort Donalson, and belonged to General Morgan's command when he entered Kentucky. I have assisted and taken many prisoners and have always treated them kindly. I was wounded at Cynthiana and cut off from my command. I have been in Kentucky ever since; I could prove that I am a regular Confederate soldier, and I hope in, and die for, the Confederate cause." A white cap was placed over his face and at the word three the prop was pulled from under the trap. The fall was not more than three feet and it did not break his neck; he was choked to death. His sufferings were of short duration. Thus ended the career of the notorious Sue Mundy. He was captured on Sunday, taken to Louisville on Monday, tried on Tuesday and executed on Wednesday, all of the same week.

His body was left hanging for about twenty minutes before it was cut down; immediately a crowd gathered around it, some were trying to cut off a button while others were trying to get a piece of the rope as a memento. A rumor was started that his jacket contained a lot of greenbacks, carefully sewed in the lining; before he was placed in the coffin a general search was instituted but nothing was found.

Just a few moments before he was taken to the place of execution he wrote a letter to a young lady, in which he said:

> "My Dear: I have to inform you of the sad fate which awaits your true friend. I am to suffer death this afternoon at four o'clock. * * * I send you from my chains a message of true love; and as I stand on the brink of the grave, I tell you, I do truly and fondly and forever love you, I am ever truly yours,
>
> "M. JEROME CLARK."

There are two traditions in reference to this lady. One is, that she is still living near Bloomfield and that she has remained true to her first and only love, and is still a maiden lady. The other is, that she married in a few years after the death of Sue Mundy and that she is still living near Bloomfield, Kentucky.

Marcellus Jerome Clark (Sue Mundy) was born in Simpson county, Kentucky, in August, 1845. He was a son of Brigadier General Hector M. Clark. He was not the son of Governor Clark as stated in some of the papers, and a first cousin of Hon. Beverly Leonadus Clark, a former

Congressman and Minister to Gautamala under the Buchanan administration. His father, Hector M. Clark, came from Virginia to Kentucky, in 1815. He married Miss Mary Hail of Simpson county, Kentucky.

Marcellus Jerome was the youngest of seven children. His mother died when he was two years old, after which his father moved to Logan county, but Jerome remained with his aunt in Simpson and attended the common schools of the county until he was about nine years of age and then went to his father's in Logan county, soon after which his father died and he was left in care of his brother who remained on the farm. He was regarded as a bright boy with a mild lovable disposition.

In 1861 he joined the Confederate army at Camp Cheatham, in Robertson county, Tennessee, being scarcely sixteen years old.

Clark was in the engagement of Fort Donelson, this is accounted for by the fact that in December, 1861, his company was detached from his regiment to serve in the field battery of Captain Rice E. Graves of Graves county, Kentucky. Capt. Graves was commissioned to organize a company of field artillery and he took charge of a squad of soldiers at Bowling Green and in order to make a full company as quick as possible one whole company of the fourth infantry, under Captain Ingram was detailed to Captain Graves. Jerome Clark was a member of Captain Ingram's company. By this change he became a member of Company B, Fourth Kentucky regiment. He was at that time a private, sixteen years of age and very boyish in appearance; he was drilled for some time as a cannoneer. He served with distinction at Fort Donelson on the 13th, 14th and 15th of February, 1862. In the late afternoon of February 14th, Captain Graves' company made a charge against the enemy and in the smoke and darkness the company became bewildered and Captain Graves called for a volunteer to go ahead and locate the company and find the way out; though Clark was one of the youngest men in the company he volunteered to do this service and he succeeded in a very satisfactory way. He surrendered at Fort Donelson with the rest of his company and was imprisoned at Camp Morton, near Indianapolis, Indiana. At that time he was very quiet and unassuming in disposition and he was well thought of by his comrades.

On one occasion Clark showed his sweetheart's picture to some of his fellow prisoners, one of them, a large man, by the name of Crow threw it in the fire, Clark immediately made an assault upon him and a fight ensued. His personal courage was never questioned after that.

He escaped from Camp Morton in May, 1862, in the following way: It was the custom at the prison for a couple of guards to take a certain number of prisoners to a small river, near by, and have them take a bath while the guards would sit on the bank with their guns and watch them. On this occasion Clark made it up with a fellow prisoner to get in a sham fight in the edge of the water. The guards enjoyed seeing the rebels fight so much that they laid their guns down and clapped their hands and urged them on, each applauding his favorite in the fight. In their struggle, they finally got out on the bank near the guns, and before the guards realized the situation, Clark grabbed up their guns and threw them into the river, as far as he could, he then jumped in and swam across to the opposite shore before they could go to the camp and secure more arms and assistance.

He made good his escape running through the woods without any clothes. He spent the night under a corn pen and early the next morning an old negro came out to feed the hogs when Clark took his clothes from him and afterwards made his way back to his brother's in Logan county. For a time he remained on the farm assisting his brother.

One evening while visiting a neighbor he and his brother were captured by some Federal soldiers and taken to the woods where his brother was shot and killed, but Jerome broke away from them and made his escape. The neighbors were afraid to render any assistance, so he went alone, and secured the body of his brother and carried it to his home. The next morning while he and his sister were alone in the room with their brother's corpse the house was surrounded by a company of Federal soldiers. Jerome made a desperate resistance and after wounding several of them the remainder retreated to a place of safety, and he again made his escape. It was said that this was the turning point in his life, that he was changed from a timid, bashful boy to the terror of the Federal soldiers, in the sections of the country where he operated.

He made his way to John Morgan's command and joined James E. Cantrell's regiment and Judge Cantrell often said that Jerome Clark was one of his bravest and most trusted scouts. He continued with him until he was wounded at Cynthiana and was left behind. From that time on nothing further was known of Clark by his relations and friends at his home. They frequently heard of the numerous operations of Sue Mundy, but none of them knew who Sue Mundy was, until his capture and incarceration in the Louisville jail, which was followed by a hasty trial by court martial and conviction at which time his identity was disclosed.

After his execution his body was shipped to his aunt, Mrs. Nancy Bradshaw, at Franklin, Kentucky, and it was buried in the old Clark or Hopkins graveyard, by the side of his father, one and one-fourth miles north of Franklin. The farm on which his unmarked grave is located is now owned by A. H. Hill, County Clerk of Simpson county.

It was thought by many that on account of his assumed name—Sue Mundy—he operated in the guise of a woman but such was not the case. This name was given to him in fun by his comrades at a May-day festival they were holding while in camp, on account of his smooth girlish looking face and long black wavy hair, which he permitted to grow down on his shoulders, they crowned him Queen of the May and give him the name of Sue Mundy, so he adopted this name through the remainder of his life.

Thompson-Daviess Tragedy.

In June, 1867, Theodore H. Daviess, Sr., borrowed from Richard Meaux, twenty-five hundred dollars for one year. As evidence of this, he executed his note to Meaux for two thousand seven hundred and fifty dollars; the increase of the two hundred and fifty dollars, over the amount actually borrowed, was intended to cover the charge of ten per cent interest. Afterwards, in order to cover usurious interest, Daviess executed another note for two hundred and fifty dollars. When suit was brought by Meaux, Daviess, in his answer, which was drawn by P. B. Thompson, Jr., set up and pleaded payment, and filed as a part of his answer the original note of $2,750.00. Meaux obtained a rule against Daviess to show cause why he should not make his answer more definite and state to whom he had paid the note. In response, Daviess stated that he had paid it to P. B. Thompson, Sr., agent for Meaux. This response to rule was filed by P. W. Hardin, at which time J. B. & P. B. Thompson, Jr., declined further to represent Daviess, and they had their names stricken from the docket.

C. A. & P. W. Hardin and T. C. Bell became the attorneys for Daviess. Kyle, Poston, M. J. Durham and W. B. Allen were the attorneys for Meaux.

Daviess stated on the witness stand that he had paid off the note and produced two receipts to the amount of eight hundred dollars signed by Thompson and which were admitted by Thompson. Daviess also produced a check for eighteen hundred dollars which was payable to Thompson and which Daviess claimed was to go on the note. This Col. Thompson denied, stating that he had paid this eighteen hundred dollars to the creditors of Daviess at his request.

A large number of old suits, executions and other court records were produced by both sides. At the conclusion of the evidence in the case, while the lawyers were preparing the instructions, P. B. Thompson, Jr., and Larue Daviess started towards the court house door, and in a moment the firing commenced, by which party, it was not known; thirty or forty shots were fired. Theodore Daviess, Sr., and his son Larue, were instantly killed and Theodore Daviess, Jr., was mortally wounded. P. B. Thompson, Sr., and P. B. and J. B. Thompson, Jr., were wounded, but none of them fatally.

W. E. Keller, Judge of the Mercer County Court, held the examining trial of the Thompsons under the following warrant: "The Commonwealth of Kentucky; to any peace officer of Mercer county: It appearing from the oath of J. C. Wilson that there are reasonable grounds for believing that Phil B. Thompson, Sr., Phil B. Thompson, Jr., John B. Thompson, Jr., and Davis M. Thompson have been guilty of murder in Mercer county, on the 26th day of November, 1873, these are therefore to command you to arrest the said Thompsons and bring them before me to be dealt with according to law. Given under my hand, this 26th day of November, 1873.

"W. E. Keller,
"Judge of Mercer County Court."

The Commonwealth was represented by Captain W. B. Allen, County Attorney; Ben Lee Hardin, W. O. Bradley, afterwards Governor of Kentucky and United States Senator, and Judge R. M. Bradley, his father, and J. C. S. Blackburn, afterwards United States Senator.

The defense was represented by Judge O. S. Poston, C. A. Hardin, Judge John J. Kyle, T. C. Bell, Gov. T. E. Bramlette and J. B. T. Davis.

There were seventy-five witnesses called, sworn and

placed under the rule; among the witnesses was ex-Governor Beriah Magoffin. The cases were called at ten o'clock, December 30th. The first witness for the Commonwealth was Samuel Harding, of Danville. The main statements made by him, were as follows: "I was present in the court house the day of the Thompson-Daviess difficulty. I was sitting near the table looking at attorney C. A. Hardin, when Judge Wickliffe spoke to the officers and said: 'Stop those men.' I looked around and saw some of the Thompsons and Daviess near the door. Theodore Daviess, Jr., was struggling with Bud Roberts, the jailor. I looked at him till a shot was fired, when I got down behind the bench. I had been present throughout the trial; I mean the trial of Meaux v. Daviess. I never thought of a fight and cannot tell how the parties were located at the time it started. There had been no firing when Judge Wickliffe said, 'Stop those men.' I saw some of the parties near the door and the remainder on either side going in that direction. Young Theodore Daviess was just outside the bar, Bud Roberts was holding him; in a few seconds the first shot was fired; I don't know who fired it. There was first a single shot, others followed in rapid succession. From the report, the first shot seemed to come from near the door, outside the bar, towards the left of the aisle going out. I did not notice the position of Theodore Daviess, Sr., nor of young John B. Thompson."

During the examination of Theodore Daviess, Sr., reference was made to the twelve hundred dollar payment and the attorney for Meaux objected; young Phil remarked, "Let him go on—I want to know what he has to say about me." Theodore H. Daviess replied that he meant no reflections.

"I can only tell where young Theodore Daviess stood at the time the fight commenced. After the fighting was over, inside, I heard a shot on the outside, and I saw Captain

Thompson running towards the bank. He was running after someone. I do not know where the second shot came from, young Theodore Daviess did not fire the first shot. At the time I saw Captain Thompson running towards the bank, there was no one with him. I saw young Phil standing outside the door, his face and shirt bosom stained with blood.''

Judge Wickliffe's instruction to the jury was that, '' The simple question in issue was payment or non-payment. His instructions to the officers of the court was; that the case was an exciting one and might beget a difficulty therefore he ordered the officials to suppress any outbreak at all hazards—even to the taking of life if necessary.''

T. J. Polk said in part: '' I went in the court room just a few seconds before the difficulty commenced. As I came towards the bar I saw P. B. Thompson, Jr., and Larue Daviess near the stove, in conversation, they started towards the door, young Phil, in front, Larue Daviess seemed excited; as they started out, some person caught hold of Larue; young Phil remarked, ' Come on.' Young Phil was not excited. As Larue passed me I took hold of the lapel of his coat, but let go before the Judge ordered, ' Stop those men.' The first shot was fired somewhere near the door. I then kicked out six panes of glass and went out to the yard; after getting out I saw Theodore Daviess, Jr., running across towards the bank, P. B. Thompson, Sr., in pursuit and firing at him with a pistol, he was about twenty feet behind him. I don't think he fired but one shot. Theodore neither turned nor looked back, while Captain Thompson was in pursuit of him. I have known T. H. Daviess, Sr., about thirteen years. I know his reputation. He was considered a very dangerous man when stirred up.''

P. Watt Hardin (Attorney General of Kentucky for many years) one of the attorneys for Daviess in case of Meaux v. Daviess, was asked: '' Would not the termination of the civil suit, if the verdict of the jury had been in favor of the Daviess, ruined the professional character of Captain Phil Thompson?" to which he answered in the affirmative. Mr. Blackburn said: the object of the question was to show a motive for putting the Daviesses out of the way. Governor Bramlett then asked, whether if the jury had decided in favor of Thompson, it would not have established the fact that T. H. Daviess had sworn to a lie, which was also answered in the affirmative. It was the theory of the prosecution that John B. Thompson, Jr., fired the first shot, the one that killed Theodore H. Daviess, Sr.

One witness testified that the first notice of the fight was; little Eugene Daviess ran to his father and said, "Father young Phil Thompson and Larue are going out to fight." Theodore Daviess then rose from his seat and started towards the door when the firing commenced.

County Attorney W. B. Allen, testified: "I was present in the court house the day of the difficulty. Phil Thompson, Jr., seemed excited during the delivery of Theodore Daviess' testimony. He walked to the stove where Larue Daviess was standing and the two got into a conversation. I saw them start towards the door together, when young Caldwell Daviess took hold of Larue, saying, 'Don't go Larue.' Larue replied, 'Yes, I will.' After going a few paces, Phil turned half around and said, 'Come on.' Just then Judge Wickliffe called out: 'Stop those men.' I ran to the window and jumped out. As I jumped, I heard a shot fired and I saw Larue Daviess stagger out of the front door and fall. Little Phil was the next to come out, following Larue. I next saw Young Phil and Theodore Daviess, Jr., in a hand to hand struggle, each had a pistol, so I continued my retreat. I then saw Captain Phil Thompson, Sr., come upon the ground and Theodore Daviess turned to flee, with Captain Thompson in pursuit. Captain Thompson said, 'Kill him.' Little Phil threw his pistol at Theodore, Jr., as the latter ran away, when Captain Thompson said, 'Kill him G—d d—n him.' Theodore Daviess made a half halt and turned partly around and raised his pistol, at this Captain Thompson fired. John Thompson, Jr., was near his father and he picked up something and threw at Theodore Daviess. I don't know who fired the first shot in the court room; eight or ten shots were fired before I got out."

P. Watt Hardin said: "During the close of the trial of the civil suit, I was sitting near T. H. Daviess, Sr., Charles A. Hardin was writing instructions for the jury. Ex-Governor Thompson (John B. Thompson, Sr.), was sitting close by; while in that position at the lawyers' table, little Eugene Daviess, the youngest son, age about ten years, came up to Theodore Daviess, Sr., and said, 'Pa, little Phil and Larue have gone out to fight.' I said, 'No, stop, I guess not,' Theodore Daviess, Sr., then arose from his seat, but at my words, he paused for an instant. 'Ah, yes Pa, I know they have,' repeated little Eugene. Mr. Daviess, the father then sprang from me as I threw my hand towards him, and knocking over a chair he started towards the door, at that instant Judge Wickliffe said, 'Stop those men,' whereupon general confusion ensued and a promiscuous firing began. Thirty or forty shots were fired within fifteen seconds and everybody was running for a safe place. There were three or four men shooting, but I am not able to specify who fired a single shot, so quickly did the promiscuous fusilade follow. I know the four defendants named in this warrant were shooting, but am unable to specify any particular shot. I saw Abe McMurdy with a pistol out during the fight, he either fell over, or on top of Judge Wickliffe. I know McMurdy had a pistol from the words of Judge Wickliffe, who was piled up behind the desk, he said, 'For God's sake take that pistol away.' I did not see McMurdy shoot or try to shoot, but I thought

Judge Wickliffe's eyes would pop out of his head when McMurdy came tumbling over him with a pistol in his hand. The first and second shots were fired near the door. I saw Theodore Daviess, Sr., as he got near the door, turn and sink down, pistol in hand as if he had received his death wound.''

Beriah Jones said: '' He could not tell who fired the first shot, as the firing was promiscuous. He saw young Phil B. Thompson fire a shot at Theodore Daviess, Sr., and soon after the latter fell to the floor, John shot but twice that witness saw.'' It also came out in Jones' evidence that Phil B. Thompson, Jr., and John B. Thompson, Jr., were twin brothers and that they looked very much alike.

Caldwell Daviess, seventeen years of age, said: '' My brother Larue Daviess was standing near the stove, inside of the bar and little Phil approached him and said, '' I want to give you a d—n good kicking.' He spoke very distinctly. I said, ' Larue don't go out,' he replied, ' I will be bluffed by no Thompson,' as the two started out, John B. Thompson, Jr., drew his pistol and fired; when the first shot was fired I got under the table. Father was standing near me, talking to Mr. Hardin. He got up and started out; when just outside the bar he was shot. John B. Thompson, Jr., fired the first shot I noticed. I remained under the table until the shooting was over. I had no pistol. I was not present when Jack Chinn testified. I did not hear Chinn when he told father, he had sworn to a d—n lie. As father passed towards the door I saw no pistol in his hand. Abe McMurdy, John Thompson, Jr., and Dr. Davis Thompson had their pistols out; this was at the commencement of the difficulty. Father has always worn a pistol and bowie too, all his life. Larue nearly always carried a pistol. When I and Larue were in Missouri, father wrote us to stay there; said he expected to be assassinated by the Thompsons and for us to remain there. I saw Davis Thompson on the morning of the day the fight came up, with a pistol in his overcoat pocket.''

Eugene Daviess testified: ''I am a son of Theodore Daviess, Sr., and a brother of Theodore and Larue. I was standing by the stove when Phil said to Larue, 'What do you want?' Larue said, 'Nothing, what do you want?' Phil said, 'I want to give you a d—n kicking, and if you will go out I'll do it.' I ran and told father. The first shot I saw, was fired by John Thompson, Jr., I got down behind the bench; when I rose I saw Phil Thompson, Sr., go out the window. I think John Thompson fired over some man's shoulder. I then went over to where father was lying. I saw Davis Thompson with a pistol in his hand. I had no pistol, neither did Caldwell. I don't know who John Thompson shot at, he shot towards the door. To the best of my knowledge John Thompson fired the first shot, one shot was fired out in the yard after I got to father.''

Rev. W. P. Harvie saw the difficulty which took place outside, saw Phil Thompson, Sr., shoot and heard him say, ''Theodore Davis, Sr., had sworn to a d—n lie and that now his soul is in hell for it.'' On cross-examination, witness said that Captain Thompson was limping, pale and very much excited immediately after the shooting of young Theodore Daviess, and was leaning on the arm of someone.

B. A. Taylor saw the trouble outside of the court house. Saw Larue Davis fall out of the court house door, young Phil Thompson just behind him. Theodore Daviess, Jr., then came out and he and young Phil clinched, just then some one jumped out of the window and said, ''Run or I will kill you.'' Captain Phil then started in pursuit, as Daviess ran out of the court yard; he had a pistol in his hand. Just before he was shot by Captain Thompson, who had two pistols, Theodore turned his head, Captain Thompson said, just as he shot, ''Kill the d—d son of a b—h.''

James C. Willson was Town Marshal and was present

and saw the trouble. After giving a statement about the civil trial and shooting, he said: "As I went out the door after the shooting, Theodore Daviess, Sr., was lying near the door dying, with a pistol in his hand, only one of the chambers was empty. I saw Larue lying on the pavement just outside the front door; I saw a pistol near him; it was a six inch Cooper's self cocker, two chambers empty and caps off of four barrels. There was blood on the wall in the vestibule as if someone had spit it out. The first man I met was Phil, Jr., the next was John B., Jr., and Captain Phil soon came up; they gave their pistols to me, all three of them were empty."

There were various statements made in reference to the character of Theodore Daviess, Sr., and Larue Daviess, but there was only one sentiment expressed as to Theodore Daviess, Jr., he was esteemed in the community of Harrodsburg above almost any other young man in Mercer county. It was in the proof that he was honorable, true, quiet and modest. Larue was hasty, impetuous and quarrelsome, but Theodore had all of the heroic elements in his composition. After his father fell in the court house and his brother outside, Theodore exhausted his pistol, then clinched with Phil, Jr., and used it as a club until Captain Phil Thompson came up and someone called to him to run, he realized that he was fighting with an empty pistol, the odds were against him and that a retreat was necessary. When he reached the bank corner he was shot in the back by Captain Thompson who pursued him to that point. Captain Thompson said afterwards, that he would give the world if he had it, to recall that last fatal shot. When the last shot was fired Captain Thompson turned back and Theodore continued down Main street to the express office, in which he was engaged and over which he had his room. When he reached his door he found it locked, after breaking it open, he fell upon the bed where he died the next morning at 11 a. m. Before he died he sent assurances of forgiveness to the Thompsons.

The friends of Captain Thompson claimed as extenuation of that last shot, that he had just a moment before seen Theodore and his son Phil engaged in deadly conflict, the face and shirt of his son, were covered with blood and he himself had been severely wounded. The whole fight had not lasted longer than two minutes.

Theodore Daviess, Jr., had a wound in his left hand and one in the lower part of the back passing through the abdomen, which caused his death. Theodore Daviess, Sr., was shot in only one place, the ball entered about an inch and a half below the left nipple and ranging through to the right side of the spine. Larue Daviess had four wounds, one through the left wrist lodging under the skin, another higher up on the same arm, another in the breast just under the collar bone and the fourth in the right side of the back near the spine; he was shot by balls of different size, the shots in the arm were of the same caliber and the other two were from a different pistol.

The prosecution examined only twenty-eight of the forty witnesses subpoenaed for the State.

The main witness for the defense, and he presented practically the whole theory of the defense, was Hon. J. C. Wickliffe, Circuit Judge of the Seventh Judicial dictrict. He said, " I am Judge of this Circuit. I was presiding here on the 26th of November and saw a portion of the conflict between the Thompsons and the Daviesses. I had taken precaution to suppress any outbreak, after one of the officers of the court had warned me that there was bad feeling between the parties on account of the suit of Meaux v. Daviess. On Monday the 13th day of the court, I directed Mr. Cummins, the sheriff, to arm himself and six other good men and suppress any outbreak. I gave the warning in open court just after swearing the jury. During the progress of the trial I noted the bearing of the Daviesses and the Thompsons. Phil Thompson, Sr., and his two sons testified in the case. I saw nothing offensive in their manner, though Captain Thompson seemed a little excited but not offensive in his manner. The manner of Theodore Daviess, Sr., while testifying, I thought rather offensive to some of the witnesses; after Mr. Daviess, Sr., had been introduced a second time as a witness, he began some remark, when Judge Durham stopped him. Young Phil rose up and turned towards me and said, 'Let him go on and state all he knows about it.' I remarked, 'I'm running this machine,' at this moment Captain Thompson was sitting on a table or chair near the railing. My attention was first attracted to the difficulty in this wise: I saw young Phil going towards the door and just behind him was Larue and Theodore Daviess, Jr. I thought it boded no good, so I looked around for the sheriff. Theodore Daviess, Sr., jumped up and started towards the door, pistol in hand, when I said, 'Bring those men back.' Just then three shots were fired in the aisle leading towards the door. I did not see young Phil any more until the fight was over. When the three shots were fired I protected myself behind the desk. A volley of five or six shots soon followed. Davis Thompson was on my right side, inside the bar and near the stove, when I got behind the desk I saw him facing towards me; I saw a shot strike him just above the hem of his pants across the abdomen. I afterwards saw the rent, his hat was also perforated, I saw the dust fly from his pants when struck; about the same time he returned the fire, using the pistol in his left hand. At the time young Phil was testifying Larue Daviess was standing near the stove with his hand in his pocket as if he had a pistol.

"The trial commenced on Tuesday and I kept my eyes on both parties, pretty close. When the firing ceased on the inside, some one called to Captain Thompson and told him there were two on little Phil outside. Captain Thompson went out of the window, followed by young John and Davis Thompson. I went up to where Theodore, Sr., was lying and made the jailor take the pistol out of his hand. I passed out and saw little Phil, his head, face, bosom and collar were very bloody, one of his hands was powder burnt, his left hand, I think; and the skin was cut or abraded. Soon after this little Jack came up and surrendered himself. His hand was shot and bleeding, I saw a bullet hole through his clothing, there was also a bullet hole through the rim of his hat.

" Captain Phil was shot through the right thigh, he remained on the inside of the bar until the fight closed in the room. I did not see that he had a pistol. None of the Daviesses were lawyers and all the Thompsons are lawyers except Davis M. I don't think Theodore Daviess, Sr., fired any one of the three first shots. When Abe McMurdy got on top of me, he had a pistol in his hand; this was while I was concealed behind the desk."

The defense proved that Theodore Daviess, Sr., had made several conditional threats against Captain Thompson, which were conveyed to him. It was in proof that Theodore Daviess, Sr., had proposed to Captain Thompson, some days before, that they should fight their matters out between themselves without involving their sons, that they should enter into an agreement to such effect. Captain Thompson, he said, refused to accede to the proposition and Daviess, Sr., thereupon said, " It would be henceforth man to man and clan to clan."

A large number of witnesses testified to the good character of Captain Phil Thompson and his boys and also that Theodore Daviess, Sr., and Larue Daviess were desperate dangerous men. A conflict between the two families was generally expected, all the parties were expecting the fight and were looking for a chance to bring on the difficulty.

W. F. Robards did not know who fired the first shot but he knew that John Thompson, Jr., fired the second shot, and that twenty-five or thirty shots were fired in the court room and he pointed out where fifteen bullets had made marks on the walls in the court room. He took the pistol from Theodore Daviess, Sr., who said, "Don't take my pistol." These were the last words he uttered, only one chamber was empty.

Out of the thirty or more shots which were fired the condition of their pistols showed that the Daviesses fired only eight shots.

After the conclusion of the evidence, Judge Keller gave the attorneys to understand that he had his mind made up and that an argument of the case would be useless.

He held Phil B. Thompson, Sr., over to the grand jury, and fixed his bond at five thousand dollars. The cases against Phil B. Thompson, Jr., John B. Thompson, Jr., and Dr. Davis Thompson were dismissed. The court said in reference to Captain Thompson: "It is a pity that the last unfortunate shot was fired; but as regards this part of the fight, the court believes that Captain Thompson ought to be held over; the court has no doubt Captain Thompson would have refrained from firing it had he known all the circumstances; but seeing his son engaged in which he thought was a mortal conflict, seeing his face and shirt bosom covered with blood, he fired the last shot in hot blood, yet this court is only a court of inquiry and the defendant should be held over." Though Captain Thompson was held over, he never was indicted and no further prosecution was made.

The Daviesses and Thompsons were among the most prominent families in Kentucky. Captain Phil Thompson was known as one of the best criminal lawyers in the State, for many years; his brother Hon. John B. Thompson, Sr., was elected to the Kentucky Legislature in 1835. In 1840 he went to Congress where he served several terms; in 1849 he was elected Lieutenant Governor of Kentucky and in 1851 was elected to the United States Senate. He was a brilliant man and a great orator; his speech on Cuba rivals Governor Proctor Knott's speech on Duluth. He died January 7, 1874, while the Thompson trial was in progress.

Assassination of Judge John M. Elliott.

On Wednesday, March 26, 1879, at about one o'clock p. m., in front of the ladies' entrance to the Capitol Hotel, in Frankfort, Ky., Col. Thomas Buford, of Henry county, Kentucky, shot and killed Judge John M. Elliott of the Court of Appeals of Kentucky. The weapon used was a double-barreled shot gun loaded with twelve buckshot in each barrel.

Judge Elliott in company with Judge Thomas M. Hines, of the Court of Appeals, was coming up Ann street, from the court room of the Old State House, when they were met at the steps of the side entrance to the hotel by Buford who was equipped for hunting. Buford spoke to Judge Elliott and said, "Judge I believe I will go snipe hunting; won't you go along?" Judge Elliott replied, "No." "Well, then," said Buford, "won't you go and take a drink?" At this point Judge Hines turned away and had gone about six feet when the gun was fired and Judge Elliott fell upon the sidewalk without uttering a word. Buford looked down upon him and said, "I'm sorry." He then lifted his head and put his (Buford's) hat under it. Judge Hines turned back and tried to raise the body but life was extinct. He thought it was an accident until Buford spoke to the deputy sheriff and a policeman who came up immediately. Buford gave up his gun and said to the policeman, "Be careful with that gun, I put twelve buckshot in it for Pryor." He was arrested and taken before Esquire Guinn, and committed to jail.

Buford gave a letter to the deputy sheriff which was addressed as follows: "Whosoever may get this note I ask earnestly to deliver it to the person to whom it is directed." The contents of the letter were as follows:

"Capitol Hotel, March 26, 1879—Whatever may happen to me, I desire that my niece, Annie O. Wallace, shall have everything both in equity and law that belongs to me. I only ask that my body shall be laid by my sister, Mary F. Buford, whom I loved so well, whose robbery and assassination I wish to try.

"THOMAS BUFORD."

The body of Judge Elliott was taken to a room in the Capitol Hotel and a coroner's inquest held. The following verdict was rendered:

"We, the jury find that the dead body now before us is that of John M. Elliott, of Boyd county, Kentucky, who was at the time of his death, a Judge of the Court of Appeals, and residing temporarily at Frankfort, was killed and murdered in said city on the 26th inst., by being shot through the body by Thomas Buford with a double-barreled shotgun."

In a short time after Buford was lodged in jail, he was asked abut the tragedy, and he commenced to tell about the case which was decided by the Court of Appeals, only a few days before, of Buford's administrator v. Guthrie; he said that his sister Mary F. Buford had been robbed and murdered by the decision of the court. He said further: "I made up my mind to kill him. I thought on Monday I would kill both him and Judge Pryor, but I thought of Judge Pryor's children and took a walk to see if I could not save him on account of his children. I finally concluded to do so. Twelve months ago, I came to Frankfort, determined to kill Judge Pryor. I had twenty-four buckshot in a flannel bag for him and somebody else but I changed my mind. Judge Pryor knew all the particulars of my case; he knew how my sister had been wronged and could have controlled the decision but the case was not yet decided and

I determined to wait. I made up my mind to kill Judge Elliott, not because he was the first to decide the case against me, but because he gave me a Judas kiss. He came to me after the decision and said, ' Colonel, I did all I could for you.' I knew that was a lie, I knew that the profession was against me.'' He said, '' My gun was loaded with twelve buckshot in each barrel; I thought this morning I would go snipe hunting; I met Judge Elliott and said to him, ' Judge, I believe I will go snipe hunting, won't you go along.' He said, ' no,' I then asked him if he wouldn't take a drink, and raised my gun and pulled the trigger; it went off clear as a bell. He fell upon the pavement and then I was sorry. I leaned down and placed my hat under his head, I wished to treat him with as much courtesy as he had shown in the robbery and assassination of my sister by his decision. It was the most ignominious game that my gun ever killed. I did not intend to kill Judge Hines or Judge Pryor. I killed Elliott to try my case, to show that they could not rob and assassinate with impunity. Last week I was down in Henry and knelt on my sister's grave and swore to gain this suit or die with her. I know what I have done, I made up my mind and I am ready to take the consequences. I had a pistol in my pocket and intended to use it, if the shotgun failed.''

When it was learned through the city that Judge Elliott had been assassinated, there was great excitement, the streets soon became crowded with people, business was at a standstill; continued and persistent talk of a mob, caused the sheriff to summons a large posse of citizens to guard the jail and the officer of the local military company was directed to hold his company in readiness for orders in case of trouble. Judge Elliott's wife was in the Capitol Hotel at the time of his death.

The shot took effect in the right side near the lower rib and passed through to the other side, causing instant death.

Buford was only a few feet from him and the whole charge entered, making a wound about the size of a silver dollar.

At a meeting of the citizens of Frankfort, which was called in view of the death of Judge Elliott, on motion, Chief Justice Pryor was elected to preside and General John Rodman was elected secretary. On motion, it was ordered that General J. P. Nuckols, Hon. Alvin Duvall and W. P. D. Bush be appointed a committee to request the Mayor of Frankfort to issue his proclamation, ordering that all places of business be closed on the 27th, in view of the great calamity which had fallen upon the State, in the death of Judge Elliott. The Court of Appeals was adjourned until the 8th day of April.

Governor James B. McCreary issued the following proclamation:

"State of Kentucky, Executive Department.

"Frankfort, Kentucky, March 27, 1879.

"The announcement of the death of Hon. John M. Elliott, Judge of the First Appellate District, which occurred at Frankfort, March 26, 1879, will cause sorrow and regret in every section of the Commonwealth. His long career of usefulness and the many positions of public trust which he so honorably filled, won for him the respect and confidence of the people of the entire State. As a citizen he was beloved for his integrity, patriotism and fidelity, as a representative in Congress he was energetic, prompt and distinguished, and as a Judge, he was able, incorruptible and impartial. In token of respect for his memory I recommond that all public offices be closed at 12 m. and remain closed the rest of this day, and that all the State officers and their clerks attend the funeral in a body.

"James B. McCreary, Governor."

THE MAYOR'S PROCLAMATION.

Office of Mayor of the City of Frankfort.

"March 27, 1879.

"The citizens of Frankfort are hereby requested to participate in the funeral services of the late Hon. John M. Elliott, at the Christian church in this city at 3 o'clock p. m., and it is further requested that all business houses be closed commencing at the hour of 12 m. for the remainder of the day, as a testimonial of our respect and esteem for the memory of the deceased.

"S. I. M. MAJOR, Mayor."

Rev. C. W. Miller, D. D., of the Methodist church preached the funeral sermon which was published in full in the Courier-Journal of March 29, 1879.

Judge W. S. Pryor and other lawyers at Frankfort believed that Buford intended to kill Judge Pryor, at the same time he did Judge Elliott. Both of these Judges boarded at the Capitol Hotel and they generally returned from the court together; this fact was well known to Buford, who had, evidently, prepared himself to kill both of them. It was thought that a very small incident saved Judge Pryor. He was invited by a friend to stop with him, and take a toddy, which invitation was accepted. Judge Elliott refused the invitation, which was also extended to him; the result was, Judge Elliot was killed and Judge Pryor escaped. Years afterwards he told how the taking of a drink had saved his life.

The substance of the case which was the alleged cause of the killing is as follows:

On December 31, 1867, George J. Roland and wife conveyed to Mary F. Buford a tract of land in Henry county, Kentucky, consisting of four hundred acres, for the sum of ten thousand dollars cash and three notes, one for ten thousand dollars which was paid and two for six thousand two hundred and fifty dollars each. The last notes were assigned to James Guthrie of Shelby county, who brought suit on them, asking that the lien be foreclosed and the whole tract sold for the lien debts. Miss Buford filed her answer and set up the fact that the title to the land was not good and she prayed that the contract be rescinded. A change of venue was granted to Fayette county and the Judge of that court ordered the land sold for the debt, and the plaintiff bought the whole tract, for the amount of his claim, and Miss Buford thereby lost her $20,000 which she had paid on the place. The case went to the Court of Appeals and in the year 1878, the judgment of the lower court was affirmed, Judge Elliott delivered the opinion. A petition for re-hearing was filed and the previous judgment of the court was affirmed on the Saturday prior to the killing. In the meantime, Miss Buford had died and Thomas Buford was appointed her administrator.

On March 28th, Buford was brought before Judge W. H. Sneed and Esquire Quinn and waived examination and was sent to jail without bail. Gen. Green Clay Smith, afterwards a Baptist preacher of note, represented Buford and the Commonwealth was represented by Warren Montfort, Commonwealth's Attorney and Ira Julian, County Attorney.

The petition of Col. Buford for a change of venue was granted and the case was sent to Owen county for trial.

Hon. P. U. Major, the regular Judge, declined to sit in the case, and thereupon Judge W. L. Jackson, of Louisville, was appointed a special Judge to try it. The Hon. A. D. Dejarnett, Commonwealth's Attorney, declined to prosecute and Judge O. D. McManama was appointed Commonwealth's Attorney *pro tem.*

There was a strong array of counsel on each side. The attorneys representing the Commonwealth were Judge O.

D. McManama, Col. W. C. P. Breckinridge, Gen. John Rodman and his son, Hugh Rodman, Col. Jerry Lillard and Judge Orr.

The attorneys representing the defendant were Judge Geo. M. Curtis, of New York; Major W. R. Kinney, of Louisville; Col. Phil Thompson, of Harrodsburg; Theodore Hallam, of Covington; Mr. Hardin, of Eminence; Mr. Proll, Congressman Evan E. Settle, Judge Thomas Gordon and Judge J. W. Perry, of Owenton.

For a defense Col. Buford plead insanity.

On January 11, 1881, the jury was completed; all of the jurors were farmers. Judge McManama made a most excellent statement of the case for the Commonwealth.

Jack Long was the first prosecuting witness. He stated that he was on the police force of Frankfort and with deputy sheriff M. H. P. Williams, arrested Buford. He testified to the admissions made by Buford, and said that Buford kissed the gun with which he did the killing.

L. B. Holloway said that he heard Buford say on several occasions, that if the Court of Appeals rendered a decision against him he would have money or blood. The State introduced eleven witnesses for the prosecution.

Hon. E. E. Settle stated the defendant's side of the case. Col. Thomas Taylor testified that he had known Col. Buford for many years, and that one of his brothers, Sinclair Buford was insane and he believed Buford was. Some of the most prominent witnesses who thought Buford insane were Rev. Gilbert Gordon, of LaGrange; Dr. W. H. Painter, of Midway; Dr. J. Slemmons, of Henry county; Dr. R. H. Gayle, superintendent of Anchorage Asylum; Dr. Renfro, Dr. Bright, Dr. T. S. Bell, Gen. Green Clay Smith and many others.

Some of the prominent men who did not think he was insane were J. W. Tate, Henry T. Stanton, Judge William Lindsay, M. H. P. Williams, Capt. Thomas C. Jones, Gen.

D. W. Lindsey, Judge Alvin Duvall, Judge W. L. Jett, Col. W. L. Crabb, Judge William Carroll, etc.

There were forty-four witnesses for the defense, and forty-one witnesses for the prosecution used in rebuttal.

Judge McManama had frequent tilts with opposing counsel, on one occasion he said to the presiding Judge, "Your Honor, I wish you would have the sneezing in the court room stopped." Judge Jackson said, "I can hardly do that at this time of the year Judge." Judge Jackson allowed ten hours to each side for arguments in the case.

Nearly all the women of Owenton were present during the argument.

Breckinridge, Rodman and McManama spoke on the side of the prosecution and Judge Curtis, Perry, Settle and Col. Phil Thompson for the defense. Judge Curtis in a very able plea for the defendant said in part:

"Come down to this tragedy. If he (Buford) had been a sane person, would he have invited the world to witness that he intended to take the life of Judge Elliott? If he had been a sane person, would he have communicated the deadly purpose of his mind as has been testified to you? His mind was diseased upon the subject of this suit. Not for one moment in his waking hours could he drive its dread presence from the temple of his reason. Is not that abundantly proven over and over again? It is proven that he saw but one thing; that is the conclusion from the evidence, and it is resistless. Believing himself despoiled, seeing his property wrested from him, and despairing of any relief, it was in that diseased state of mind that these threats, having no particular purpose or relation to any particular individual, issued from his lips.

"One thing while I remember it. General Rodman told you that when his sister died the case had been reversed. Not so. The case had been decided against her, and she had simply gained a rehearing. It was simply the privilege to go the old thorny path over again, with this *ignis fatuus* of possible justice and relief at the end of it. It was the harassing character of that litigation from the beginning that broke her bright and sensitive spirit. I say that was the central domination of his mind. He goes to Frankfort. Why? He was dispossessed of his Henry county home. He was ejected from the soil on which he had hoped to live, and in which he had hoped to lay his bones. His sister is dead. He is alone in the world. Like an irresistible attraction and fascination, this suit pending in Frankfort drew him there, because outside of that place he had no interest. That is what brought him there, and I do not believe, except in a general way, that the intention and the design to slay this man ever entered his mind until the adverse decision came.

"The fact of his sparing Prior on account of his children, while it indicates a choice, does not establish sanity. It was some relic of that old generous and chivalrous nature that caused pity to find a lodgment in the shadowed chambers of his mind.

"This theory of Dr. Kennedy, of the gradual working of insanity, like heated lava in a volcano, with its consequent 'explosion,' was adverted to by Messrs. Beach and Brady, in the famous Cole case, and their views have been adopted in England *in extenso.* Such an 'explosion' did occur when he fired the fatal shot at Judge Elliott, and when insanity had relaxed its hold upon the will power and organs of his mind, pity entered his heart. He put his hand under him saying, 'I am sorry; I had to do it'—showing not that he had singled him out to die; showing not that against him he treasured up the vials of wrath, but showing, as was the truth before God, that that rudderless mind had made its voyage and struck upon a rock. His kissing the gun; his cool, calm demeanor, as Dr. Kennedy says, are marks of an insane person. I imagine it was the same nonchalance, the same apathetic indifference, that have distinguished him through this trial. He is fast approaching that time when he will be insensible —his intellect lost in dementia.

" In the case of General Cole, indicted for the murder of Speaker Hiscock, Mr. Beach and Mr. Brady, two of the greatest advocates that ever lived in any country or in any age, contended with success that the overpowering presence of sudden and uncontrollable frenzy acting upon a diseased mind, not simply right and wrong, not the frenzy of passion simply, but that mad, irresistible impulse, which comes when reason is overthrown, the will is subdued and the conscience palsied, constitutes a legitimate defense of insanity in a trial for homicide. In this case the deceased had dishonored the wife of the accused, who had brooded in melancholy over his disgrace, and coming suddenly upon the violator of his honor, slew him in the midst of his friends, and within the very shadow of the capitol of Albany. The sight of Hiscock caused in the mental constitution of General Cole that explosion, of which Dr. Kennedy so graphically speaks. The same doctrine was upheld in the case of Wagner, and it is now the admitted principle that controls this class of controversies. The same rule of law is declared in Willis v. People, and many others.

" As I have before observed, the sudden sight of Judge Elliott by Buford, the deceased Judge being associated in the deranged mind of the prisoner with all the latter's woes and calamities, the homicidal frenzy seized upon the faculties of Buford, and he immolated Judge Elliott almost upon the very steps of the tribunal of the law.

" You must not forget, gentlemen, in the consideration and determination of this august issue, the plain principles of law and medical jurisprudence that control it; remember that it is established science and settled law that lunacy may be produced by profound and protracted emotion, that grief and sorrow, as well as love and hatred, can corrupt the mind with disease until the grasp of reason upon the will is relapsed, the passions are unloosed, and man becomes a wild and unconscious demon. Such are the views expressed by Mandesley, Deane, Ray, Gray, Hammond, Beck, Taylor, Shelford, Brown, Marc, and the great Esquirol. Such a wild and unconscious demon was Buford on the twenty-sixth day of March, raging and violent in the streets of Frankfort. Behold in his shattered reason pity struggling with ferocity, his horrible laugh, his words of tenderness, his invocation of fate, his utterance of regret and his act of blood.

"Over the dead body of the august victim, he waved his hand in silent and eternal adieu, feeling in his distempered fancy and fate had sealed with an act of tragic horror that which had been decreed from the beginning. 'Canst thou minister to a mind diseased,' is the question put by the first of poets and philosophers into the mouth of one of his greatest conceptions. Can you, gentlemen of the jury, reconcile the act of this man's life, so painfully panoramic in the shifting scenes of this trial, with any theory save that of positive madness?

"You must remember, also, gentlemen of the jury, that the legal test is ability to comprehend the moral character of the act committed and the power of will to govern one's action in obedience to the judgment. Dr. Bell tells you in startling and almost dramatic tone that Buford's mind is rudderless. You must also remember that it has been declared as the law of this country, in the case of General Sickles, who was tried for the murder of Philip Barton Key, that the legal rule does not require that the insanity which absolves from crime should exist for any definite period, but only that it exist at the moment when the act occurred with which the accused stands charged. You will not fail to remember that in this case the insanity of Buford is proven to have been active for the last two years, and to have been latent, sleeping like a serpent in his blood ever since the moment when in infancy and innocence he opened his eyes in his mother's arms. And I beg you not to forget that in the case of Commonwealth v. Rogers, tried in the Commonwealth of Massachusetts, in 1843, before Chief Justice Shaw and a jury, and which is, I repeat, a pioneer case in this country, it was declared as the law of the land and the settled rule of science that a person laboring under the hallucination of communicating with the spirits of those who had 'gone to that bourne whence no traveler returns,' was not a sane person, and could not be punished for acts stimulated and provoked by the mental affliction of which, as in this case, the accused is the unhappy victim. Much has been said about existing differences between the law of Kentucky and the law of the rest of the world, upon the subject of mental alienation. I am not one of those who believe that any such disparity exists, for I can not but remember the noble and exalted sentiments expressed upon this subject by the great Chief Justice Robertson, who now sleeps amid the 'clods of the valley,' and who has found his eternal rest. But if what has been said on this subject really be true, let legislation and adjudication in the name of humanity wipe out so foul a blot upon the administration of justice in Kentucky. Hugo says, in that incomparable work, 'Les Miserables,' 'our joys are shaded, the perfect smile belongs to God alone;' as it is with the moral so it is with the mental world. Lord Bacon and the great Dr. Haslam may have been correct when they declared that all men were more or less unbalanced in their minds, and perhaps the idea is more felicitously described by Lord Erskine in the words, 'reason had not forsaken her throne, but unreason went up and jostled her in her seat.'

"I do not contend, gentlemen of the jury, that a slight

departure from the ordinary conduct of an individual, or an eccentricity as it may be termed, constitutes or typifies the condition of mental unsoundness. Acts of eccentricity in themselves are but rivulets that feed the mighty stream of madness, but in this case we have proven that the great central idea in the dominion of Buford's mind was that he had been wronged, pillaged and despoiled; and around the central delusion of his mind, with fascinating, hideous planetary regularity, revolved all the conceptions of his soul; and when he saw by the last adverse decision of the Court of Appeals his last hope on earth disappear, his mental battallions broke in panic and dissolved. Then came the cataract of the frenzy that overthrew the will power; then came with its resistless rush that stream of frenzy that carried to death and eternity the life of Judge Elliott, that startled all mankind with a tragic horror unexampled in the history of the jurisprudence of the world.

"Lest I may forget it, gentlemen, let me warn you against anything that may be said on the other side, after I shall have closed in relation to the perfect physical health (apparently) of the accused. You remember that Dr. Chipley was forced to admit that he never dissected a human being, and if I remember rightly, he could not name a single occasion on which he had been present when the knife of the surgeon opened up to the enchanted eye of the medical student the wonders and secrets of the human anatomy. But bear in mind that if anything is sought to be said on that subject, to our prejudice, that *post mortem* examinations of insane subjects have failed to reveal, in many instances, any evidence of physical disease or organic disturbance; furthermore, there is no proof in this case whatever as to the real physical condition of Col. Buford, consequently, the relation of physiology to mental condition will not enter into your deliberations.

"Gentlemen, did you ever see a phonograph invented by

that sublime genius Edison; by its instrumentality he causes a piece of tin-foil, wound round a brass cylinder, to speak the language of joy, pathos and human pity; to utter words of hope, despair and human sorrow. And how does this letter, written by Buford on that day of blood, his foot on the brink of eternity, speak to us to-day? It tells us that the o'ermastering monomania of his life had conquered the shattered remnants of his reason. It speaks to us of that undying, unfaltering, eternal love for that wronged and sainted sister who now sleeps in the Lord. It tells us that his last earthly provision was for one who in the days of anguish and pain, had soothed, caressed and cheered him. Christianity forbids that you immolate this man. Salvation bursting from the sepulchre of the Lord westward has belted the earth, and it is now returning to the cradle of its birth. The principles taught by the Redeemer in that sacred land, within whose limits are the pool of Bethesda, the brook of Kedron and the cedars of Lebanon, forbid the sacrifice to human vengeance of one afflicted by the inscrutable power and will of the Diety.

"One other topic, gentlemen, and I will close this discussion, as the weather is most sultry, and I have no doubt your patience is well nigh exhausted. All the medical experts on both sides, including Dr. Chipley, concur in the opinion that sleeplessness, chronic and long-continued, is one of the most positive indications of a diseased mind.

"And the proof in this case demonstrates beyond controversy or contradiction that for a long time anterior to this tragedy, Col. Buford's nights were sleepless, and were passed in mental anguish and disturbance. He walked the floor, muttering to himself, cursing and denouncing real or imaginary foes, and, in wierd communication with the spirits of the departed in the land of shades, listening to voices from an unseen world. In the language of some of the witnesses, great scalding tears rolled down his cheeks, and the strong man of dauntless heart was convulsed in the paroxysm of sorrow—and I ask you, gentlemen, is not the story of his life one that justly causes the tear of human sympathy to flow down the marble cheek of justice. Behold him upon the highway, astride his horse, talking loudly to himself and gesticulating to the air.

"It was not in this mood that Daniel Webster composed those prophetic and sublime sentences that saved the American Union and destroyed Governor Hayne. It was not in this mood that Henry Clay, the Great Pacificator, the Great Commoner, composed those magnificent sentiments that enthralled the American Senate and fascinated the world. So you see that Col. Breckinridge in this illustration and comparison was not in his usual happy vein.

"I think I have now said all that need be said on our side of this case. It is in your hands. I thank you for the kind consideration and attention with which you have deigned to honor me. I am speaking here as it were for the dead friend of my youth, and if it is possible that he be conscious of what I have done it is a consolation to me to know that he at least understands that I have never forgotten the ancient friendship that existed between us. I have demonstrated in this proof that this man's life can not be taken without a judicial murder. I have shown you the acts and influences that operated upon his mind and the reason why, in the view of the law, in the view of medical science, in the view of Christianity, in the view of humanity, you should not lay your hands on that life.

"In the name of our Heavenly Father, whose service is perfect justice, in the names of your wives and children, to whose embrace you will soon return, in the name of Christianity, humanity, science, progress and the law, lay not audacious and sacrilegious hands upon this mentally-benighted man, from his very infirmity under the protection of heaven. In the progress of the ages this country may become only the subject of the antiquary, but let not the historian of that distant day have it to record that a lunatic, o'ermastered by his fate, afflicted with the direst infirmity with which God has ever chastised any of his children, was, in obedience to the bestial voice of popular ignorance, clamor, prejudice, and revenge, in the gaze of the civilized universe, strangled to death on the scaffold and inhumanly rushed, soul unprepared, into the presence of his Maker.

"Col. Breckinridge, in his beautiful and eloquent peroration, brought before you the State of Kentucky holding in her hand the record of her list of crimes, and with her he brought the body of the dead judge. And upon this spectacle he demanded judgment for the people. I bring you, the dead judge, the mad assassin, and assaign all before Kentucky, and demand, in her sacred name, her traditions and her laws, that you be true to the solemn oath you have taken to true deliverance made between the people and the prisoner.

"I stand in the land of Boyle, Crittenden, Clay and Robertson, and in their name, in the name of that law which they so nobly vindicated while upon the earth, I demand that this mad captive go free and unscathed from this temple of justice; and, in the sentiment of the sublime prayer of the common law, 'May God grant him quick deliverance.'"

* * * * * * *

On the first ballot the jury stood six for conviction and six for acquittal on the ground of insanity. The jury finally agreed that he was insane.

On the following day after the verdict of the jury, Judge Jackson convened court and made the following order: "The jury in this case has returned a verdict of not guilty on the grounds of insanity and the court after hearing the testimony given in the case as well as the evidence which was called and being of the opinion that if he, the prisoner, was insane at the time of the commission of the act charged, he is now insane, orders that he be taken to the asylum for the insane at Anchorage, and that he be treated as an insane person."

Buford said that he did not see any use in sending him to the asylum, that six weeks further confinement might compell him to pass in his checks and that he would a great deal rather be out hunting and fishing. Col. Buford was confined in the Anchorage asylum for a short time, when he made his escape and went to Indiana, where our requisition laws were not sufficient to have him returned to Kentucky.

Col. Buford was about fifty years of age, and was a breeder of fine stock. His father raised a family of twelve children, Gen. Abe Buford being one of his sons. Several of Col. Buford's brothers were prominent in their sections of the State. He was a man of very high temper, stubborn and revengeful. In 1885, he shot and wounded George Thomas at the Lexington fair. He was considered wealthy but he lost most of his property. He was one of the most reckless, daring and dangerous men in Kentucky, a perfect desperado. He was not afraid of anything. On one occasion the sheriff with a posse of twenty-five men went to his house to levy an execution on some of his property. When the men arrived at his gate he walked to the door and pointed his gun at the man in front and told them, he would kill the first man who entered his gate. He then invited several members of the posse to take dinner with him saying, that as friends he was glad to see them, but as officers they could not come in his house. When dinner was over, he told them that they must leave. He had extended the hospitality of his farm and he was done with them. Not one of the twenty-six men had the pluck to disobey or disregard what he said, they did not levy on anything or offer to do so after his threat.

Judge John Milton Elliott was born in Scott county, Virginia, May 16, 1820. He was a son of John A. Elliott, a farmer, who served in both branches of the Kentucky Legislature.

Judge Elliott located in Floyd county, Kentucky, and began the practice of law in 1841. In 1847, he was elected to the Kentucky Legislature. In 1852, he was elected to Congress and was re-elected in 1855-57 and 59. In 1861, he was again elected to the Kentucky Legislature from Floyd and Johnson counties, but he was indicted in the United States Court, Judge Bland Ballard presiding, and he was expelled for, " directly or indirectly giving aid and comfort to the enemy." He then cast his fortunes with the South and represented the Ninth district in the Confederate Congress which assembled in Richmond, February 18, 1862, and he represented the Twelfth district in the two succeeding terms and until the downfall of the Confederacy. After the war he settled in Bath county, Kentucky, and was elected Judge of the Circuit Court, his term expired in 1874, and two years later he was elected to represent the First Judicial district in the Supreme Court of the State.

He was a man above medium height with a clean shaven full face, genial in manner and social by nature. He was a brave and true man in every sense of the word. " He acted well his part in the great drama of life."

There seemed to have been a fatality which marked the course of the Elliott family. Judge Elliott's father once killed a man. One of his brothers was shot through the stomach and killed at the battle of Princeton, Virginia. One of his brothers killed another brother, and a fourth one blew his own brains out in a fit of insanity.

Judge Elliott was buried in the State Cemetery at Frankfort; a beautiful marble shaft marks his last resting place. The subbase is of stone, the base is marble about three feet square and about six feet high on which is a marble column about fifteen feet tall and on which is the Goddess of Liberty, blindfolded and holding in her hand the scales of justice. On the east side of the base, facing the driveway is inscribed the following:

"John Milton Elliott,
Born May 16, 1820.
Assassinated for having done his duty as a Judge
March 26, 1879."

On the South side is found:

"A statesman of stainless honor. He became a member of the Legislature of Kentucky, served three terms in the Congress of the United States and two terms in the Confederate Congress.

"A Judge of pure heart and strong intellect, fearless, faithful, kind and efficient. As Circuit Judge and Judge of the Court of Appeals, he was without reproach."

On the West side:

"As a man, he was ardent, social, genial; by nature a philanthropist. He won the love of his fellowmen by his generosity and worth. Devoted as a husband; as friend, faithful and just. A dutiful citizen and upright official. His crowning virtues were candor, integrity and love of truth."

On the North side is the bust of Judge Elliott which is said to be a very fine likeness.

The Grandson of Gov. John J. Crittenden.

In December, 1882, and for some time prior thereto, Thomas Crittenden was living with his father, United States Marshal R. H. Crittenden, at Anchorage, Ky. Rose Mosby, a colored boy about nineteen years of age was employed as a dining room servant at the Crittenden home. On Friday, December 8th, Crittenden went to the railroad station at Anchorage under the influence of liquor. While there he became involved in a quarrel with the colored porter of the station, named Philip Young; after a few words had passed between them, Crittenden struck Young in the face with his fist several times and bruised his face to considerable extent.

The next day a warrant was issued against him for assaulting the negro and the trial took place at Middletown on Friday morning, December 13. Rose Mosby was present at the time of the difficulty and he was the chief witness against Crittenden; on the statement made by Mosby Crittenden was fined one cent and cost. Mosby testified that the colored boy Young did not call Crittenden a white son of a b—h as Crittenden claimed. After the conclusion of the trial, as Mosby passed out of the court room Crittenden said to him, "I will see you later about this," or, "I will see you this evening." He immediately left for his home and Mosby accompanied by a colored man named William Butler, followed, some time afterward.

Crittenden's home was near the railroad about two hundred yards above Anchorage station; the two colored men passed it on the way back. Mosby stopped and walked around to the kitchen where he met the cook. She told him he had better leave as Crittenden had been around three times looking for him. Mosby knew well the character of the man, and acting on her advice, immediately walked out on the road and rejoined Butler, who walked down to Anchorage station with him. The two went on the platform, at the Southeast corner of the station and remained in conversation at that place. In a few moments Crittenden walked up on the platform and seeing them, came up to Mosby and asked: "Aren't you going up to the house and clean up the dishes?" He replied, "No, I don't think I'll go back there any more." Crittenden simply remarked, "All right," and turning he walked up the railroad to his home, entering his front door. He took down his double-barreled breech loading shotgun and placed a cartridge into each barrel and put several more in his pocket and walked out the back door, going down to the stable. His actions were seen by the two colored men on the platform. Butler remarked to Mosby, "You had better leave for I see him coming with a gun." The victim however, felt no fear and replied, "He is only going hunting as he does every evening." Crittenden walked through the barn lot and making a short circuit approached the station from the rear, carrying the gun carelessly under his arm. He walked up on the platform at the fartherest point from where the two men were standing, they were around the corner of the building from his approach. Butler stepped, so that he could see around the corner, just as Crittenden got up the steps and he said to Mosby, "You had better run, here he comes," the warning was not heeded, Mosby made no attempt to escape. Crittenden walked up the porch and around the corner where the two colored men stood, he looked at Mosby for an instant and then presented his gun and said, "You son of a b—h you swore a d—n lie against me in court"; at that instant he pulled the trigger, the two men were standing about three feet apart and the full charge of shot struck Mosby in the left breast just over the heart, killing him almost instantly; Mosby staggered against the wall of the building and partly turned around, and as he did so Crittenden fired the second shot which struck him in the shoulder. With the gun still in his hand Crittenden turned facing Butler and said, "You are another one of the sons of b—s"; at the same time throwing out the empty shells and placing a loaded shell in one of the barrels. Butler had seen enough to convince him that it was time for him to leave and he quickly disappeared around the corner of the house. Crittenden reloaded the second barrel and walked around the corner, as if looking for Butler, but the frightened negro had made good his escape. Crittenden seeing that his man was out of reach, placed the gun under his arm and returned up the railroad to his home.

In a short time a crowd gathered around the dead body, a blanket was thrown over it and a telegram was sent to Louisville for the coroner and police officer. When the officer arrived the body was carried into the station and his clothing removed sufficiently to show the two wounds, either of which would have been fatal; one was in his left breast just over his heart, and large enough to insert three fingers at a time. Some fragments of shattered ribs were protruding from the hole. The coroner took out one large piece of a rib. The hole in the back was behind the right shoulder blade near the spinal column. The coroner summoned a jury and held the inquest; there were only three witnesses examined, William Butler gave his version of the whole affair, as above stated and two other witnesses who testified as to the threats made at the court house. The jury found that Mosby came to his death from a wound, inflicted with malice aforethought by the hand of Thomas Crittenden.

Crittenden was committed to jail without bail. At the January term, 1883, he was indicted for willful murder.

He was tried on that charge in April of that year and the result was a hung jury. After the jury was discharged, on motion of the defendant he was admitted to bail in the sum of two thousand dollars. In February, 1884, the second trial was had. Hon. Asher G. Caruth was Commonwealth's Attorney and prosecuted the case. The attorneys for the defendant were Judge P. B. Muir, Isaac Caldwell, Major W. R. Kinney, Muir & Kayman and Marc Mundy.

The evidence for the defense disclosed the following facts: After Thomas Crittenden returned from the trial at Middletown he went to the station, and there received an express package for his father, which he carried to his home, where Harry and Burnley Crittenden, his brothers, were awaiting dinner. The dining room was upstairs and the kitchen was below. Susan Johnson testified, "When Thomas Crittenden came back from Middletown, where the trial was held, he came into the kitchen and asked for Rose, if he had come. I said, 'No,' and he asked me if Rose had come and then he said to have dinner, that Harry would set the table." She said nothing about Crittenden being in good humor or making any threats. She said further, "When I was carrying the soup up I had on Rose's apron; Mr. Thomas came out of the room when I came up the steps, I did not know whether he was going to the dining room or going out. He ran up against me; he said, 'Is that you Rose,' and I said, 'Yes.' He said, 'Excuse me.' I did not go over to Ellen Barnett's and take Rose Mosby out and tell him not to come back to Crittenden's, that he would be killed." She was asked: "Were you not, when you went to Ellen Barnett's, in an alarmed and disturbed condition, and did you not go there to warn him not to come back to Crittenden's?" She answered, "I don't know whether I was disturbed or not, after he said he was not coming, I just told him not to come."

The Commonwealth proved by Henry Nichols that Susan

Johnson said that she told Rose not to come there; that Mr. Tommy was looking for him and looked mad and she thought he would be hurt. That Mr. Crittenden had come down twice to look for him; he came into the room where she was, looking for Rose, and he looked mad and she got excited and ran up to Mrs. Barnett's to tell him not to come there, that Mr. Tommy would shoot him. About the time Crittenden left the house after he ate his dinner, Mosby came into the kitchen and began eating, and when asked by Susan Johnson why he did not set down and eat his dinner as he ought to, he said that he had not time; "that Mr. Thomas wanted to see him and he wanted to see Mr. Thomas," and he then went out. Shortly afterwards, Crittenden met him at the railroad station and said, "Are you going over to the house and wash the dishes?" Mosby replied, "No, I don't think I will go there any more." Crittenden said, "Very well" or "you won't, very well," and went back to the house. Just after he left, Mosby picked up a rock and put it in his pocket. Crittenden was at the house for some minutes, he got his gun and loaded it with bird shot saying, he was going hunting, there having been some blackbirds in the neighborhood shortly before that time. He passed out the back way, and as he went towards the stable, his brother says that he told him to pay the expressage, which Crittenden said he had forgot, but would do so, and went on to the stable where he staid some five minutes, then he went to the west end of the depot, the route he took being further than the usual way. He got on the platform which led to the express office. He walked down it until near to Mosby, presented his gun and said, "You son of a b—h, you swore a damn lie against me in court," and shot him in his breast. Mosby turned and Crittenden shot him under and between the right shoulder and spinal column. Mosby staggered twenty or thirty feet and fell dead or died soon after his fall.

Brumbley Crittenden testified that he came in a few moments afterwards and took the gun from his brother and unloaded it. He said, when he got there Mosby still had a large rock in his hand. The Commonwealth claimed that Mosby had only one rock and that was in his pocket. Several witnesses testified that they saw no rock in or near Mosby's hand after he fell, and that none was on the platform.

The theory of the defense was that several colored boys who were present at the time of the shooting, belonged to and were members of a secret order and that they were at or near the depot, to assist Mosby in his contemplated assault on Crittenden; that Mosby had armed himself with rocks and when Crittenden came up he drew the larger rock to throw at him and was shot in the act; that Mosby went to Crittenden's home after he had been at Barnett's showing no fear of Crittenden, but hurrying through eating so he could find him, as he said he wished to see him.

After receiving instructions from the court and hearing the argument in the case, the jury returned into court the following verdict: "We, the jury, find the defendant guilty of voluntary manslaughter and fix his punishment at confinement in the penitentiary for the term of eight years.

"G. B. SHIPP, foreman.'

Thereafter an appeal was taken to the Court of Appeals and the case was reversed because of incompetent evidence which Judge W. L. Jackson, the presiding Judge, permitted to be introduced to-wit: "Did you not tell Ellen Barnett that while the Crittenden's were awaiting dinner that you went over to Ellen Barnett's and took Mosby out and told him not to come back to Crittendens; that he would kill him"? She answered, "No, sir; I did not think he would be killed, I did not know." She was asked, "Did you not tell Henry Nichols, that you went to Ellen Barnetts and took Rose Mosby out and told him not to come back to Crittendens that he would be killed "? Her answer was, " I don't know whether I told Henry that or not."

The Commonwealth was then permitted to prove by Henry Nichols that she said she told Rose not to come there, that Mr. Tommy was looking for him and looked mad and she thought he would be hurt, that Mr. Crittenden had come down twice to look for him. He came into the room where she was, looking for Rose, and he looked mad, and she got excited and ran up to Mrs. Barnett's to tell him not to come there. Commonwealth proved by Ellen Barnett that she said, " She had told Rose not to come down there, that Mr. Tommy would shoot him."

The Court of Appeals said: " This testimony was illegal, because it was an effort, substantially, and in effect, to show that the witness had stated, out of court, facts which she failed to prove in court, and thus to transform the hearsay testimony of Nichols and Barnett into substantive evidence which did not have the oath of Susan Johnson to support it. She failed to state in court facts which, it is said, she admitted out of court, and it was illegal to supply the omission by hearsay testimony."

When the mandate of the Court of Appeals was filed, Crittenden made an application for a change of venue, and thereupon the case was sent to Spencer county. Judge James Morris was Prosecuting Attorney of that district at that time, and he made a hard fight to convict Crittenden a second time, but the jury acquitted him. Some time after the last trial the court house of Spencer county was burnt and with it all the records of this case.

Thomas Crittenden was at the time of this trouble about twenty-nine years of age. He was a very handsome man, and a good baseball player. He was the son of United States Marshal R. H. Crittenden and a grandson of the famous ex-Senator and ex-Governor John Jordon Crittenden. He had an excellent education and was surrounded by wealth and refinement all his life. He had a reckless nature and a dare-devil spirit. He had the reputation of being a fighter and a desperate man. His associates were young men of good families, who having plenty of money to back them were guilty of all kinds of escapades. He was always regarded as a brave man but prior to the killing, his fighting had always been done with his fists, he never drew or used a weapon. When his father was appointed United States Marshal, Tom was made a deputy and he became noted throughout the State as a determined and successful officer. At one time there was a prize fight, in which he was engaged, at the old race course near Louisville with a member of the police force and in which he was badly beaten up. For two years prior to the killing he had been living with his parents near Anchorage, Ky.

Thomas Crittenden was a member of one of the most illustrious families in the State. His father, R. H. Crittenden, was United States Marshal for Kentucky. His grandfather, John Jordon Crittenden, served in the lower house of Congress and as United States Senator from Kentucky. He was Governor of Kentucky and was in the Federal Cabinet under President W. H. Harrison and under President Fillmore as Attorney-General. He was one of the great lawyers of the nation, a compeer of Clay, Calhoun and Webster. His great grandfather, John Crittenden, was an officer in the Revolutionary war. His uncle, George Bibb Crittenden, lawyer and soldier, served as an officer in the war between Texas and Mexico. He was captured by the Mexicans and was a prisoner for nearly a year. While he was in a Mexican prison, the Mexicans having determined upon a retaliatory measure, declared that a certain number of prisoners should be shot and to that end designated which should be the victims by requiring that lots should be drawn. A box containing a certain number of white and black beans was produced, those who drew the white beans were to be spared and those who drew the black were to be shot. General Crittenden, being an officer, was among the first to draw and he got a white bean, one of his intimate friends, who came later, was a man of family, having a wife and several children. General Crittenden gave him the white bean and risked his life by another draw which fortunately resulted in his drawing another white bean. He was an officer in the Mexican war. In the war between the States he was a Brigadier General and was promoted to the rank of Major General on the side of the South. After the war he was State Librarian for several years. Another one of his uncles, William Crittenden, was in the filibustering expedition to Cuba in 1850, and was captured by the Spaniards, and in short time afterwards he was ordered to be shot. The Captain of the squad who had the duty to perform, ordered Crittenden to kneel with his back to his executioners. He refused to obey the orders and said, " A Kentuckian never turns his back on an enemy and he kneels to none save God."

Thomas L. Crittenden, another uncle, was a Major General in the Federal army and held other positions of honor and trust. Lieutenant John J. Crittenden, a cousin, was on the staff of General Custer and was one of the sixteen officers who died with General Custer and his three hundred men on the 25th of June, 1876, at the Little Big Horn, and since known as the Custer massacre by Sitting Bull, leader of the tribe of Sioux Indians.

Thompson-Davis Tragedy No. 2.

Hon. Phil. B. Thompson, Jr., Congressman from the Eighth Congressional district of Kentucky, met Walter Davis as he was entering a train near Harrodsburg Junction on the morning of April 27, 1883, and accused him of debauching his (Thompson's) wife and thereupon drew his pistol, and as Davis attempted to make his escape from the train, Thompson shot him in the back of the head killing him instantly.

The deceased, Walter Davis, was not related to Theodore Daviess, who was killed, with his two sons, Theodore, Jr., and Larue Daviess, by Phil B. Thompson, Sr., Phil B. Thompson, Jr., John B. Thompson, Jr., and Davis Thompson at the court house in Harrodsburg in December, 1873.

Walter Davis and his family had been on intimate terms with the Thompson family for many years, and he had always been a warm political supporter of the Thompsons. Davis had been especially active in his support of Phil B. Thompson, Jr., in his race for Congress.

In December, 1882, Mr. Thompson went to Washington, D. C., on official duty and his wife went with him as far as Cincinnati where she stopped for a visit with some friends and relations who were boarding at the St. Clair Hotel. While there she was met by Mr. Davis, who, it was claimed, enticed her from the hotel and who drank with her until she was drunk and then took her to her room while in that condition.

When Mr. Thompson heard of his wife's conduct he refused to live with her again, and he never saw Davis any more until the time of the killing.

The shooting took place on a passenger coach on the Cincinnati Southern road at the Harrodsburg Junction.

Mr. Davis had started to visit his brother at Chicago,

and Mr. Thompson had started to Lexington, Ky., with Mr. J. W. Chinn, to witness the speed of Mr. Chinn's horses. Mr. Thompson rode from the Harrodsburg station to the junction in the passenger coach and Mr. Davis rode in the baggage car, which was also used as a smoking car, and they did not meet until they reached the junction. Mr. Thompson changed cars and had taken his seat in the Cincinati Southern coach near the door. Mr. Davis went in the same coach and seeing Thompson started towards him holding out his hand and said, " How are you Phil? " to which Thompson replied, " You damn son of a b—h, do you dare to speak to me after debauching my wife? " and at the same time rising from his seat. Davis turned quickly and went out; he slammed the car door and started down the steps; at that moment the car started. As he passed the front window to the steps Thompson drew his pistol and fired through the glass, the ball entered the back of his head and he fell from the train and rolled twelve or fifteen feet down an embankment. After the shooting Thompson got off the train and returned to Harrodsburg upon the same train which carried him out. The body of Davis was also taken back on the same train.

Thompson went to the residence of John B. Thompson, his brother, and there remained until the Circuit Court convened, a term of which, was at that time being held at Harrodsburg. He went to the court room and walked into the bar and addresed Hon. C. A. Hardin, the presiding Judge as follows:

" May it please your Honor: I know it is not customary, on occasions of this kind for the person appearing before the court, to make any statement of the facts surrounding an affair like this, but I deem it due to myself, the position I occupy, the community in which I have lived so long and who have so often honored me, that I should say something in reference to this unfortunate affair. I need not point to my long life and unblemished character for honor before these people as a justification of what I did, but feel that they should know from me or hear from me a history of the case or a portion of it. Last December, being called to Washington City by the duties growing out of my position, I was accompanied by my wife to Cincinnati; and being anxious to go to Washington as soon as possible, I left on Monday, the same day of my arrival in Cincinnati, and left my wife with friends in that city. The next day Mr. Walter H. Davis, the deceased, came to Cincinnati, and having met her upon the street, registered himself at a hotel and learning from her and the lady who accompanied her that she was stopping at the St. Clair Hotel, he followed them down to the hotel, sought her out and registered again there under an assumed name and took a room at the St. Clair. He then carried her out, under the protest of friends and having plied her with drink until she was utterly besotted, well knowing her infirmity in that respect, and continued his application until he carried her to his room, debauched her, making her the victim in her unfortunate condition of his degraded lusts; then turned her out to wander where she would until picked up by the night watchman, who carried her to her friends.

"Having accomplished my dishonor, he left the house before breakfast. While I had been informed of some of these facts relating to her intoxication, and that he was the cause of her public exposure at the hotel and her degradation, I did not know the extent of the wrong until last Tuesday night as I returned home, when I was fully informed of the infamy which he had heaped upon her and my family. I do not believe that I will receive the censure of this people, but whatever is the will of the court, I bow to it and submit as becomes a good citizen. This has broken up and destroyed my domestic relations and my peace and happiness. My daughter, dearer to me than all else on earth, is an exile from home and an outcast from society. She has sobbed herself to sleep on my bosom under this great calamity, only a part of which, she knew. His blood is but a feeble atonement for her tears, and had he an hundred lives, all of them would not atone for this great wrong.

"For the first time, this morning, I met him and I feel that I did what any man, who had a home that he loved and a daughter dear to him, would do, if he has courage to defend them from wrongs. In this I hope and feel that I receive the sympathy of the good and the virtuous and now submit to the action of the court."

When he concluded the Judge said: "It is, perhaps improper for me, occupying the bench, to express the sympathy I feel for Mr. Thompson as a man, but I deem it my official duty to hold him to bail to await any indictment the grand jury now in session, may find against him and fix his bail at five thousand dollars."

The bond was promptly given and he was released from custody.

During the speech of Mr. Thompson the court house was packed and every word was listened to with earnest attention.

In many respects the trial of Phil B. Thompson, Jr., was one of the most interesting ever held in the State. There have been very few instances where such eminent legal talent had been arrayed on opposing sides in any one case in Kentucky or elsewhere.

The attorneys representing the Commonwealth were Finley Shuck, Commonwealth's Attorney; James E. Cantrill, who was Lieutenant Governor at that time and afterwards Circuit Judge and Judge of the Court of Appeals; W. C. Owens, Congressman from the Seventh district of Kentucky, at that time Speaker of the House of Representatives; Judge Jerry R. Morton, of Lexington; Col. George Denny, of Lancaster, and B. S. Robbins, of LaGrange.

For the defense were United States Senator Daniel W. Voorhees, of Indiana; Senator J. C. S. Blackburn, of Versailles; Gen. D. W. Lindsey, of Frankfort; Col. R. P. Jacobs, of Danville; Col. Phil B. Thompson, Sr., and Col. T. C. Bell, of Harrodsburg.

On May 8th, the case was called at Harrodsburg, Ky., the Hon. Charles A. Hardin presiding. A large number of prominent people from other sections of the State were present to hear the trial.

The case was called in the morning and passed until two o'clock at which time both sides announced ready and the great legal battle was begun.

The first question of importance was raised when the Commonwealth moved the court to commit the defendant to jail during the intermissions of the court, and the defense moved the court to permit the defendant to remain on the bond which had been given, during the progress of the trial. His bondsmen consenting, the court permitted him to remain on bail during the progress of the trial until the case was finally submitted to the jury.

The next question which produced much oratory was a motion made by the prosecution to excuse one of the jurors, who had not been sworn, but who had been accepted by both sides. The Commonwealth stated that since the juror had been selected it had been discovered that he had an indictment for unlawfully shooting pending against him.

The Judge ruled in favor of the Commonwealth and the juror was excused.

Judge Jerry Morton stated the case for the Commonwealth.

The first witness was Mr. K. C. Smith, ex-Town Marshal of Harrodsburg, who testified in words or substance as follows: I was on the train the morning of the killing; when we reached the junction with the Southern road, while I was waiting for the Southern train, I saw Davis at the door of the baggage car of the branch road. He spoke to me and asked where I was going. I said to Lexington. He said that he was going to the same place. The train then came up and I went into the smoking car. Mr. Thompson and Mr. Chinn were standing up talking. I went on several feet beyond them. When Davis came in with his satchel and coat on his left arm, he held out his right hand to Mr. Thompson; Mr. Thompson said, "Have you the impudence to spêak to me, you damn son of a b—h, after ruining my wife and family?" and reached for his revolver. Davis threw his right hand back, but I don't know whether for a pistol or the door knob. Mr. Thompson drew his pistol as he spoke, and as Davis slammed the door, Davis *sorter* dodged. Mr. Thompson fired and I saw Davis no more until the train was stopped and we found him on the ground dead. He was shot in the rear of the right ear. There was a lightning Colts revolver, thirty-five caliber, self cocker, in Davis' pocket, partially out. I helped carry him up the platform, holding the pistol in as best I could; when we laid him down, the pistol fell out of his pocket. I saw cartridges in the chamber of the pistol.

Pat Nester, a newsboy, saw practically the same as Mr. Smith; when Davis came in he heard Davis and Thompson quarreling. Mr. Chinn was near them, the witness said: "I heard some one say, 'For God's sake don't.' I saw Davis back out of the car, and his valise got caught on the door and then it caught a second time, he pulled it a third time and slammed the door so hard that it broke the glass; about the time the door was shut, Thompson was getting his revolver out. He stepped towards the window and as Davis passed the window, Thompson fired, with the revolver about six inches from the window glass. The next time I saw Davis he was dead, and was lying twelve or fifteen feet from the track. When Davis came into the car he had his right hand on the door knob and never let go of it at all, as I saw; I did not see him extend his hand to Mr. Thompson."

John Wilson, conductor on the branch road, after telling about the killing said: "After the shot was fired Mr. Thompson stepped off of the train onto the platform opposite the body of Davis, I turned Davis over and said, 'Phil you have killed Walter; why did you do it?' Phil said, 'Davis had gotten his wife drunk, at Cincinnati, took her to his room and turned her out into the hall of the hotel to be picked up by the watchman, and that he could never look his daughter in the face again while that man lived.' Mr. Thompson twice alluded to his daughter, saying that she was an outcast from society, and he must kill Davis before he could look her in the face again."

Dr. Forsythe said: "I saw the wound; the ball entered the brain in the rear of the right ear and ranged from right to left; then to the front and downward. It was a deadly wound for any man."

The first witness introduced for the defense was Col. Jack Chinn, the noted turfman and politician. He was with Thompson at the time of the killing; his evidence was along the same line of the prosecution. He gave a detailed account of the trip from Harrodsburg to the junction and a very minute account of the killing.

After the introduction of several other witnesses, Mrs. Roth, a handsome French lady, about thirty years of age, wife of the hotel proprietor in Cincinnati, was introduced; nearly a whole day was taken up by the opposing counsel in the case. The Commonwealth claimed that her evidence was not competent, but Judge Hardin permitted it to go to the jury.

She said in part: "I am the wife of the proprietor of the St. Clair Hotel and housekeeper. I am a native of Louisville; Miss Buckner boarded with us. Her room was number forty-nine. It could not be seen from the elevator.

Mrs. Thompson occupied room forty-nine with Miss Buckner. She came from the Burnett House. She remained one or two nights. I first saw her the afternoon of the last night. I asked her what she wanted, she said Miss Buckner's room. Next time I saw her, was in the hall at night. I was attracted by talking in the hall, and went out and saw Mrs. Thompson and Davis standing in front of Davis' room. She was very much intoxicated. I asked her what she wanted, and she said she wanted to go to Miss Buckner's room. I said, I would take her. Davis said, very well, good night. I took Mrs. Thompson to Miss Buckner's room and rapped on the side window and awakened her. I wanted to see if Miss Buckner would notice Mrs. Thompson's condition and what she would say. Miss Buckner said, 'I thought you said you were going to the theater?' Mrs. Thompson said, 'We did go.' Miss Buckner said, 'When I go I don't get back this early.' Mrs. Thompson said that she left before the theater was over. The night watchman told me that he had tried Miss Buckner's door but could not arouse her and that she was not there. I said, I know she is, but she is sick. Then I went and aroused her, taking Mrs. Thompson with me. I had been out visiting and came in that evening at nine-thirty when John told me, as I went up the elevator, that the man who had room nineteen had come in with the lady who was with Miss Buckner, and they had been drinking and had gone to room nineteen and all was not right.

"When I saw Mrs. Thompson in the evening in the hall, she was staggering drunk. I asked her if she was sick; she said, 'no,' and tried to straighten up, but she was too intoxicated and bumped against the wall and struck her head against the door and finally got to Miss Buckner's room. When I first came in and John told me about Davis and Mrs. Thompson going up intoxicated and that they both went into Davis' room, I passed by room nineteen and the door was closed. Davis opened it to take Mrs. Thompson to Miss Buckner's room, when I found them in the hall, but I said, I would take her. I told Miss Buckner the next day that neither Davis nor Mrs. Thompson could room there any more."

John Maurer corroborated Mrs. Roth. He said that Davis and Mrs. Thompson had come in at nine o'clock, both of them had been drinking. When they left the elevator, Davis said, "Come this way, this is our room over this way." Davis took her to his room. About eleven o'clock I went up to put out the gas and Mrs. Thompson came out of room nineteen followed by Davis. I said, "Lady, what do you want?" She said, "I want to go to Miss Buckner's room." Davis said that he would go with her, but I would not let him. Mrs. Thompson was very drunk and staggered along holding to the wall.

The defense proved that Davis registered at the St. Clair Hotel on the 28th of November. Mrs. P. B. Thompson's name was found registered November 27th, and assigned to Miss Buckner's room. Davis was assigned to room nineteen as shown by the register.

Mr. M. T. Threlkeld was in Cincinnati at this time with Davis. He said: "Davis, on separating from me in the afternoon, said that he would see me again that evening. I put up at the Gibson House and ordered a room with two beds. Davis did not register. He told me he was stopping at the Emery. I expected he would stay with me over night and that was my reason for ordering two beds. Next morning I saw him and asked him why he didn't come around. He said he had some business which delayed him. I jokingly combatted that excuse and he then said, 'To tell the truth I drank a little wine and got a little full.' He may have said that he got as drunk as a fool, but my recollection now is, he said, 'I acted the fool.'"

After several hours argument on the question, Judge

Hardin gave John B. Thompson, Jr., the twin brother of the defendant, permission to tell the jury what he had found on investigation. He stated in substance: that he went to Washington City to see the defendant and he found that a letter had been received by him from Miss Buckner in which she had told him about his wife being drunk while in Cincinnati and that the defendant had written to Miss Buckner and his wife asking all the particulars and that his wife refused to tell anything that took place at Cincinnati. The defendant had stopped in Cincinnati as he came home, a few days prior to the killing and had investigated the report in regard to his wife, and he said, "I investigated and verified the worst what we heard."

On the fifth day of the trial, Miss Jessie Buckner, from Cincinnati, was placed on the stand and while she was testifying, three ladies dressed in black came into the court room for the first time. One of them was the widow of Walter H. Davis, another one of them was her sister and the other was the mother of Mrs. Davis and who was the wife of Governor Robinson. Miss Buckner told about Mrs. Thompson being drunk in the afternoon, and about Davis being with her. She said: "In spite of my protestations that evening the two left the hotel to go to the theater and I did not see her again until about eleven o'clock that night. Mrs. Thompson was at that time as drunk as she could be and fell on the floor in a heap; the next morning she left for Harrodsburg. The next time I saw Davis, I told him that he took his life in his own hands when he went home where he would see Phil, who would be sure to avenge the insult to his family."

The witness then made a detailed statement of the whole matter which she said she told the defendant, after he had insisted on her telling it to him. At the close of Miss Buckner's evidence the defense rested, and the Commonwealth introduced twelve witnesses in rebuttal.

The court instructed the jury: First, as to the murder; second, manslaughter; third, if in doubt the jury should find for the lessor offense; fourth, as to self-defense; fifth, if the jury believe from the evidence that Phil B. Thompson, Jr., at the time he killed Walter Davis, if they believe from the evidence that he did kill him, was so mentally insane as not to know that such an act was either legally or morally wrong, or not to have sufficient power or control to govern his actions, they should acquit him; sixth, if there is a reasonable doubt of the defendants being proven to be guilty he is entitled to be acquitted.

The court gave each side seven hours in which to argue the case to the jury.

B. S. Robbins commenced the argument for the prosecution, followed by W. C. Owens. Senator Voorhees made an eloquent plea for the defense, while he was describing the meeting at the time of the killing he said, it was more than man could do to restrain himself; James Garnet, the brother of Mrs. Thompson called out, "You are a G—d—d liar." The Judge ordered Garnet removed from the court room.

Governor James E. Cantrill, Judge Jerry Morton, Judge Denny and Finley Shuck made arguments for the prosecution, and Col. Thomas C. Bell and Hon. J. C. S. Blackburn for the defense.

Judge George Denny made the strongest argument which was made for the prosecution and Hon. J. C. S. Blackburn made the best for the defense. Many people who heard him said, "he made the best speech that was ever made in Harrodsburg." During the trial Mr. Blackburn received the following telegram: "Guthrie, Ky., May 10th.—Twenty thousand men in Southern Kentucky say, 'Little Phil' did right." (Signed) "Soldier."

After about two hours consultation the jury returned into court the following verdict: "We, the jury, find the defendant Phil B. Thompson, Jr., not guilty as charged in the indictment.

"SMITH OVERSTREET, foreman."

The last words had not been uttered, before a shout went up which shook the court house to its foundation, and it was repeated over and over again, in spite of the Judge's gavel and the sheriff's cries for order. The crowd made a rush to shake hands with the defendant and the lawyers who defended him.

Walter H. Davis was a prominent business man at Harrodsburg; he had been on intimate terms with the Thompson family and this friendship had been made closer by his marrying a close friend of Phil B. Thompson, Jr. He left a wife and two small children. The friends of Davis claimed that he found Mrs. Thompson on the streets of Cincinnati, in an intoxicated condition and that he took her to his room in order to get her sober and to protect her while she was in a helpless condition and that his conduct towards her was honorable and in keeping with the excellent character of the man.

Phil B. Thompson, Jr., was a bright young man under thirty-eight years of age at the time of the tragedy. He was a son of Phil B. Thompson, Sr., one of the best criminal lawyers in Kentucky at that time. He was known as "Little Phil," he had many striking qualities of his father and also of his Uncle John B. Thompson, Sr., who was Lieutenant Governor, and later was United States Senator from Kentucky, and who was also one of the great criminal lawyers of the State.

Phil B. Thompson, Jr., served with his twin brother John B. Thompson, Jr., as a Confederate soldier under General John H. Morgan. It was said that the twin brothers were so much alike in personal appearance that it was very difficult for their best friends to distinguish one from the other. They were only boys when the war closed and when they returned to their homes both of them studied law. Phil B. Thompson, Jr., was elected Commonwealth's Attorney in his district and he won distinction as a prosecutor. They were so much alike, not only in personal appearance but they had the same expression from the eye and the same tone of voice to such an extent that, when it was not convenient for Phil B., to attend court and perform the duties of Commonwealth's Attorney his brother John B., would take his place and neither judge nor juror would know the difference.

Phil B. Thompson, Jr., was elected to the Forty-Sixth, Forty-Seventh and Forty-Eighth Congress. He was serving in the Forty-Eighth Congress at the time of the unfortunate killing. In his first race for Congress he defeated William O. Bradley, one of the brightest lawyers in the State and who was afterwards Governor of Kentucky and United States Senator. In his second race he defeated Speed S. Fry who was a very popular man.

Judge Richard Reid Cowhided by J. J. Corneilison.

RICHARD REID was born in Montgomery county, Ky., October 3, 1838; he was of Irish descent; his immediate ancestors were substantial, worthy people. His mother was a woman of strong character; she died when Richard was only three years old; his early education was in the public and private schools of Montgomery county. His collegiate education was at the Baptist College, at Georgetown, Ky. He commenced practicing law at Versailles in 1860, and in a short time thereafter, formed a partnership with Governor Porter. In 1861, he was engaged to be married to Miss Sarah T. Jameson, a handsome, cultivated woman, who died two weeks prior to the day set for the marriage. He afterwards married Mrs. Elizabeth Jameson Rogers, November 12, 1873. In 1864, he returned to Mt. Sterling and formed a law partnership with his brother Davis Reid. He became a member of the Christian church in early manhood. He was kind hearted and generous. Rev. George Darsie, pastor of the Christian church at Frankfort, Ky., said of him, "I do not think I ever knew a purer, truer, better man than Judge Richard Reid."

In the session of 1881-2, the Legislature passed an Act providing for the "Superior Court of Kentucky to supplement the Court of Appeals." Judge Reid received the Democratic nomination of the district convention which was held in Lexington, in May, 1882, and was elected without opposition at the regular election. The Superior Court was organized in September of that year and Judge Reid became known in a short time as a clear thinker and strong writer.

In 1884, he became a candidate to succeed Judge Hargis

to the Appellate bench. His nomination was almost assured; his friends in all sections of the district were confident of his success. On Tuesday, April 15th, he returned to his home in Mt. Sterling, from a trip through the mountain section of his district; many of his home people called at his office to see him, and to assure him of their hearty support, among them was J. J. Corneilison, who was a brother in the church and a supporter of Judge Reid in his political aspirations.

On Wednesday afternoon, April 16th, Judge Reid went to the law office of John J. Corneilison to meet an engagement which was made the day before. Corneilison met him at the foot of the steps, they joined in pleasant conversation and ascended the steps together. John J. Corneilison was a muscular man of considerable strength. He weighed about two hundred pounds. Judge Reid was also a tall well built man, weighing at that time one hundred and seventy-five pounds. When the two men reached the office, Judge Reid was invited to take a seat; without taking off his hat or overcoat he sat down to examine some papers which Corneilison looked for but said that he could not find. "But here," said Corneilison, "Is a petition for rehearing by Judge Lindsey in the case of Howard v. Corneilison. I should like you to examine this and give me your opinion of it."

Judge Reid took the paper in his right hand and turned the leaves with his left. While leaning forward engaged in the examination of the petition in the office of his supposed friend, Corneilison struck him a severe blow with a hickory walking stick; this was followed by a great many other licks with the same instrument, until not less than five and possibly as many as twenty blows had been inflicted; in a dazed and bewildered way Judge Reid made his escape to the open street. Corneilison followed him with a cowhide which he had secreted about his person and continued the assault on the public street until he became almost exhausted and Judge Reid sought protection in the storeroom of Mr. John E. Bean. Judge Reid was unarmed. He had been a student and a gentleman all his life and he never had a personal difficulty with anyone in his life.

Corneilison gave two reasons for the assault. One was that Judge Reid had influenced Circuit Judge Riddle to remove him from the position of Master Commissioner of the Montgomery Circuit Court and the other charge was that Judge Reid had betrayed him while acting as his lawyer in the case of Howard v. Corneilison, which case was appealed to the Superior Court, and decided against him. From the evidence in the case, it was evident that neither charge was well founded. While a number of lawyers at the Mt. Sterling bar had signed a petition to Judge Riddle, requesting him to remove Corneilison, Judge Reid had refused to sign the petition or have anything to do with it. There was no proof to the effect that Judge Reid had ever mentioned the subject to Judge Riddle.

When the case of Howard v. Corneilison was heard in the Superior Court, Judge Reid was not present and the accusation of Corneilison that Judge Reid had written several words on the margin of the record was denied by both Judge Bowden and Judge Richards. Judge Bowden said: " Judge Richards wrote the opinion of the court in the case of Howard v. Corneilison, and I afterwards examined and read the record and concurred in the opinion. Reid never mentioned or talked to me about the case or tried to influence my opinion in any way. I have now before me the original record of the case of Howard v. Corneilison and the words in red pencil on the margin ' why ' on page 36 and ' his fee ' on page 37 and ' to his own statement ' on page 38, are all in my handwriting, and those in the blue pencil are in the handwriting of Judge Richards. The defendant came to my room and got the time extended in which to file a petition for rehearing, which was nearly thirty days after the opinion had been delivered. The defendant never at any time asked me whose handwriting said pencil marks were in, on the margin of said record. There are no words or memoranda on the margin of said record in the handwriting of Judge Reid or on or about the record anywhere.

Judge A. E. Richards swore to the following facts: " I wrote the opinion in Howard v. Corneilison. I made the blue pencil marks on the margin of the record and those in red pencil, the word ' why ' and ' his fee ' and ' to his own statement ' are in Judge Bowden's handwriting. Richard Reid never mentioned anything to me about the case before rendition of said opinion. He never in any way, directly or indirectly, tried to influence me in the opinion. There is not a word or any writing of any kind on said transcript from beginning to end in Judge Reid's handwriting. No inquiry was ever made of me by defendant as to whose handwriting said marginal memoranda were in. When I wrote the statement at the foot of the original opinion written by me, I wrote ' Judge Reid not sitting,' because of the fact that Reid's and Stone's names were to the petition. My recollection is clear that Judge Reid was not in Frankfort when this case was taken up and decided by Judge Bowden and myself."

This decision reflected upon the character of J. J. Corneilison. The Courier-Journal and other papers published the opinion in a few days after it was rendered.

Judge J. H. Hazelrigg, who represented him in the case of Howard v. Corneilison, and also defended him in the case of the Commonwealth against him stated that Judge Reid took no part in the case, either in its preparation or argument.

Col. Stone stated that he and Judge Hazelrigg prepared

Corneilison's case, and that he alone briefed it for the Superior Court, and that Judge Reid had nothing to do with it.

Judge Reid said: "Neither as attorney, or Judge did I have anything to do with the case in either court.

Corneilison's charge was: that professing to be his friend, being an elder in the same church to which he belonged, he had almost conclusive evidence that Judge Reid was traitor to his interests, and in an underhanded manner was doing all in his power to defame and slander him to the fellow members of his court. In the light of all the facts given to the public both prior and subsequent to the death of Judge Reid, it is hard to believe that he had anything at all to do with the case of Howard v. Corneilison.

Judge Reid's public statement was: "There are times in the lives of men when silence would be criminal; crises which Providence, for some wise and often inscrutable purpose sends upon us.

"The people of my home county have, in unmistakable terms, denounced the wanton causeless and inexcusable assault that was made upon me. They have resolved that the issue is now upon the people of Kentucky, whether the law is to be defied or obeyed. Whether a judicial officer should be required to avenge a wrong done him by taking summary vengeance in his own hands or is to be commended for forbearing to resort to violence and for upholding the majesty of the law.

"The circumstances of the attack upon me are well known to most of you. They have been properly characterized by the people of Montgomery county, and by the people and press of the entire State and of the United States.

"Utterly unsuspecting, I was in the law office of my assailant on a matter of business. I had always been friendly with him and supposed he was with me. The very day of the assault we met as usual. In the morning, on my way down town, I had a pleasant talk with him on the street, in front of his office, and addressed some kind words to his little boy at his side. We then made an appointment to meet at Stone's office and we met at or about the time named. He was in and out of the office several times engaged in conversation. He appeared as usual. I went to his office by appointment, and upon his invitation. When seated in a chair, turning over with my right hand the leaves of the pamphlet he had handed me to read, he began a furious assault upon me with a cane striking me, before I could rise up, a powerful blow on the side of the head, which paralyzed and stunned me, and left only my left hand disengaged to parry his blows. So swift and stunning were they that no means of defense were left me. I was stunned and bewildered. He was armed with a cane, a cowhide, and as I believed from his motions, words and threats, with a pistol. I was unarmed and all I could do was to struggle with him to the door between which and me he stood all the time, and escape his insane fury. This I did, and reached the street. I was dazed and bewildered by the assault, and was then unable to think or reason. I have no distinct memory of anything that occurred after I reached Main street and I did not come to myself until I came around opposite Stone's office:"

He said in explanation of his conduct: "I did not want the blood of my assailant on my hands. I knew that if I killed him it would wreck my life and destroy my usefulness. I did not want the spectacle of his prostrate form and the mournful procession of his wife and eight helpless children marching constantly before my eyes and haunting me day and night. I did not want the gloomy shadow darkening the windows and dimming the light in my own home."

On the day of his death Judge Reid arose about six

o'clock, after a good night's sleep, ate a hearty breakfast and seemed in better spirits than at any time since the assault. He had several conferences with friends in reference to his campaign. A large number of his friends were at his office. About nine o'clock he left Judge Brock's office. He talked with Judge Brock about a business matter for a short time, then complained of a severe pain in his head and asked Judge Brock if he could go upstairs and lie down. (Judge Brock roomed over his office.) The latter replied he would go up and see if the bed had been made. He took Judge Reid to his room and left him lying down. Two hours after that he returned to his office and went upstairs. He found Judge Reid lying upon his back, on the floor, his right hand at his side, his left upon his breast, a pistol on the floor to his right and a pool of blood near his head. A wound was found in the head where a pistol ball had entered back of the right ear, coming out back of the left ear.

The verdict of the coroner's jury was: "We, of the jury, find that the deceased Richard Reid came to his death by a pistol shot from his own hand between nine and eleven a. m., May 15, 1884."

He was buried in the Machpelah Cemetery at Mt. Sterling, Montgomery county, Kentucky.

The indictment charging the assault was as follows:

"Commonwealth of Kentucky,
v. Indictment for an assault and battery.
John J. Corneilison.

"The grand jury of Montgomery county in the name and by the authority of the Commonwealth of Kentucky, accuse John J. Corneilison of the offense of malicious assault and battery committed as follows, to-wit:

"The said John J. Corneilison of the county and circuit aforesaid, did on the 16th day of April, 1884, unlawfully, wilfully and maliciously and with the intent to wound and kill Richard Reid, in and upon the person of said Reid, make an assault and battery with a cane, stick, cowhide and did then and there unlawfully, wilfully and maliciously with the intent aforesaid, strike, beat, bruise and wound him the said Reid with the cane, stick and cowhide and inflict upon his head and body divers grievous and dangerous blows, whereby the said Reid was cruelly and dangerously wounded and his life greatly endangered and against the peace and dignity of the Commonwealth of Kentucky.''

The attorneys for the Commonwealth were C. R. Brooks, Commonwealth's Attorney, who was assisted by W. R. Patterson and Col. H. L. Stone, of Montgomery; Gen. John Rodman, of Frankfort, and Gen. William J. Hendricks, of Fleming.

The defendant was represented by Thomas Turner and son, Chas. C. Turner, who was later Judge of the Court of Appeals of Kentucky; A. T. Wood, Henry Woodford, B. F. Day, R. A. Mitchell, J. H. Hazelrigg, later Chief Justice of Kentucky; S. S. Gaitskill, H. Clay McKee, M. S. Tyler, W. P. Thorne, who was later Lieutenant Governor, and Judge William Lindsey, who had also been Chief Justice of the Court of Appeals, and was later United States Senator from Kentucky.

The instructions which were given by the court were as follows: '' The court instructs the jury that if they believe from the evidence beyond a reasonable doubt that the defendant J. J. Corneilison, in Montgomery county, Kentucky, and within twelve months before the finding of the indictment unlawfully, wilfully and maliciously with the intent to beat, wound or kill Richard Reid, making an assault upon the said Reid with a cane, stick or cowhide by striking, beating or wounding him, the said Reid, with such cane, stick or cowhide, then the jury will find the defend-

ant guilty of an assault and battery and fix his punishment by a fine in any sum or by imprisonment in the county jail for any period of time, one or both in their discretion.''

The Commonwealth proved by Jeff D. Cockrill that on the 16th day of April, 1884, in the afternoon between two and three o'clock, he (witness) was in the store of John E. Bean, in Mt. Sterling, Kentucky, and there were several persons present and that Richard Reid came running into Bean's store pursued by the defendant Corneilison, who had in his hand a cowhide and was lashing Reid over the head and shoulders with it. Reid said, "John," speaking to John Bean, "Stop him; make him quit," and witness rushed up to defendant and took hold of him, and said, "What the devil do you mean?" Defendant replied that he was thrashing the son of a b—h or d—d son of a b—h, don't know which. Defendant struck Reid four or five times over the head and shoulders with the cowhide in Bean's store and witness then took hold of defendant by the arm, who made no resistance and walked with him from Bean's store to defendant's law office, a distance of about seventy-five to one hundred yards and defendant was very much excited and exhausted and very weak; and when he and defendant got to defendant's office witness found the room in great disorder, showing evidences of a struggle and upon the floor not far from the door, witness found and picked up two walking canes, etc. Witness swore that defendant struck Reid five or six times in Bean's store. Bean swore that he struck him several times. No testimony was offered as to what took place on the street between Corneilison's office and Bean's store.

The substance of J. D. Cockrill's evidence was: That Reid came to Corneilison's office on his own business; that while sitting at the table, Corneilison showed him a paper and asked him if that was his writing. Reid said, "No," and Corneilison called him a liar. After some words, Corneilison struck him once with a stick, afterwards he drew a cowhide from under his clothing and struck him with that a number of times. Reid finally ran out of the office and into Bean's store.

Corneilison said he did not hurt him much and did not give him half enough; that Reid had betrayed him as his attorney and had, in some way influenced or procured the court to render an infamous opinion against him, which reflected upon his character, etc.; that he had no doubt of Reid's treachery to him and that he had evidence of it in Reid's handwriting.

It was in proof that Corneilison said: he told Reid he held him responsible for an opinion of his court; that Reid said to him, "John, I told you before that I had nothing to do with that"; that they then got into a stiff quarrel which got warmer and warmer for three or four minutes when he struck at Reid and struck a gas jet, and the blow hit Reid on the side of the neck; that he told several witnesses he did not intend to kill Reid. He claimed to have thoroughly investigated the matter and had found that Reid had betrayed him as his lawyer in the Howard-Corneilison case and had caused his court to render an opinion which was intended to disgrace him, and that Corneilison said he had gone to Frankfort and got the record in the Howard-Corneilison case and had found Reid's handwriting on the margin of the record; that he knew Reid's handwriting as well as he did his own; that he had shown the writing to H. Clay McKee, Judge J. H. Hazelrigg, R. A. Mitchell and J. R. Tucker, and they all pronounced it Reid's handwriting.

Corneilison avowed that he could prove by R. A. Mitchell that Reid was acquainted with his financial condition and knew him to be a very poor man with a wife and eight small children, all under fourteen years of age.

Corneilison offered to plead guilty to the offense of a malicious assault and battery but the court refused to permit that plea to be entered. The jury brought in a verdict as follows:

" We, of the jury find the defendant guilty and fix his punishment at a fine of one cent and cost and imprisonment in the county jail for three years," and the court rendered a judgment accordingly.

Corneilison was committed to the Montgomery county jail, there to remain for a period of three years. After he had been in jail for several months he was taken out on a writ of habeas corpus which was issued by Esquire Silas Stoper during the temporary absence of the Circuit and County Judge from the county. Esquire Stoper very promptly decided that Corneilsion was not legally held and he ordered his release, which order the jailor obeyed; but his freedom was of short duration. In a few days thereafter the Circuit Judge directed that the defendant be rearrested and he was forced to serve out the full term which had been adjudged against him.

The Tolliver-Martin or Logan Feud.

On June 22, 1887, the battle was fought which settled for all time the controversy between the Tolliver faction and the Martin or Logan faction in Rowan county. No other feud in Kentcky had given the State officials so much trouble. The Governor sent the military arm of the government to Morehead on several occasions; so long as the company of soldiers remained there everything was quiet, but immediately upon its withdrawal the trouble between them was renewed. Governor J. Proctor Knott did everything he could to settle the feud but all efforts failed. At one time he sent the Attorney-General, P. Watt Hardin to prosecute the cases which were tried before a special judge. All that General Hardin succeeded in doing, was to get some of the Tollivers indicted for carrying concealed deadly weapons.

The Governor succeeded, at one time, in having a treaty of peace signed by the leaders of the factions in which they swore that they would keep the peace for all time and which they did actually keep for nearly a year. This peace was terminated by the fight in which young Will Logan was killed. After this, Cook Humphrey and Craig Tolliver agreed to leave the State forever, and this agreement was kept for about four months.

During the session of the Kentucky Legislature in the year 1887, there was a joint resolution passed by the general assembly, for the purpose of investigating the troubles in Rowan county.

The joint committee from Senate and House, appointed pursuant to this resolution, made its report through Hon. John K. Hendricks, chairman, on March 6, 1888. This report was in part as follows: "Your committee finds from the evidence that the feud and lawlessness in Rowan county commenced in August, 1884, and grew out of the election of W. Cook Humphreys as sheriff of the county. On the day of the August election, one Soloman Bradley was killed in a street fight and a dispute arose as to whether Floyd Tolliver or John Martin did the killing. Bradley was a Republican and a friend and partisan of said Humphrey, and from the date of that killing and for some months afterwards the feuds partook of a political nature. Cook Humphrey and his followers representing a Republican faction and Craig Tolliver and his followers a Democratic faction.

"On December 2, 1884, Floyd Tolliver was killed in a barroom difficulty by John Martin. Martin at the time being a member of the Humphrey faction.

"On December 10, following, John Martin was assassinated at Farmers, in Rowan county, while in charge of the officers of the law under a forged order to bring him from the Winchester jail, in Clark county, to Morehead, to stand his examining trial.

"From that time forward, open murders and secret assassinations followed in quick succession until June 22, 1887, when the principle leaders of one faction of the marauders and murders were killed in an attempt to arrest them.

"From August, 1884, to June 22, 1887, there were twenty murders and assassinations in the county and sixteen persons wounded who did not die, and all this in a county whose voting population did not, at any time, exceed eleven hundred, and during this period there was not a single conviction of murder, manslaughter or wounding, except for the killing of one Hughes who was not identified with either faction."

In the year 1884, Cook Humphrey, a young man of twenty-five and a Republican, and Sam Gooden, a Democrat, were candidates for sheriff of Rowan county which county was ordinarily Democratic. The contest was very bitter, Gooden lived in Morehead and Humphrey lived on his fathers farm about seven miles from town. Humphrey was elected by a majority of twelve votes. On election day a man by the name of William Trumbo and a man by the name of Price quarreled, this quarrel ended in a fist fight; while the fight was in progress, John Martin, a son of Ben Martin, a well-to-do farmer, was struck in the face with a heavy instrument and one of his teeth was knocked out and his head badly bruised. He afterwards said that John Day and Floyd Tolliver struck him and knocked him down; when he got up he drew his pistol and the other men also drew their pistols; in the battle which followed, Solomon Bradley, a middle-aged man with seven children who was standing near, was shot through the head with two bullets. The Martins claimed that John Day killed him and the Tollivers claimed that John Martin did it. Ad Scyremore, another man who was not connected with the trouble, was shot in the neck but was not fatally wounded. It never was decided who did the shooting. From this killing the Tolliver-Martin feud originated, the relatives of each family allied themselves to their kindred until almost the entire county became involved, with reinforcements from Elliott and Carter counties.

Old man Martin, who resided a short distance from Morehead, had three sons, John, Will and Dave who resided near him. There were also several Tollivers, Marion and Craig at that time lived in Morgan county and Floyd lived in Rowan. Bud, Jay and Wiley Tolliver were their cousins and they lived in Elliott. Mace Keeton, Jeff and Alvin Bowling, Tom Allen Day, John Day, Boone Day, Mitch Day, Jim Arksley, Bob Messer and others who were engaged in the feud were Democrats and lived in Rowan. The Martins were Republicans and they were the friends and supporters of Cook Humphrey. The Logans were also

Republicans and friends of Humphrey. Matt Cary, the county clerk, was also a Republican. All of these parties resented the death of Solomon Bradley.

In December following the August election, John Martin went to Morehead where he met John Day, Sam Gordon and Floyd Tolliver. Tolliver went up to Martin and said, "John, you have been wanting to bulldoze me, but I am not going to permit it." Martin said, "I have not tried to bulldoze you Floyd." Tolliver said, "Yes, by God, you have and I am not going to permit it, I want you to understand me." Martin left him and went into the barroom of the hotel, then called the Galt House, and Tolliver followed him; on the inside Tolliver repeated his threats and at the same time he put his hand in his pocket. Martin then said, "Well if you must have a fight, I am ready for you." Both of them drew their pistols at the same time but Martin fired first and Tolliver fell mortally wounded. His friends rushed to his assistance and Tolliver said to them, "Boys remember what you swore to do, you said you would kill him and you must keep your word." Immediately after the killing Martin gave himself up to the lawful authorities. The members of the Tolliver faction were greatly enraged at the death of Floyd, and Martin was hurried off to Winchester to prevent a mob from hanging him. He had been there six days, when five men arrived with an order signed by the proper authorities, commanding the return of Martin to the jail at Morehead. It was claimed by the Martins that these five men were Alvin Bowling, Edward and Milt Evans and two other men named Hall and Eastman. The order they had was forged. The jailor gave Martin to them although he prayed to the jailor, not to do so. Martin's wife was in Winchester and she went back to Morehead on the same train which took her husband but she did not know at the time, that he was on the train. When they reached Farmers, a small town a few miles from Morehead, the train was boarded by a large body of masked men. Martin was handcuffed and was perfectly helpless. The mob filled him with lead. No one was ever arrested for the crime.

The third victim was also a Martin man and a deputy of Sheriff Cook Humphrey, his name was Stewart Bungardner. He was a native of Elliott county, but he had lived for a few years in Rowan. In March, 1885, he was riding along the public road, about six miles from Morehead, when he was shot from ambush and killed. The names of the assassins were never known; when the body was examined it was found torn to pieces, several charges of buckshot had been fired into the neck and chest and numerous bullet holes were found in other portions of the body. The Martins charged the Tollivers with the murder, but no arrests were made. In the following month Taylor Young, the County Attorney of Rowan county was the father of Allie Young who was afterwards Circuit Judge and of William Young, who later, was also Circuit Judge of the same judicial district, was shot from ambush and severely wounded. Young was a man of more than ordinary ability and much superior to the other men who were recognized as members of the different factions. He was a lawyer of ability and of good standing in the community. He disclaimed any connection with either the Tolliver or Martin faction, but the Martins claimed that he was a Tolliver adherent.

Some time after the bullet was fired into Taylor Young's shoulder, Ed Pierce was arrested in Montgomery county on the charge of highway robbery. He was tried in the Montgomery Circuit Court and sentenced to seven years in the penitentiary. While he was in the Montgomery county jail Pierce confessed that he and Ben Rayburn ambushed Young but he claimed that Rayburn fired the bullet which lodged in Young's shoulder. He said that Cook Humphrey had promised them two dollars a day and all the whiskey they wanted while watching for Young, and two hundred and fifty dollars when they killed him.

The fourth man killed was another deputy of Cook Humphrey. He was a visitor at the Martin home. The Martin home was a substantial two story building, the front of which was frame and the balance of logs; it stood about thirty feet from the public road and about seventy-five feet from the C. & O. Railroad. There was a steep hill back of the house which was covered with trees and undergrowth.

Mrs. Martin said, " Craig Tolliver and his gang came to my house early in the morning after Cook Humphrey and Ben Rayburn. At that time there was no one living at my house except women. Beside myself there were my two grown daughters, Susan and Annie, my little daughter Rena, also my married daughter, Mrs. Tusser, was at my house the day Rayburn was killed. My husband had gone to Kansas. He had received several warnings that he would be killed if he didn't go and we women folks persuaded him to leave although he did not want to do so. My two sons, Will and Dave, had also been threatened and they too had gone to Kansas. It was Sunday when the Tollivers came. Cook Humphrey and Ben Rayburn were at my house. They spent the night there. Cook was in the habit of coming to our house and the children always treated him as a brother. The Tollivers found out that they were there because the night before Humphrey was afraid that they might want to kill him and he slipped into Morehead after his Winchester which he had left there. They saw him and the next day they came after him. They knew that there was somebody with him but they did not find out that it was Rayburn until after they had killed him. They hid in the bushes around the house. In the party was Craig Tolliver, Mark Keeton, Jeff Bowling, Tom Allen Day, John Day, Boone

Day, Mich and Jim Ashley, Bob Messer and others whose names I did not know. Tolliver was town marshal of Morehead at that time and he claimed that he had warrants for the arrest of Humphrey and Rayburn on the charge of attempting to assassinate Taylor Young, but they never had any warrants. The Tollivers came in the yard and demanded that Humphrey and Rayburn surrender; they asked them to show their warrants and as they could not, they refused to surrender. Then the Tollivers hid all around the house and began to shoot. Rayburn had no arms except a pistol. Humphrey had a Winchester rifle and a shotgun. The Tollivers were armed with Winchesters and shotguns. Craig Tolliver slipped into the yard and got inside the house. He was creeping up the stairway when Humphrey discovered his presence, seized the shotgun and discharged it into his face. Tolliver fell back down the steps and his friends rushed in, grasped him by the legs and dragged him out of danger. He was carried away and took no further active part in the seige. He was badly scarred by the load of shot but quickly recovered. The half-grown boy was at work in the field. He approached the house and two shots were fired at him. The news of the affair was taken to Morehead but no one dared to go to the relief. Sue Martin made her escape out of the house. She was met by Craig Tolliver with his face covered with blood. He threatened to kill her if she dared to go to Morehead. She made a dash through the bushes and Tolliver fired two shots at her but she escaped and hid in a ditch until nearly night when she went to town where she was immediately arrested and placed in jail. In the afternoon the Tollivers threatened to set the house on fire if the two men did not surrender. About four o'clock Rayburn made an attempt to run for the bushes. Several hundred shots had by that time been fired. Mrs. Martin attempted to assist him; she went to the stable where Tom Allen Day, one of the best marksman was ambushed and when he prepared to shoot at the fleeing man she knocked up his gun. The two men rushed out of the eastern door, leaped the yard fence and dashed across the cornfield towards the mountain and forest. The entire Tolliver band rushed after them, firing as they went. They rested their guns on the yard fence and took good aim. The fugatives were over a hundred yards off when one of them fell. It was Rayburn. Humphrey escaped into the bushes and hid. The pursuers knew that he was armed with a Winchester and were afraid to go in after him. When the Tollivers reached Rayburn's body, they fired several more shots into it; they then robbed him and divided the money. After taking the money they went back to the house and left the body where it fell. They remained around the house and after dark Mrs. Martin said they set fire to it. She put out the blaze but they fired it again and the house and all the furniture was consumed. The women ran from the house and all of them except one daughter spent the night under a tree. The daughter went to Morehead where she was arrested and put in jail with her sister.

The next night Major Lewis McKee and one hundred and fifty soldiers arrived in Morehead; the Martin girls were released; there were no charges against them.

The Tollivers and Days were arrested and had an examining trial before two magistrates. The magistrates disagreed and the defendants were released.

The Tollivers claimed that they had warrants for the arrest of Humphrey and Rayburn and that they had a right to use as much force as was necessary to arrest them.

In a few months after that Jeff and Alvin Bowling, two of the prominent participants in these tragedies were tried in other courts. Jeff Bowling killed his father-in-law in Ohio and he was hung in the following August. His brother

Alvin killed Town Marshal Gill in Mt. Sterling and he was sent to the penitentiary for twenty-one years.

After the soldiers were returned from Morehead, Cook Humphrey, Howard Logan, Mat Casey and two or three others of their friends were beseiged in the Galt House in Morehead and several dozen shots were fired, but no one was killed. The doors to the hotel were riddled with bullets and the windows were shot out. After this Craig Tolliver and Cook Humphrey signed an agreement to leave Rowan county and never to return. In about four months after that Tolliver returned but everything remained very quiet for several months and when the time came to elect a police judge of Morehead, Craig said that he was now a peaceable man and a good quiet citizen and that the people ought to encourage him in his good behavior by electing him police judge of Morehead and he thereupon became a candidate for that position and he went out canvassing for votes with a Winchester rifle and in a short time thereafter all the other candidates withdrew. At the election, Craig received about fifty votes and he was duly declared elected. On the day of the election Craig Tolliver was standing near the voting place when Boone Logan came up to vote; the officer of the election asked him if he wanted to vote for police judge; Logan asked him who were candidates, and the officer said, Craig Tolliver was the only one and thereupon Logan said, "I will vote for———," and he named the most worthless man in town. The election to the position of police judge gave him power to issue warrants and this led up to the worst crime which was committed by either side, and that was the killing of the two Logan boys which occurred about two weeks before Craig and his followers were finally settled with.

Police Judge Tolliver issued a warrant charging the two Logan boys with kukluxing and placed it in the hands of Marshal Manning who, accompanied by a posse of twelve men including Craig Tolliver, went to Doctor Logan's about two miles from Morehead where his sons were staying ana demanded their surrender. He told them that he had a warrant for them. The Logans knew the men in the posse and they were sure that their arrest simply meant their assassination and they declined to surrender. Manning and his men then attempted to enter the house, when Jack Logan the youngest of the boys fired and severely wounded him (Manning). The council of the elder Logan then prevailed and they gave themselves up to the posse under the promise that they should not be harmed and that they would be given a fair trial and that their houses should not be burnt. Thirty steps from the house, one of the posse told the boys that they must die there, and they were thereupon murdered. About twenty buckshot and pieces of slug were found in each of the bodies; after they were killed their faces were mutilated by kicking them in the face. Their bodies were afterwards buried in Doctor Logan's private graveyard. The Logan boys were considered extra fine young men. The youngest one of them was studying for the ministry. The real motive for the killing of these two excellent young men was, that Craig Tolliver wanted Dr. Logan convicted of the charge against him. Doctor Logan had been arrested on the charge of conspiring to kill Judge Cole and others and he had been sent to Lexington for safe keeping. His sons would have been witnesses in his behalf and their testimony would have doubtless cleared him of the charges and Tolliver concluded that the best thing he could do was to put them out of the way.

Up to this point seventeen men had lost their lives in the feud; among them were Solomon Bradley, John Martin, Whit Pelfrey, B. Caudelle, Deputy Sheriff Baumgartner, Mason, Keeton, John Marlow, John Davis, Wiley Tolliver, Witcher, Willie Logan, Ben Rayburn, John Day, Floyd Tolliver, John B. Logan and W. H. Logan. The killing of the two Logan boys was followed by a notification from Craig Tolliver to Boone Logan, another brother, to leave the county. Boone Logan was a lawyer and a quiet citizen. He left there and went to Frankfort to consult with Gov. Knott on the situation. Gov. Knott told him in the presence of Liteutant Governor Hindman that he was sorry that he had no official power to extend any relief to the citizens of Morehead; that everything the State could do had been tried and found unavailing as a remedy. It was currently reported at the time that Gov. Knott had told Logan that a private citizen could arrest a man if a warrant had been issued for him charging him with a felony. Whether Logan was advised what to do or whether he acted on his own intitiative made but little difference in the final result. After the consultation with the Governor, Logan got into communication with Hiram Pigman, a merchant at Morehead who had been in trouble with Craig Tolliver. These two men secured the active cooperation of Sheriff Hogg and a systematic canvass of the best citizens of the county was made and they were requested to assist in bringing the Tollivers to justice. One hundred and thirteen men in Rowan county and surrounding counties were enlisted; and to secure arms for them Boone Logan went to Cincinnati and purchased sixty Winchester rifles, the rest of the men were provided with shotguns, muskets, etc., meetings were held and plans were formed. Warrants of arrest were issued charging murder, arson and other crimes and misdemeanors against Craig Tolliver, Jay Tolliver, Bud Tolliver, Andy Tolliver, Cal Tolliver, Burke Manning, Jim Manning, John Rodgers, Hiram Cooper, Boone Day, Bill Day, Tom Day and Sam Gooden. These warrants were placed in the hands of Sheriff Hogg and Wednesday morning at ten o'clock, June 22, 1887, was the time designated for the arrest. At three o'clock that morning one hundred and thirteen men under the command of Sheriff Hogg arrived in detachments at Morehead, and were stationed at seven different positions outside of the town limits and completely surrounded the town.

Craig Tolliver was apprehensive of an attack but he felt secure. He had heard of the citizens meeting and he started the report that a band of regulators was being organized to drive him out of the county. This was likely done to strengthen his own resistance to the authorities. He evidently felt confident of his ability to repel any attack, and he claimed that he and his men could whip a thousand regulators. He had been drinking for some time and was at that time under the influence of liquor; he was not aware of the feeling which existed against him since the killing of the Logans.

At eight o'clock the Tolliver forces were gathered at the American House; they were on the lookout for trouble. They were well armed as usual; Craig had two pistols and a belt full of cartridges. It was a quarter past eight when one of the posse named Byron was seen at the depot. Byron was armed with a Winchester and the Tollivers at once opened fire on him. Byron ran and the Tollivers pursued him, keeping up the firing. This precipitated the conflict. Men sprang from behind stumps, bushes and piles of lumber. A volley was poured into the Tolliver party which caused them to make a hasty retreat. They ran past the American House and towards the Central Hotel. The other squads of the posse came up and the action became general. The Tollivers continued their retreat and all of them but one reached the Central Hotel. The one who fell was Bud Tolliver with a wound which shattered his knee. He managed to crawl through the fence and conceal himself in some tall grass. The members of the posse wore no hats in order that they might, by this means of identification, avoid shooting each other. The Tollivers soon discovered that their enemies were bareheaded and threw away their hats. By doing this several of them escaped. The battle lasted for two hours and a half and there was about two thousand shots fired. Tolliver and his men were driven from the hotel and Jay Tolliver was killed on the hill a short distance from it. Craig Tolliver ran down the street bareheaded in the direction of the Cottage Hotel, just as he reached the railroad about sixty feet from the Galt House a bullet struck him in the leg and he fell. He started to rise when he was struck by another bullet. There were at least fifteen men shooting at him. He made no effort to get up after the third attempt. As he lay there apparently dead the firing continued. He was shot through the head twice. Though the Tollivers were good shots they were not able to use their pistols with any effect. The only man in the posse who was wounded was Bud Madden, he was shot in the side by Cal Tolliver. One of the gamest fighters on the Tolliver side was Cal Tolliver, a boy of fourteen years of age. He was a nephew of Craig's. He was very small for his age. He did not seek the protection of trees and fences as many others did but he stood out boldly and fired his pistol like a veteran. One bullet passed through the seat of his trousers. When Craig Tolliver fell this boy ran to him and got the watch and pocketbook of the dead man.

Some members of the posse found Bud Tolliver in the grass where he had crawled to conceal himself. He was wounded and in a helpless condition. They placed their guns close to his head and fired several shots into his brain.

Hiram Cooper was found in a wardrobe in Allie Young's room at the Central Hotel. He was dragged from his hiding place and killed in the room.

Cal Tolliver crawled under a house near the Central Hotel and remained in hiding until late in the afternoon when he escaped to the woods. Andy Tolliver who was shot during the engagement also made his escape. The two Mannings escaped by throwing away their hats, they continued their flight until they got out of the State. John Rogers also made his escape. Allie W. Young, who was at that time, the Prosecuting Attorney for Rowan county, was at Mt. Sterling which fact more than likely saved his life.

After the battle, a mass meeting was held at the courthouse at which Boone Logan and others made speeches. A citizens protective association was formed. They adopted resolutions declaring; "If any one is arrested for this day's work we will reassemble and punish to the death any man who offers the molestation."

The bodies of Craig, Jay and Bud Tolliver were taken charge of by the posse. They were washed, dressed and laid out in the public room of the American House. Coffins for the four bodies were ordered from Lexington. The Tollivers were taken to Elliott county for burial.

Craig Tolliver left a wife and two small children. He was a good husband and indulgent father. Marion Tolliver, a brother of Craig's, was a peaceable and well behaved citizen. He took no part in the feud.

Craig Tolliver's correct name was Talliaferro. His father came from Virginia and he was a well-to-do farmer of Morgan county. However, when Craig was a boy fourteen years of age his father had a lawsuit with a neighbor in which Tolliver was successful; there was a general bad feeling against him and after the trial was over, the unsuccessful litigant and a few of his friends went to Tollivers house in the night time and shot him to death while he was in bed. Craig was present and saw his father murdered; this happened about twenty years before Craig lost his life. After his fathers death the family moved to Elliott county where Craig grew into manhood. He carried weapons, practiced shooting, drank liquor and was a tough character as a boy and he grew worse as he grew older.

He went to Rowan county about five years before his death. He was six feet tall; thirty-six years of age; had light blue eyes; brown hair and he wore a large mustache and a small goatee. He was true to his friends and cruel to his enemies. Perhaps no gamer man ever lived in the mountains or elsewhere. He was poorly educated, shrewd and cunning and mild mannered except when in action. He was a typical desperado.

While the newspapers in all parts of the United States had much to say about Craig Tolliver, about the time of his death, no mention was ever made of any man who had lost his life from his hand. It seems that he directed others to commit deeds of violence but seldom took part in them. Tolliver made his living without any visible occupation or means of support but he always had plenty of money. Shortly before his death he engaged in the whiskey business and at the time of his death he owned two saloons in Morehead and he was also engaged in the hotel business.

The Goebel-Sanford Killing.

On April 11, 1895, State Senator William Goebel shot and killed John L. Sanford, cashier of the Farmers and Traders Bank, of Covington, Ky.

The shooting occurred at the entrance of the First National Bank in Covington, at 1:30 o'clock. Mr. Sanford died about five hours after the shooting. He was shot through the head; the ball entered his forehead over the left eye at an upward range. At the same time, Mr. Sanford shot at Senator Goebel; the ball entered his coat in front and passed across his left hip ranging downward, entered his trousers and passed through cutting the flap of his cutaway coat and splitting the left flap at the hip. Though the ball passed for some distance between the clothing and his skin, the skin was not broken. Only two shots were fired, both of them almost simultaneously. The witnesses did not agree as to who fired first.

Mr. Sanford fell with his face downward, across the bank steps; Senator Goebel backed a few steps and seeing that his aim had been perfect, he placed his pistol in his pocket and walked down the street to the police headquarters. He walked in and entered the telephone booth and telephoned to his brother, Justice Goebel, of Cincinnati, to come to him at once; when he came out of the box he said to the officer in charge, "I suppose you have heard of it," and being answered in the affirmative he then said that Sanford had tried to kill him and that he had defended himself by shooting him. He thereupon surrendered himself into the custody of the officer at the same time handing to him his pistol which was a 38-caliber Smith & Wesson, which had only one chamber empty.

Mr. Frank P. Helm, president of the First National Bank, at the door of which the shooting took place, and the Honorable W. J. Hendricks, Attorney-General of Kentucky, were present at the time the shooting occurred. In a few moments after the shooting, General Hendricks said: "I am so shocked I can hardly talk about the matter, it came so suddenly, so entirely unexpected, that I have not recovered from the shock. Senator Goebel and I came up the street together with Judge O'Hara and some other friends from the court house. We separated from these gentlemen at Judge O'Hara's office. I had a check I wished to get cashed, and asked Senator Goebel to walk up to Sanford's bank with me. He assented and we were going in that direction when we saw Mr. Helm across the street; Senator Goebel said, 'Helm will cash your check, go over to the bank.' Mr. Helm assented, and we crossed the street and walked up to the bank. As we approached the bank, I saw Mr. Sanford standing there in a waiting attitude. He seemed to be leaning on the iron railing that runs down besides the steps and I think was on the steps. As we came up, he spoke to me and shook hands with me with his left hand having his right in his trouser's pocket. He then turned to Senator Goebel, saying, 'I understand that you assume the authorship of that article,' to which the Senator responded, 'I do.' The shooting followed instantly and I was so dazed and dumbfounded that I could not realize what was happening until Mr. Sanford fell face downward on the steps and Senator Goebel backed away. I declare I don't know who shot first, the shots were so close together."

Mr. Frank P. Helm, the other man who was present at the time of the shooting, said: "I was right up against them and really thought at first that I had, myself, been shot. I was on my way to the bank from dinner and as I came up Scott street I saw Attorney General Hendricks and Senator Goebel; they saw me and crossed the street, we exchanged greetings, Hendricks wanted a cigar and he and the Senator started up to Beckert's. I told Goebel that Beckert had died about noon and that his place was closed and directed their attention to Nedler's drug store, where I told them they could get a cigar. Neither Goebel nor I wanted to smoke, so Hendricks went over alone, when he came back he spoke of wanting to go to Sanford's bank to get a check cashed. Goebel said, 'Helm here will cash your check.' We then crossed the street (Madison) and turned towards the bank. As we were about at the gas office, I saw Sanford standing on the bank steps and said, 'there is Sanford now.' 'Yes,' said Goebel, 'There's the —.'' He laughed and repeated his remark. I did not pay attention to it. I did not think of any previous trouble between them and thought Goebel was speaking good humoredly though roughly. As we came to the bank entrance, I spoke to Sanford and stepped on the bottom step. Hendricks also spoke to Sanford and they shook hands. Sanford extended his left hand, his right being in his trousers' pocket. As he withdrew his hand from that of Hendricks he turned to Goebel, motioning his left hand in his direction and said, 'I understand that you assume the authorship of that article.' 'I do,' responded Goebel, and as he said it I saw him with a fumbling motion begin to draw a pistol from his right hand trousers' pocket. At the same instant Sanford drew and the two shots rang out. The shots were almost instantaneous and I can not say positively which fired first. The shots were right in succession —bang-bang, and Sanford fell forward, instantly, face downward on the bottom step. My impression is that he was standing on the steps as I was, for in falling his head struck the front part of my left leg and my left foot.'' Mr. Helm showed the blood stains on his trousers and shoes. '' The position of his fall almost threw me down and Hendricks caught me saying, 'Are you hurt?' My face was powder burned and I did not know but that I had been shot. I can't see for the life of me how Goebel escaped. We were right together, all four of us. As we came up I was on the inside of the pavement, Goebel in the middle and Hendricks on the outside, as we reached the steps I stepped upon the first step and turned facing the three. Hendricks was next, Sanford and Goebel directly in front, the width of the step possibly separating them. As Goebel replied to Sanford's question, he partially turned and as he fumbled with his pistol right under my chin, I being partially between them and fired upward. Sanford fell, as I stated, almost throwing me down. Sanford's pistol fell to the pavement and Goebel backed away a step or two, then picking up his coat, walked down to the front of the gas office and stood near the curb for a few minutes when I lost sight of him. As I turned my attention to Sanford several people rushed up and I had them carry him into the office and sent runners for physicians. While I can not say that Sanford fired first, the impression left on me by the circumstances is that his pistol was possibly first exploded. At the exchange of words both men instantly drew, and as I say, it was impossible for me to determine by actual sight, who, if either, did shoot first, but Sanford's falling impresses me that possibly his was the first shot, as he probably could not have shot after being hit.'' The circumstances are all conclusive that when the words passed both men went for their guns with fatal intent.

The article referred to which caused the fatal shooting appeared in the *Ledger,* a weekly newspaper, which was issued every Saturday. The paper had been issued by Thomas Riley until just prior to the tragedy. Riley stated that he had transferred it to Senator Goebel and at that time had severed all connection with it, but no public announcement had been made of the transfer or change in ownership and it was not generally known that Senator

Goebel had assumed the ownership and had become the editor. The article referred to was on State politics and the excerpt which provoked Mr. Sanford's indignant resentment, which resulted in his death was as follows: "Col. John Gon-h-ea Sanford claims to carry the legislative vote of the county of Kenton in the next Senatorial race, in his pocket and proposes to deliver it bodily to Senator Joe Blackburn in his effort for second re-election. 'Gon-h-ea' John owes a peculiar debt to Blackburn and proposes to pay it. When Senator Blackburn's brother was Governor, the Senator induced his brother, the Governor, to pardon a close kinsman of 'Gon-h-ea' John before trial or conviction and while a fugative from justice in Canada, because of indictment returned against him by a grand jury of Kenton county for forgery and embezzlement while city clerk of Covington. There will, however, be some music before that debt is paid in that way."

The unfriendly feeling between the two men dated back of this period for several years. Senator Goebel was regarded by Sanford as having antagonized the banking interest and in his vigorous way opposed the Senator's political ambitions. He was largely instrumental in defeating Senator Goebel's ambition or desire to become the Appellate Judge in his district. He managed to secure a split of the delegation from Senator Goebel's own county and he became the leader of the opposition at the August convention. For some time after the August convention the political warfare was abated; neither side had an occasion to make a decisive move until the campaign of Hon. A. S. Berry for his return to Congress. In this contest the two men were counted for Berry. Mr. Sanford took some active part for him and Senator Goebel was also in favor of his return to Congress. The last outbreak between them was traceable to the fact that Senator Goebel was for Clay against Hardin and Buckner and was for Brown against Blackburn. It was understood that Sanford would warmly support Senator Blackburn and that he would make an aggressive fight against the anti-Blackburn combination. Senator Goebel anticipating this and having secured control of the *Ledger* he concluded to assume the aggressive, and forestall any attack that Mr. Sanford might have had under contemplation. This is the explanation offered to his allusions to Mr. Sanford which provoked the encounter and resulted in the shooting.

The time of the shooting was the first meeting of the two men since the appearance of the *Ledger* which contained the article referred to.

Mr. John L. Sanford was the son of Cassius Sanford, a well known citizen of Covington. His mother was a sister of Capt. T. P. Leathers, of New Orleans, the noted steamboat man. Mr. Sanford was about fifty-eight years of age at the time of his death; he left surviving him, a widow, one son and one daughter. His wife was the daughter of J. Birney Marshall and the niece of Gen. Humphrey Marshall. He served in the Confederate army. For some time he was on the staff of General Preston and when that officer was appointed Minister to Mexico, he served as Adjutant General under General John H. Morgan; later he was on the staff of Gen. John C. Breckinridge in southwest Virginia, and after General Breckinridge was made Secretary of War, he served on the staff of General John Echols. He was a brave soldier and an efficient officer. After the war he returned to Covington and for a long time he was clerk and teller at the Farmers Bank. When the Farmers and Drovers National Bank was organized about fifteen years prior to his death, he became cashier and continued with that institution until his death. He was recognized as being its chief executive officer. He was an energetic business man and was successful in his business relations. He had excellent judgment and his opinion was sought upon all matters connected with investment.

He was a political leader of ability and a good organizer. He was the close friend and political advisor of Hon. John G. Carlisle from an early period in the career of that distinguished statesman. He was noted for his aggressive leadership but he never sought political preferment for himself. He was a true friend and an honest man.

In his domestic life he was a devoted husband and father. He owned a farm of several hundred acres near Covington on which he resided and in which he took great pride.

Governor Goebel was a successful business man as well as a successful lawyer. He was forty years of age at the time of this unfortunate incident. He came from Pennsylvania to Covington when he was quite young. He was never married. He was successful in politics and served for many years as State Senator. He was the author of many measures which gave him popularity among the masses and by which he also incurred the hatred of certain classes.

He championed low bridge tolls and the curtailment of other rights and privileges which had been granted to corporations. It was one of these measures regulating turnpike charges over roads in which Sanford was interested which hastened the rupture between them. Goebel was the leader of the faction against Harvey Myers and Theodore Hallam. There was bad blood in Kenton county politics for years. There have been very few State conventions in the past thirty years where there was not a contest from Kenton. At every opportunity the embittered factions have fought each other relentlessly. Sanford and Goebel were nearly always on opposing sides. Sanford was bitter against Goebel in his race for Judge of the Court of Appeals and caused his defeat.

Perhaps no other man in the history of Kentucky ever incurred so much opposition and bitterness as did Senator Goebel. He was a man of strong intellect and he occupied a conspicious position in the Senate. He was a hard fighter; even his enemies admired his ability and his fighting qualities. The Goebel election law stirred the State from center to circumference as did also other measures advocated by him. The opposition which developed through the State to some of his measures; the fierce attacks made upon him by the press; the relentless fight waged against him by the corporations which he had undertaken to control, conspired to make him more determined in his fight against them. Smarting under their attacks he became the fiercer in his opposition to measures which he did not approve and more curt toward persons whom he suspected of being unfriendly to his views. The opposition which he aroused pursued him to his death. His race for Governor, the contest which followed and his assassination were the culmination of the bitterness and hatred of the corporate greed and avarice which slew him.

Judge Stephens held the examining trial; Senator Goebel was represented by W. McD. Shaw, Mat Harbison and Richard P. Ernst; the Commonwealth was represented by County Attorney Simmons. The chief witnesses were General Jack Hendrick and Mr. Frank P. Helm. The trial was held in the court house at Covington, April 16, 1895. Several witnesses testified that Sanford shot first. J. B. Scheffer testified that when Mr. Sanford's clothes were opened a dirk knife was found upon his person.

Claude Desha, of Cynthiana, testified that in March he told Senator Goebel of a conversation between himself and Mr. Sanford at the August convention in the August preceding the shooting, in which Mr. Sanford had said he would like to kill Goebel and he intended to do so.

The trial lasted from ten o'clock in the morning until four in the afternoon. The friends of the deceased did not employ any counsel to assist the pros cution. When rendering his decision in the case, the court said: "If there is reasonable doubt of the guilt, the court must acquit, is briefly the law. In this case there is reasonable doubt in my mind; or in other words, I can not believe the accused would be held guilty by a jury on the evidence that has been here adduced. I therefore dismiss the charge and the defendant is at liberty."

In rendering his opinion, the court did not correctly state the law which applies to examining courts. In the final trial before a jury the court instructs the jury, unless they believe from the evidence beyond a reasonable doubt that the defendant has been proven guilty the jury should acquit. This rule is reversed in the examining trial, and it is the duty of the court to hold the defendant to the grand jury if there are reasonable grounds to believe that a public offense has been committed.

Though the court held that the evidence was not sufficient to hold the defendant over to the grand jury. The whole matter was examined into by the succeeding grand jury. When the Kenton county grand jury had the killing under investigation Mr. Thomas T. Riley, who formerly owned the paper in which was the publication which caused the killing, testified. Mr. Riley admitted that he was a part owner of the paper at the time, but he declined to answer the question, "Was that article written by Senator Goebel, or was he in any way instrumental in its publication?" When taken before Circuit Judge Perkins, Mr. Riley declined to answer the question and thereupon Judge Perkins sent him to jail for contempt of court, there to be held until he should consent to answer all questions asked him. In about an hour Mr. Riley concluded to tell the jury who wrote the article. It developed from his evidence and that of the typesetters in the *Ledger* office, that the article was in the handwriting of Senator Goebel.

The grand jury failed to find an indictment and some time afterwards Mrs. Sanford, the widow, brought suit against Senator Goebel for the sum of ten thousand dollars but the jury refused to find anything for the plaintiff.

Swope-Goodloe Tragedy.

On Friday afternoon, November 9, 1889, Col. A. M. Swope and Col. William Cassius Goodloe had a personal encounter in the corridor of the post office, at Lexington, Ky., in which Col. Swope was instantly killed, and Col. Goodloe received fatal injuries from which he died in about forty-eight hours.

The two men accidentally met in the corridor of the post office, each having gone there for his mail, and it happened that their boxes adjoined each other, one under the other. They were both trying to get their mail at the same time. Col. Goodloe remarked, "You obstruct the way." Col. Swope responded, "You spoke to me; you insulted me" instantly, following these remarks Col. Goodloe drew from his pocket a large dirk knife with a spring back, and Col. Swope at the same time drew his revolver, a Smith & Wesson of thirty-eight caliber. As soon as the weapons were drawn, in an instant before the movements of the two men could hardly be perceived, Col. Swope discharged his pistol and Col. Goodloe at the same time made an attack with his knife. In the fierce hand to hand encounter which followed, the advantage was with Col. Goodloe, who continued to plunge his dirk into the body of his adversary until he had gashed him in thirteen different places. Col. Swope fired his pistol a second time, the ball took effect in the lower abdomen of his enemy. The two men had clinched; as soon as Col. Goodloe released him, Col. Swope fell to the floor, face downward, and he died almost instantly from the effect of the wound under the left shoulder which pierced his heart. The doctor said that any one of the several wounds in the breast would have caused his death, they were from three to five inches in length and several inches deep. Col. Goodloe walked to the front steps, which led down to the street, where he was met by Mr. W. K. Shelby and Mr. Frank, who took him to the office of Doctors Stockdale and Young where his wounds received the necessary attention. When he reached the Doctor's office his clothes were still burning from the effects of the powder, showing that Col. Swope's pistol must have been almost against him when the shots were fired. He remained in the surgeon's office for about two hours, when he was removed to a room in the Phoenix Hotel, where he died about forty-eight hours later. The ball entered the abdominal cavity and pierced the bowels. His family was notified of the tragedy. His daughter fainted when she entered the room and saw the condition of her father, and had to be carried out of the room. She remained unconscious for some time.

Several days before the trouble, Col. Swope said, that he knew, if he and Goodloe met, it would bring death to one of them, and if such a event happened he preferred to be the slain rather than the slayer for the reason that Goodloe had a large family dependent upon him.

The remains of Col. Swope were taken to his room on Market street, where a post mortem examination was made. He received no cuts about the face, but his forehead and cheek were badly bruised, and discolored from the effects of the fall on the stone floor in the corridor of the post office; his right wrist was nearly severed from the arm, the rest of the arm being severely cut, up to his shoulder. There were two severe wounds in the breast, near the heart. The wound on the left side of the back, nearly under the left arm was the one which caused his death, it was about six inches deep; it went into the cavity and pierced the heart. In the back near the spinal column was another severe wound which would probably have proved fatal. There were four other wounds in the back, one of which was under the left shoulder and the other in the muscles of the back.

Col. Swope's remains were later taken to his rooms in Mrs. Hedges' boarding house and were dressed in a new suit of clothes which he had just received from his tailor. The only thing he was heard to say during the struggle, was to exclaim, "Oh, my God, don't."

The coroner's inquest over the dead body was held the following day. The coroner held his court in the court room of the Fayette Circuit Court. Col. John R. Allen conducted the examination of the witnesses. The weapons used in the duel were placed on a table in the presence of the jury.

Swope's nickle plated thirty-eight caliber Smith & Wesson revolver looked like a handsome top, but the knife was a terrible weapon, sharpened to a razor's edge on both sides of the point, with a blade five inches long and with a rough bone grip handle.

Attorney William K. Shelby was the first witness called. He said: "I went to the post office yesterday afternoon at about 1:30 o'clock. I walked along the street for some distance with Col. A. M. Swope. We entered the box corridor at the same time; he went to his box which was almost opposite the Main street entrance of the building, while I went into the money order office to get a postal note. Postmaster W. S. McChesney waited on me. I turned and saw Col. Goodloe and Col. Swope standing close together. Swope was standing at the same place, or very near the same place where I had last seen him. Some angry words passed very quickly between the two and I caught the words, 'You have spoken to me and that is an insult.' Both men seemed to have the instruments of destruction in their hands almost at the same moment. They were very close together and scuffling in a lively manner, making a circle of some nineteen feet in circumference.

" Swope's pistol was discharged early in the action and Goodloe almost instantly stabbed him. Swope exclaimed, ' Oh,' and reeled a little back from Goodloe and the two were now in almost the same position as when the scuffle commenced. Goodloe seemed to have a hold on Swope and was stabbing away when Swope turned and fired again, the ball missed and struck lock box 362 as I afterward located. Then Col. Swope bent forward seeming to turn toward the door to get out. He caught hold of the wainscoating with one hand, having already lost hold of his pistol by reason of a wound on his wrist which almost severed the hand from the arm. Every time Goodloe stabbed, Swope exclaimed, 'Oh.' Col. Swope fell upon his face with Goodloe standing over him; Swope was groaning loudly. Goodloe waived his hand slightly, still holding the knife. I asked him if he was hurt, and he replied, ' I am shot through and through, send for a doctor.' Mr. Swift, Çaptain Veach and several others rushed into the corridor just before this, and Captain Veach and I accompanied Col. Goodloe to Dr. Bryan's, but we met Dr. Stockdale on the way and we conducted Col. Goodloe to his office where his wound was examined.

" I could not distinguish anything said, but the remark above quoted, and I did not know which of the men used it, but I was inclined to think it was Swope's remark. I think the first time Goodloe stabbed, it was fatal or very painful, as Swope evidently began to fall. I was first attracted by loud talking."

Dr. McClure testified as follows: " I was one of the physicians who examined the wounds upon Col. Swope; they were thirteen in number, in various parts of the body, on the breast, on the arms and upon the back; all the wounds, or nearly all, were stabs. Two were deep stabs near the breast bone; one a little to the right and the other to the left; one close to the left rib; another, and the worst wound of all, a stab under the left arm. I inserted my finger into the wound and am sure that the wound reached to the cavity which maintains the heart, I am not sure whether it touched the heart or severed the main artery to the heart, one of the above must have been the case and the wound was necessarily fatal. One stab was in the small of the back and extended toward the spinal column; this was also a bad wound and in all probability would have proved fatal by itself. There were two bad wounds on the left arm making a V shaped gash. I could not tell just what wound caused death or how many of them would have been fatal alone, but was certain that the wound under the left arm, either of the chest wounds or the stab on the back running toward the spinal column could have ceaused death. All the others might have been inflicted and not produced death."

Postmaster W. S. McChesney's testimony was nearly the same as that of Mr. Shelby, and Dr. Keller corroborated Dr. McClure.

The testimony of H. C. Swift was along the same lines of the other eye witnesses. He said further: "I am the chief clerk in the post office. Col. Swope took out his mail and was stooping down to his open box talking through the aperture to me about a matter of business; while I was answering, his box suddenly closed, then reopened and he called out 'All right,' closing his box again. Col. Goodloe had not taken the mail out of his box.

The verdict of the coroner's jury was as follows: "We, the jury, find that the deceased, Armistead M. Swope, came to his death from the effects of wounds made with a knife by William Cassius Goodloe in the vestibule of the post office, in Lexington, Ky., on November 8th, about 2 p. m."

Col. Goodloe's version of the trouble was in substance: When he entered the post office he saw Col. Swope at his box and not wishing to meet him, held back to give him time to get his mail; after getting it, however, in the place of moving away, he remained talking to Harry Swift, through the post office box. At this time Goodloe approached and remarked, that Swope was obstructing the way. He retorted that it was a matter of indifference to him whether he was stopping the way or not. Col. Goodloe saw that the crisis had come—both men saw it. Goodloe remarked, "This is the second time you have insulted me." And upon the instant, both men drew. Before Goodloe could open his knife Swope placed his pistol against Goodloe's body and fired. The ball penetrated a bundle of paper under Goodloe's arm and he distinctly felt the bullet pass into his abdomen. He knew that he was shot; probably fatal. Before Swope could shoot again Goodloe struck him twice in the breast and then followed him up stabbing him until he died. Col. Goodloe said that if either of them had been unarmed and had announced the fact there would have been no trouble, but both were armed and both knew it, and both of them also knew that the time had come to fight it out.

Col. Goodloe died at 12:55 p. m., November 10th, he having survived Col. Swope nearly forty-eight hours. A few hours before his death he sent for the Rector of Christ's Episcopal church, and stated that he wanted to become a member of the church, and he was received into the membership.

When told by his physician that he would probably die, Col. Goodloe said to his son-in-law, "Tell Mary, if I die before she gets here, that I thought of her and the children and did not strike until I was struck."

Dr. M. T. Scott said that Col. Goodloe's death was caused by a "lucky piece" which he carried in his pocket and which the ball struck and ranged downwards with fatal result.

Col. Goodloe was buried in the Lexington cemetery. The remains of Col. Swope were taken by his brothers to Lincoln county and buried in the family lot in the old Buffalo cemetery.

The cause leading to the duel between the two men and which culminated in the tragedy unparalleled in the history of Kentucky, dated back several years. Col. Swope was appointed Internal Revenue Collector by President Arthur, and he removed to Lexington from the town of Paris, where he had practiced law since the close of the Rebellion. From that time, there had been a feeling of political jealousy between them, each of whom was striving to be a party leader in the State. Both of them were extremely anxious for political honors and each strove for the leadership of the Republican party in Kentucky.

Each year the bitter feeling existing between them increased, until the meeting of the Republican State convention in Louisville on the first of May, 1888, to appoint delegates to the National convention at Chicago. At that time the fight was renewed more bitterly than ever. During the convention which was a very stormy one, a delegate from Pulaski county arose and protested against his county casting its vote for Col. Swope as a delegate-at-large to the National convention. Col. Swope thereupon said, " That is right, I do not want your vote. Don't do like my county did; instruct for one man and vote for another." In response to this statement, Col. Goodloe said that he thought it ill became the gentleman from Fayette to complain of his treatment at the hands of the delegates, as 21 out of the 23 delegates from Fayette did not speak to him when they met him on the street, and that nine-tenths of the Republicans in Lexington did not speak to him. Col. Swope became very much offended at this statement and he sought personal settlement while in Louisville, but could not find Col. Goodloe at his hotel. After returning to Lexington on the 8th of May, the two men met in the Phoenix Hotel. Col. Swope denounced him in emphatic terms and he used very scathing and bitter language. Goodloe declined to attack him, stating that Swope was armed and he was not. Swope thereupon drew off his coat and turned his pockets inside out, to convince Goodloe that he was not armed.

After this meeting each of them armed himself for the fatal encounter; but through the intervention of friends it was agreed to leave the settlement of their troubles to their friends. Each of them was to select two men. After the selection was made the committee had a conference, and it was agreed, that each of them should withdraw the offensive language used by each; and thereupon Col. Swope wrote a card withdrawing what he had said at the hotel and Col. Goodloe wrote one withdrawing what he had said at the Louisville convention. It was believed and hoped by their friends that this conference had ended the difficulty, and that the bitter feeling between them had been permanently allayed, and yet it was no surprise to their inner circle of friends who knew the temperament and high spirit of the men when the fatal duel was fought.

Both men were born in Lincoln county, Kentucky, and in the same section of the county. In physical statute they were nearly the same height. Col. Swope was the heavier and stronger of the two. Swope was Goodloe's superior intellectually, but he was of more humble origin. His people were plain substantial citizens in moderately good circumstances. On the other hand Col. Goodloe was a member of an aristocratic family; he was proud of his ancestry, proud of his family relation, and he evidently resented the idea of Col. Swope's elevation to a position over him; and it was still more humiliating to him to be forced to recognize his own intellectual inferiority to the man whom he most heartily despised.

The ambitions and aspirations of the two men were along the same line. They were opposing candidates several times for Revenue Collector, each of them aspired to become the leader of the Republican party and Governor of the Commonwealth. Col. Swope was a single man, in the prime of life, of large commanding physique, about forty-five years of age, he weighed two hundred and thirty-eight pounds. He practiced law at Paris, Kentucky, until the beginning of the war when he joined the Union army and arose to the rank of Colonel and served on the staff of General Buell. He fought under the United States flag which floated over the government building and died beneath it. After the war he went to Paris and resumed the practice of law. He held several positions of trust within the gift of the National administration and was regarded as one of the ablest men in his party. In 1877 he was appointed Collector from the Seventh Kentucky district and resigned in 1883. He was an applicant for the same position under President Harrison but was defeated through the enmity of Col. Goodloe. He was never elected to any position by the popular vote.

Col. Goodloe was forty-eight years of age; he was attractive in appearance and popular with the people. He was the third son of D. S. Goodloe and was descended from a line of distinguished Virginians. He was educated at the Transylvania University being a member of the senior class in the spring of 1861, when he withdrew to accompany his uncle Cassius M. Clay, to St. Petersburg, Russia. While there he acted as Secretary of Legation until the summer of 1862, when he returned to the United States, and entered the Union army, and was appointed Assistant Adjutant General of volunteers by President Lincoln. In January, 1864, he withdrew from the army, and commenced the practice of law in Lexington. On January 1, 1867, he commenced the publication of the *Lexington Statesman.* In 1868, he was elected as a delegate to the National convention at Chicago, which nominated General Grant for President. In 1871, he was elected to the Legislature from Lexington, and was his party's nominee for speaker. In 1872, he was chairman of the Kentucky delegation at the Republican convention in Philadelphia, and was elected the Kentucky representative on the Republican National Committee. In 1873, he was elected to the State Senate from his Senatorial district, and in 1875, was a candidate for Attorney-General. He was minister to Belgium under President Hayes and was elected representative to every Republican national convention from that time until his death.

He was married in June, 1865, to Miss Mary E. Mann, of Rhode Island, and they had six children. A short time prior to his death he was appointed Revenue Collector for the Lexington district and in which capacity he was serving at the time of his death.

The Colson-Scott Tragedy.

COL. DAVID COLSON, of Middlesboro, and Lieutenant Ethelbert D. Scott, of Somerset, met in the lobby of the Capitol Hotel at Frankfort, Ky., on January 16, 1900, and the pistol fight which ensued resulted in the deaths of Lieutenant Scott, Charles Julian, of Franklin county, and Luther W. Demaree of Shelbyville. Lieutenant Scott was shot seven times. Col. Colson was wounded in the arm. Harry McEwan of Louisville and Capt. Ben Golden of Barboursville were wounded, and Mr. C. D. Redpath of Chicago, a traveling salesman, was seated in the lobby of the hotel near the railing which protected the entrance to the basement having his shoes shined. When the shooting commenced he jumped over the railing and fell to the bottom of the steps and broke his leg.

Col. Colson and Lieutenant Scott were both army officers and both of them Republican politicians. The quarrel between them originated during the encampment of the army at Anniston, Alabama, during the Spanish-American War. Each of them was an officer in the Fourth Kentucky Regiment which was encamped at that place. They had a fight at Anniston during that encampment in which Col. Colson was wounded by Scott and from the effect of which he was partially paralyzed and which finally resulted in his death a few years later. An exciting contest for the position of Governor, and other State officers, was being waged between the Democrats and Republicans. The contests were before the Legislature of Kentucky which was at that time in session. Strangers from all parts of the State were congregated at Frankfort and at the time of the shooting the lobby of the Capitol Hotel was crowded. Groups of men were standing in the large room, and others were seated and leaning against the walls and others were lounging in the easy chairs around the columns in the rotunda. Members of the Legislature, State officials and politicians had congregated there after the adjourned session of the Legislature. Women were passing in and out of the dining room where dinner was being served. Col. Colson was seated in the front part of the lobby of the large office, leaning against the wall and engaged in conversation with some friends, when Lieutenant Scott came through the right hand door leading from the dining room to the lobby, the two men seemed to have seen each other about the same time and each of them immediately made preparation for the duel which followed. The question as to which of them fired the first shot has never been settled. Eighteen shots were fired by them in less than a minute, thirteen of which found lodgement in human victims, resulting in the death of three men and the wounding of four others, one shot went through the large glass window in front, one struck the wall near the window, one went near the head of Richard Paxton, afterwards Representative of Anderson county and who was at that time talking to Mr. Charles Julian, and another struck the letter case in the hotel office.

Lieutenant Scott came to Frankfort the day before the difficulty and Col. Colson came on the morning of the trouble. The first meeting between them took place in a short time after Col. Colson reached the city. It occurred on the sidewalk near the Capitol Hotel, at that time Colson gave Scott a defiant stare in the eye and he almost stopped until Scott passed him. Each of them claimed, to their friends, that the other was pursuing him.

The evidence at the coroners inquest which was held January 17th, disclosed the following facts:

Mr. Kitt Chinn, son of Col. Jack Chinn, said: "I was standing near the cigar counter at the Capitol Hotel about twelve thirty o'clock when Scott and Golden went in the hotel at the woman's door leading to the lobby and stopped at the cigar counter where I was standing and Scott asked me to go down in the basement to the bar and have a drink. I declined; he insisted and I said that I would go with him though I did not want anything to drink. We reached the center of the lobby, which it was necessary to cross in order to get to the steps leading down to the basement. I stopped in the center of the lobby and told Scott to go on, that I would wait for him upstairs; Scott turned his head to hear what I had to say, while Golden advanced a few steps further away. I turned to go back to the cigar counter and in a moment I heard the shots."

Mr. J. C. C. Mayo, at that time election commissioner, and later the National Democratic Committeeman from Kentucky and who had come to Frankfort as a witness in the Goebel-Taylor contest case, was sitting by the side of Col. Colson and he too was leaning the back of his chair against the wall near the front window and was facing the entrance from the dining room, when Scott, Golden and Chinn came in and stopped near the center of the room. Mr. Mayo said: "All of a sudden I saw an expression of unusual excitement on Col. Colson's countenance. He arose from his chair, and either, while rising or just after rising he drew a long revolver and after he had advanced a step or two the firing began. I could not say who fired first. The shots were close together. While I was looking directly into Col. Colson's face just before he arose, I thought I could distinguish, outside of my eye, as it were, two men approaching, but I paid no attention to that as the lobby was full of people. Colson steadied his pistol with his left hand, after firing several times, he circled around so as to put himself nearer the center of the lobby, while Scott got nearer the corner farthest from the stairway leading from the basement. I think Scott got behind a man who must have been Demaree, as Demaree quickly fell to the floor. I found that I was getting in range, so I dropped to the floor to escape the bullets."

Mr. J. N. Kehoe of Maysville said: " I had just started toward Colson and Mayo, I was going to speak to Mayo. I saw Colson get up, draw his pistol, steady it with his left hand and begin shooting. I do not know who fired the first shot." From all evidence adduced in the case, it appeared that Scott and Colson saw each other about the same time and each of them realized that the time had come for a final settlement between them. Each of them knew that the other was dead game and that one or both of them must die. Each of them drew his pistol and they evidently fired simultaneously. Out of the half hundred men who were present and saw the duel, not one of them could state which one of the two men fired first.

Eighteen shots were fired in rapid succession. Col. Colson emptied two revolvers and Scott emptied one. Col. Colson first drew a forty-four caliber Colt's long barrel target pistol from his belt at his left side and after emptying it he very cooly and deliberately laid it in one of the long leather office chairs and then drew a thirty-eight caliber Smith & Wesson and advanced on Scott who had by this time exhausted the loads in his pistol. Col. Colson had been shooting towards the corner where Scott had placed himself and they were only a few feet apart. During the fusillade and after Colson had circled around to Scott's original position in the center of the lobby, Scott stepped behind Demaree, who was talking to some friends, and threw one arm around him and held him as a protection, so that three of Colson's bullets pierced Demaree's heart in quick succession. One of the bullets went through Demaree's heart and his entire body and having spent its force went through Scotts clothes and lodged against the skin on his breast; at the post mortem examination of Scott this bullet was found in the skin but it was not deep enough to hide it.

Col. Colson had been wounded in the left arm, when he was laying his forty-four Colts in the leather chair as stated; when he drew his thirty-eight Smith & Wesson, Scott ran across the lobby to the opposite corner; he was trying to get down the stairway to the basement. At that time he had emptied his pistol and had been severely wounded and he evidently realized the danger he was in, when he saw Colson draw his second pistol and knowing his own was exhausted, he attempted to make his escape by way of the basement. Col. Colson followed him across the lobby with his fresh pistol and fired the first shot from his thirty-eight just as Scott reached the first step leading to the basement; the ball struck him in the back of the head. At that time he had already been struck in the front of his neck and twice in the abdomen. The bullet in the back of the head sent him headforemost down the stairs on top of C. D. Redpath, who had jumped over the banister and broken his leg, in his effort to get out of the range of bullets. Colson looked over the balustrade and fired another shot; he had fired two shots into Scott's back as he fell down the stairs and then followed down the stairs and fired one more shot into Scott's body after he had fallen across Redpath. Colson then stepped over the bodies of the two men and went out through the basement door which opens on the east side of the building and went up the street with the empty pistol in his hand. When he reached Mrs. M. H. P. Williams' boarding house, located about one square from the hotel, he went to the room of a mountain friend and borrowed a pistol from him. He then went to the room of another friend and had him send for a doctor. Dr. E. E. Hume was summoned and he extracted the bullet which had badly shattered the bone near the elbow of the left arm. In a short time the chief of police arrived and placed him under arrest and he was taken to the county jail, and there confined on a charge of murder, without bail. The Franklin county grand jury was in session and it very promptly returned three indictments against him for murder; one of which was for killing Ethelbert D. Scott, one for killing Charles Julian and one for killing Luther W. Demaree and he was also indicted twice for carrying concealed deadly weapons.

Col. Colson claimed that Scott and Captain Golden had been following him all morning and he claimed that Scott was the first to draw a pistol. He was of the opinion that Capt. Golden also fired several shots at him. Capt. Golden was present at the time the shooting commenced but no one seemed to know that he was wounded until after the fight was over. He said: that when the two men began firing at each other, he started to grab Colson's arm but he at once concluded that since he and Colson were not on good terms, he might get shot, so he turned and ran toward the hall door and when he was about half way across the lobby a bullet struck him in the small of the back near the right button of his Prince Albert coat; he shouted "I am shot," and ran into the hall and up to the parlor, where he met Governor McCreary and others who took him to a room in the hotel and sent for a physician. Capt. Golden claimed that he did not have a pistol and that he did not fire a single shot. Hon. Milton Hager, a former Representative was coming up the steps from the basement of the hotel, when Scott fell against him and came near knocking him down. He said: "Colson looked over the balustrade, fired once and then followed Scott in hot pursuit. He fired two shots into Scott's back as he fell down the stairs." Col. Colson said that he tried to shoot around Mr. Demaree, who was his friend, but whom Scott held tightly.

Col. Colson was tried on the indictment for killing Ethelbert D. Scott at the April term 1900, of the Franklin Circuit Court, and on April the 21st, the jury brought in a verdict of not guilty, and on April 24th, the Commonwealth's attorney filed a statement and moved the court to dismiss the other cases, which was done. There was also an order entered at that date, directing that the two pistols used by Col. Colson on that occasion be turned over to him and that the one used by Scott was directed to be delivered to Thomas Scott, brother of the deceased, Ethelbert D. Scott.

Lieutenant Scott was about thirty years of age. He was a son of Dr. Scott, a former superintendent of the Eastern Asylum at Lexington. Dr. Scott had married a sister of Governor William O. Bradley and Lieutenant Scott was their son; he was also a nephew of Judge Z. T. Morrow, for many years Circuit Judge and at one time the nominee of the Republican party for Governor.

Lieutenant Scott was a young lawyer, located at Lexington, when he persuaded his uncle, William O. Bradley, to appoint him an officer in Col. Colson's resgiment.

The original cause of the trouble between Scott and Colson dated back about a year before the tragedy.

In February, 1899, Col. Colson preferred charges against Lieutenant Scott on the questions of competency, capacity and good conduct. Both of the army officers were present during the whole proceedings. Col. Colson's arraignment of Scott was very severe and costic, notwithstanding the rumor that Scott had said he would kill Colson if his (Scott's) character was assailed.

The evidence taken by the military board showed that Scott had acted the part of a spoiled child, that he was without military experience, training or discipline and that several witnesses stated that Scott was in the habit of drinking and loitering around saloons, remaining out of camp and that he had never drilled with his company more than twice in six months. Col. Colson testified that Scott had visited saloons. Scott asked him how he knew that fact.

Colson replied: "Because I saw you there." "What were you doing there sir?" said Scott. Col. Colson said: "I went there to get a drink sir." Several times during the proceedings the two men were restrained from shooting each other. The Board recommended that Scott be discharged on the grounds of incompetency and the papers were sent to Washington. Lieutenant Scott secured a leave of absence and after ten days he returned and said he had been to Washington and had got it fixed, that he would stay with the regiment. After that Col. Colson preferred other charges against him for disobedience of orders, insubordination, etc., and asked that he be tried by another court martial, but some of the friends of the two men saw that serious trouble was impending and knowing that the regiment was to be mustered out in a short time, they prevailed on Col. Colson to withdraw the charges. It was generally known that both men were fearless and serious trouble was expected by their friends, but there was no further trouble until after the regiment was mustered out. The next day after it was mustered out, Scott was dining in a restaurant with a party of friends, Col. Colson entered and giving his order for dinner proceeded to the only vacant seat at the table where Scott and his friends were seated, apparently not noticing the presence of Scott until some remark, made by Scott, attracted his attention. Col. Colson thought it was intended as an insult and he made a statement to that effect. Scott thereupon arose from his seat and very deliberately and quietly laid down his napkin, pushed his chair to the table and stepping behind it, he raised his pistol and fired and as he did so Colson fired at about the same time. Colson's ball missed its mark but Scotts lodged in Colson's groin from the effects of which he never fully recovered. Neither the military nor the civil authorities took any notice of the difficulty. Col. Colson was taken to his room and Scott left for Kentucky on the next train. The order for the mustering out of the regiment was dated January 11, 1899, only a few days more than a year before the shooting in Frankfort. Ethelbert D. Scott was a large handsome man with dark curly hair; he was a great favorite with the people who were well acquainted with him. He was a witness in the Goebel-Taylor case. Col. David G. Colson was a lawyer, thirty-nine years of age. He had served two terms in Congress; he had served in the Kentucky Legislature and had been pension examiner for one term. He was a Colonel in the Spanish-American war and at the time of the trouble was a prospective candidate for the Court of Appeals.

Luther W. Demaree was a lawyer about thirty-five years of age. He lived at Shelbyville, Kentucky, where he had been assistant postmaster. He owned a fine Shelby county farm and was supposed to be worth forty or fifty thousand dollars.

Charles H. Julian, another victim, was shot with a thirty-eight caliber ball, but as Colson and Scott both used a pistol of that size it was impossible to say who shot him, but it is more than probable that Scott shot him for the reason that he and Colson were seated near each other when the shooting commenced and at one time Colson must have been nearly in the line between Scott and Julian. Julian was shot in the calf of the leg. He ran out of the lobby and said that he was shot. He was taken to a room in the hotel and seated in a chair; an artery had been severed, and he was bleeding a great deal. Several physicians were sent for who did all they could for him but in twenty minutes he was dead. The physicians thought that the loss of blood was not sufficient to cause his death, but that the loss of blood and the shock resulted in heart failure. Mr. Julian was a farmer, he owned a fine farm a short distance from Frankfort. He had been married only a few years. He left a wife and a baby boy only a few months old.

The Goebel Assassination.

THE several trials of the accused men who were charged with the assassination of William Goebel, continued through a period of about eight years. If a full transcript had been made of all the evidence produced at the trials, of all the arguments of counsel and all the instructions and statements made by the several courts which tried them, perhaps, twenty thousand pages would not contain it all.

The year 1899, marked the closing days of the Bradley administration; it had been a disappointment to the Republicans and a surprise to the Democrats; it was worse than the Republicans had claimed it would be and it was better than the Democrats had predicted.

The Democratic State convention was held in the city of Louisville in 1899, there were three candidates for Governor. General P. Watt Hardin lacked only a few votes of having enough instructed for him to nominate him on the first ballot. The other two candidates, Senator William Goebel and Col. W. J. Stone, saw that it was necessary for them to unite their strength and organize the convention, any other course would have simply deprived them of all chances for nomination. While they were criticised for "pooling" their interests it was recognized later to have been a shrewd political movement, not only calculated to bring success, but which ultimately, resulted in the nomination of Senator William Goebel.

The music hall convention was stormy and the result was unsatisfactory to a large number of the Democrats in the State. The acrimony and bitterness engendered at that convention brought discontentment and strife to every section of the Commonwealth and the regular November election of 1899, was the natural result and outcome of the conditions then existing. For many years prior to this time

Senator Goebel had been active in securing what was termed " reform " legislation. He had secured the passage through the Kentucky Legislature of the franchise tax law and the anti-lottery law. He was an advocate of the American railway rate legislation, the school book legislation, the fellow servant law, the employers' liability law, the law regulating the toll rate on bridges and turnpikes and other measures of like nature. He said, " The question is: are the corporations the masters or servants of the people?" He was a member of the State Senate from 1886 to 1900. The one thing which brought more opposition to him than all else was the Goebel election law. In this law, the Republicans contended that the civil rights of the people were abridged and that the passage of the Goebel election law was a menace to the liberties fought for and secured by the patriots of the Revolution. By reason of his position on these questions he had united these several interests against him. No man had ever before been fought with so much bitter hatred and with such a determination to defeat him at any cost.

The face of the returns showed that he had been defeated by 2,383 votes, and the whole Democratic State ticket by approximately the same vote. The majority in the Legislature was very small; the House was almost a tie while the Senate was Democratic by a small majority.

The Democratic candidates for State positions, with Senator Goebel as leader, at first concluded to accept the result as shown by the face of the returns, without any protest, but after several consultations they agreed to a contest. On January 2, 1900, a notice of contest for the office of Governor was served on W. S. Taylor by William Goebel, and that of Lieutenant Governor was served on John Marshall by J. C. W. Beckham. The grounds specified that in thirty-nine mountain counties, " All the official ballots used in all of the said counties were printed upon paper so thin and transparent that the printing and the stencil marks thereon made by the voters, could be distinguished from the backs of said ballots, that none of the said ballots used in said counties were printed upon plain white paper sufficiently thick to prevent the printing from being distinguished from the back of the said ballots whereby the secrecy of the said ballot was destroyed and said election in all of said counties rendered void, etc.''

(2) The election in Louisville was void because the Governor William O. Bradley called out the militia on the day before the election and the said militia was in charge of the polling places in said city on said election day in command of W. O. Bradley, Governor, etc.

(3) Because Sterling B. Tony, one of the Circuit Judges, issued a mandatory injunction in said city and required the officers of election to admit many people in said polling places who were not entitled to be there, etc.

(4) That the employees of the L. & N. Railroad Company were intimidated by the chief officers and superior employees and prevented from voting and that enough of them were deterred in that way to change the result, etc.

(5) That the leaders of the Republican party entered into a conspiracy with the officers of the said railroad company and the American Book Company, and other corporations and trusts in which the said corporations and trusts furnished large sums of money to be used in defeating contestants, etc.

(6) That certain mountain county election boards were compelled by mandatory injunctions, issued unlawfully, to make false certificates.

(7) On account of threats made by United States marshals to intimidate voters, etc.

(8) On account of a conspiracy between the L. & N. Railroad Company and John Whalen and others who brought a large number of armed and desperate men to

Frankfort for the purpose of intimidating the State Election Board, etc.

A joint committee of four from the Senate and seven from the House was drawn in each case. In the Goebel-Taylor contest all of the committeemen were Democrats except one and in the Beckham-Marshall contest all of the committeemen were Democrats except two. The Republicans had committees of leading Republicans in both House and Senate to stand by the clerks and see the ballots prepared and placed in the box and that the box was properly prepared and well shaken before the drawing. There was no fraud detected at the time of the drawing, but on January 11th, the Republicans asked that the contest committees be discharged on account of fraud in the drawing and they stated that the ballots in the boxes were fraudulently arranged in both Houses. It has since been stated that the fraud consisted in securing a certain kind of paper upon which the names of the members were written and when this paper was placed in a roll, it remained tight or loose according to the will or desire of him who rolled it; the paper on which the Republican names were written were rolled tight and the Democrats loose. In this way the clerk easily detected, by feeling them, whether they were Democrats or Republicans. When the Republican committee insisted on shaking the box each time after a name was drawn, the Democrats readily agreed to it, because when shaken the loose rolls were inclined to come to the top and the tight ones go to the bottom.

As the contest progressed the interest increased. At the same time there were sixteen seats contested in the House and a corresponding number in the Senate. These contests brought hundreds of people from all sections of the State to the Capitol. On January 26th, there were nine hundred and sixty well armed mountaineers arrived in Frankfort and more than a thousand men were camped on the

State house grounds. About the same date a letter was received by a Judge of the Court of Appeals, dated at Middlesboro, January 24th, and in which Judge J. P. Hobson, Judge J. H. Hazelrigg and Senator William Goebel were designated as the men who would be assassinated by the mountain men and the request was made that each of them be notified of the impending danger. All kind of rumors were being circulated on the streets of Frankfort; threats on both sides were openly made and the feeling had become so intense that every one recognized the fact that a riot was likely to be commenced at any moment. The attorneys for the Republicans were W. O. Bradley, T. L. Edelen, W. H. Yost, W. H. Sweeney and W. C. P. Breckinridge. The attorneys for the Democrats were Louis McQuown, Aaron Kohn, Jack Phelps and James A. Scott.

By the last week in January all the politicians of the State had congregated at Frankfort, and most of them were drunk from excitement or bad whiskey and many of them were well under the influence of both. This condition was especially the case with the mountain men who came from local option counties, but this feeling was not confined to visitors. The people of Frankfort, who had formerly been good friends, passed each other without speaking, men who had never been known to carry a pistol were seen with their pockets well filled; double-barreled shotguns were borrowed and shells filled with buckshot were purchased by men who were never known to have any trouble with anyone. Frankfort was on the verge of civil war and every one was shocked and horrified when it was announced that William Goebel had been assassinated but no one was surprised; the greatest surprise was that only one man lost his life. The Democrats at once denounced the act as the greatest outrage that was ever perpetrated in a free country and many of them desired to wreck vengeance on the Republicans, regardless of whether or not they had anything to do with the killing.

The Republicans generally deplored the killing but most of them thought that Senator Goebel had brought it on himself and that it was a just punishment summarily inflicted. Many of them openly admitted that they thought it was a just retribution.

On the morning of his last fatal walk to the capitol, Senator Goebel was accompanied by Col. Jack Chinn from Harrodsburg and Col. Eph Lillard, warden of the Kentucky penitentiary. Senator Goebel wore a chinchilla overcoat, a gray suit of clothes and a soft black hat. Col. Chinn said: "I went to the Senator's room about ten o'clock this morning, Warden Eph Lillard and Mr. Aaron Kohn, one of Mr. Goebel's attorneys were in his room, Parlor A, at the Capitol Hotel. We all left the room about the same time, Lillard, Barclay and myself came down the stairs with Goebel; Lillard and myself accompanied him to the capitol. Lillard and Goebel walked about twenty feet in front of me, as I was holding back for Mr. Barclay. I caught up with them at the capitol gate. Goebel fell back with me while Lillard walked about thirty yards ahead of us through the yard towards the General Assembly building. I was on Goebel's right and he was about two feet ahead of me when the first shot was fired. When we were about half way between the fountain and the steps I heard the report of a rifle, at about the same instant Goebel bent double, groaned harshly, clutched at his right side and fell to his knees. I said, 'My God Goebel, they have killed you,' I was a little too far away to catch him. 'I guess they have,' he said as he was falling. He fell to his right and then forward rolling over on his back. I think his right knee struck the pavement first. He raised in a moment as if to get up on his elbow, when I said, 'Lie still Goebel, or they will shoot you again.'

"The first shot struck Goebel and it was fired from one of the floors of the Executive building just east of the General Assembly building to which we were going. The first shot was followed in quick succession by four others. Mr. Lillard was almost to the door ahead of us when the shooting occurred."

Senator Goebel was shot from a window in the Secretary of States' private office, the ball passed entirely through his body and lodged in a hackberry tree which stands near the Western front gate. He was picked up and carried to the office of Dr. E. E. Hume and from there he was taken to his room in the Capitol Hotel where he languished and died, the third day thereafter. In the meantime the General Assembly voted on the contest cases and declared that he was duly elected Governor and that J. C. W. Beckham was elected Lieutenant Governor. He took the oath of office on the same day he died, the third day of February, 1900. J. C. W. Beckham also took the oath required of the Lieutenant Governor and immediately following the death of Governor Goebel he took the oath as Governor.

Dr. E. E. Hume said that Dr. J. N. McCormick, Dr. J. G. Furnish, Dr. J. G. South, Dr. U. V. Williams, Dr. H. L. Tobin and Dr. J. R. Ely helped to examine the wounded man. He said: "We opened his clothing and found that he was shot two inches to the right of the right nipple in the edge of the arm pit; we found that the ball had ranged downward passing through and across his chest and made its exit two inches to the left of the spine and about two inches lower down than the entrance on the chest. When I first saw him he was bleeding considerably. We injected a normal salt solution of a quart under the skin on the chest to keep up the circulation and supply the place of the lost blood."

Harlan Whittaker was arrested immediately after the

shooting; Henry Youtsey and others a few days afterwards.

On April 16, 1900, the grand jury of Franklin county returned into court indictments for the willful murder of William Goebel against Henry Youtsey, James Howard, Berry Howard, Harlan Whittaker and Richard Combs. On April 17th, Charles Finley, John L. Powers, William H. Culton, Caleb Powers and F. Whorton Golden were indicted for being accessory before the fact to the willful murder of William Goebel.

On April 18th, true bills were returned against Green Golden, John W. Davis and W. L. Hazelipp. On February 2nd, a true bill was returned against Garnett D. Ripley for being accessory, etc. On May 5th, a true bill was returned against former Governor W. S. Taylor for being accessory before the fact and on February 1, 1902, Frank Cecil and Zack Steel were likewise indicted.

On the petition of Henry Youtsey and Caleb Powers their cases were transferred to the Scott Circuit Court.

Captain Garnett D. Ripley was the first to be tried on the charge of being accessory to the murder of Gov. Goebel. He was tried at Frankfort and was acquitted by the jury. He was prosecuted by Col. R. B. Franklin, the prosecuting attorney of the Frankfort district, and who was assisted in the prosecution by Mr. Thomas Campbell, of New York, and Judge Ben G. Williams, of Frankfort; Ripley was defended by Judge J. T. O'Neal, of Louisville; Col. William Cravens, of New Castle; Judge P. U. Major and L. F. Johnson of the Frankfort bar.

There were nine trials of those accused of the assassination of William Goebel; two of whom, Garnett D. Ripley and Berry Howard were acquitted; Henry E. Youtsey was convicted and sentenced to the penitentiary for life, he accepted the sentence as just and took no appeal. James B. Howard was tried three times; the first trial resulted in a conviction, with the penalty at death. The Court of Appeals reversed the case and the second and third trials the jury fixed the punishment at confinement in the penitentiary for life. His case was reversed the second time and the third time the Court of Appeals affirmed the lower court and Howard was serving a life sentence when the Republican Governor Augustus E. Willson pardoned him.

Caleb Powers was also tried three times, the first and second trials resulted in conviction and the punishment fixed at confinement in the penitentiary for life. Each time the Court of Appeals reversed the case and in the third conviction the punishment was fixed at death. The case was appealed the third time and it was pending before the Court of Appeals when Governor Willson pardoned him. Governor Willson also pardoned W. S. Taylor and John W. Davis.

In the trial of Ripley the attorneys for the defense admitted the conspiracy and joined with the prosecution in the charge against the leaders of the Republican party for causing the assassination, claiming of course that the defendant was not in the conspiracy. In the defense of Berry Howard the attorneys followed the same plan and accomplished the same end. In the defense of James B. Howard on his first trial, the attorneys who represented him, to-wit: W. C. Owens, J. B. Finnell and Carlo Little, undertook to defend the leaders of the Republican party and so thoroughly did they commit him to that defense that the attorneys who undertook to defend him the second time were unable to get away from the line of defense used in the first trial. The attorneys who defended Howard at his second trial were James A. Scott, James A. Violett, Carlo Little and L. F. Johnson, all of whom were Democrats and these Democratic lawyers found themselves in the anomalous position of defending the Republican party, and by reason of that fact some of them refused to defend him at his third trial. Without expressing any opinion as to whether James B. Howard was guilty or innocent of the charge, it is safe to say that if the attorneys who defended Ripley had been employed to defend Howard when tried the first time, he never would have been convicted. The facts and circumstances connecting him with the case were of such a nature that notwithstanding the confession of Youtsey, it would have been most a difficult matter to convict him if his attorneys had undertaken to defend him in the place of defending the leaders of the Republican party. The defense of Youtsey was a different proposition. His confession before and after he was arrested and his conduct were such that his conviction necessarily followed. The only thing which saved him from the gallows was the fact that he " threw a fit " at a very opportune time.

Youtsey was ably defended by Major R. W. Nelson, Judge James Askew and Col. Crawford, a half-brother of Youtsey. He was strongly prosecuted by Col. R. B. Franklin, Mr. Thomas Campbell and Victor A. Bradley. Judge James E. Cantrill was the presiding judge. In the trial of Caleb Powers there were different conditions to meet. He had so identified himself with the leaders of the Republican party that he had become its brain and backbone and there was no defense that he could make that was separate from his party. His attorneys soon realized that his defense was almost a hopeless task.

The attorneys for the prosecution in the Powers case were R. B. Franklin, Thomas Campbell, Victor F. Bradley, B. G. Williams, John K. Hendricks and T. S. Gaines. The attorneys who defended him were J. S. Simms, Jere Morton, J. B. Finnell, L. F. Sinclair, A. T. Wood and James A. Violett. Judge Robbins was the presiding judge.

Henry E. Youtsey was tried at Georgetown in October, 1900. On October 9th, he " threw a fit " in the court room.

It was near the close of the Commonwealth's evidence. Mr. Arthur Goebel, brother of William Goebel was placed on the stand and the question was asked him, "Have you ever had a conversation with Henry E. Youtsey, the accused?"

"I have."

"Where, and what time?"

"On the day of his arrest and on the second floor of the county jail."

"Will you repeat the conversation?"

"I was out of the city at the time he was arrested; when I returned that afternoon I——."

"It is a lie," said Youtsey, as he started towards Mr. Goebel. "I never had a conversation with that man in my life, at the jail or anywhere else; I will not—" Here he was stopped by his attorney, but in a short time he continued, "I will not stand here and hear my life sworn away. I have no blood on my hands; I am innocent; he can not swear my life away." At this juncture Mrs. Youtsey threw her arms around him and tried to stop him. "Let me go," he said, "I won't stop," and in his struggle he struck his wife; as he sank into his chair Mrs. Youtsey turned to Mr. Goebel and said, "I hope you are satisfied now, you have killed him," and she fell fainting into her mother's arms. Two deputy sheriffs had taken hold of him, he struggled desperately for a short time and then broke down and cried like a child. The court room was full of excited people, several ladies had to be carried out. The sheriff was not able to keep order. The sobs of Mrs. Youtsey were in concert with those of women from all parts of the room. Attorney Crawford had taken hold of Youtsey to quiet him when he called out, "I tell you that Goebel is not dead, all the demons in hell could not kill him." Judge Cantrill said, "Mr. Sheriff, if this defendant can not behave himself put the handcuffs on him." Youtsey fell to the floor and apparently became unconscious. After a few moments Judge Cantrill became impatient and said, " Proceed with the trial."

The prosecuting attorney said, "Mr. Goebel will you detail the conversation you had with Mr. Youtsey?" Mr. Goebel resumed his statement as if nothing had happened. In a short time Mr. Crawford requested the court to suspend the trial until the following day; he said, " It is but simple justice to our client." Judge Cantrill said, " I think it would be justice to his counsel." Mr. Franklin agreed to pass the case until the next day. Youtsey had to be carried from the court house to the jail. On reaching the jail he cried three times, " Hurrah for Goebel." He was examined by Dr. R. L. Carrick, who said that he was in a state of nervous collapse. Youtsey had another fit after he reached the jail and the following morning he failed to appear in court, his physician claimed that he was too ill to be present. The court continued the case until the following day but he gave the attorneys for the defendant to understand that he believed Youtsey was shamming and he said that Youtsey would be tried it mattered not what condition of his mind or body might be. The following day the physician said that Youtsey was threatened with brain fever and that he was still in a stupid condition and that his malady might terminate fatally. His case was continued from day to day until Monday, October 15th, at which time his counsel said that his condition was unchanged and that they could not proceed with the trial, but the court ordered the attorneys to proceed. Col. Crawford asked that Youtsey be permitted to remain in the jury room during the remainder of the trial. Mr. Franklin objected to that and after some delay the court ordered Youtsey to be brought into the court room. He was brought in on the wire bed upon which he was lying. He gave no sign of being conscious.

The examination of Arthur Goebel was proceeded with.

On the day prior to the murder of William Goebel, Henry Youtsey was on his knees in front of one of the windows in the Secretary of States' office. He had a rifle with the barrel pointing from the window. On the morning Goebel was killed Youtsey was seen in his office cleaning the same rifle. One minute after Goebel fell Youtsey announced in the Assistant Secretary's office that " Goebel's shot." After the argument of counsel the case was submitted to the jury. In a short time the jury came in with a verdict of guilty and fixed his punishment at confinement in the penitentiary for life. Judge Cantrill pronounced judgment in accordance with the verdict and from which judgment Youtsey did not take an appeal. For the past fourteen years he has been confined at hard labor in the penitentiary at Frankfort. There has been some effort made to secure a pardon for him but the general impression seems to be that he is not getting any more than he deserves and if he serves the remainder of his life behind prison bars he will never be able to fully atone for the horrible crime of which he was convicted.

The trial of Caleb Powers was the most interesting one of the " Goebel cases." He was tried the third time in August, 1906. Judge Jos. E. Robbins presiding. A large number of witnesses were introduced and every phase of the case was gone into. Several men who were under indictment and Youtsey who had been convicted, testified in the case. The scope of this work will permit of only a very small part of the evidence being reproduced.

Golden testified that the plot of Powers, Finley and others was not only to kill Senator Goebel but to also kill Speaker South Trimble, Willard Mitchell and the Democratic Judges of the Court of Appeals. He said, " Finley said, ' that the mountain feudists will kill off enough Democrats to make a Republican majority in the Legislature,' and in response Powers said, 'By God, that's what we will do.' "

Frank Cecil testified that he had a conversation with Caleb Powers the night before the day of the murder in which Powers told him that he was seeking a man who could be relied upon to murder Goebel, the next day, and offered him the job of assassination. Powers said that Youtsey had offered to do the killing, but he was not willing to trust him to do it and he had sent to the mountains to get a man and that this man was expected to arrive the next morning. Later in the day Powers went with Cecil to the private office of Governor Taylor and he said that Governor Taylor made him the same proposition and told him that he had twenty-five hundred dollars of the Republican campaign fund left over which he would give him and a full pardon if he would do the killing. On his refusal to take the job, Cecil claimed that Taylor threatened him with death if he ever told of the conversation between them.

Cecil testified that he assisted in the organization of the "mountain army" of January 25, 1900, and he said that he was instructed to bring with them the "toughest s— of b—s" he could find and that he brought more than a hundred from Bell county who answered that requirement. He also said that Powers made the statement that if the plan should fail they would all get their necks broken as conspirators.

Henry E. Youtsey was placed on the witness stand in the Power's case. He testified in substance as follows: "I have been indicted, tried and convicted of the murder of William Goebel. I was born in Campbell county, Kentucky. I am twenty-nine years of age and am by profession a lawyer. At the time of the killing I lived in Frankfort. The first conversation any one had with me in reference to the killing was by the chairman of the Republican county committee of Trimble county. He came to my office and we talked about Goebel. In the course of the conversation he said he understood that Goebel wore armor of some kind but that he did not wear it about his G—d d—d head and he ought to be met at the State house gate some morning and swing him to a limb. Dr. W. R. Johnson was the next man who talked to me about the matter. He told me what a good shot he was and he said that he could do the killing. After this conversation with him I sent to Cincinnati for some smokeless cartridges with steel bullets to be used in Grant Roberts' 38-35 Marlin rifle which I had borrowed. Before the cartridges arrived Dr. Johnson came to my office and said that he was anxious to kill Goebel as he approached the Legislative building. He had his pistol in his hand and he said, ' G—d d—n him, I can kill him with my pistol.' I told him he must not do that, because we had information that on the 25th there was to be an army of mountain men and the contest would be settled in favor of the Republicans on that day, and that nothing of that kind should be undertaken until after the 25th. In the afternoon of the 25th I went in the general reception room and knocked at the door leading to the Secretary of States' private office. I heard a noise of some kind in that room and Dr. Johnson opened the door, when I went in I saw that the corner window was raised and that there were two chairs facing the window and a Marlin rifle was lying across the back of the chair and the chairs were so arranged as that Dr. Johnson, or anyone, could take aim across the back of one chair and sit on the chair in the rear and shoot out of the window in the direction of the walk leading to the capitol building. Culton was in the reception room; when they saw that I understood the situation, Culton asked me to go up to the Senate chamber to see if Mr. Goebel was there. I went up and came back and reported that Goebel was still there. I had several talks with Dr. Johnson about the gun. I had it in my office for some time and he decided that it should be used for the killing of Senator Goebel. I went around through the general reception room into the secretaries private office and opened the glass door which leads into the hall. As soon as Johnson saw that the door was open, he slipped the gun under his arm. He had on a long overcoat and he could entirely conceal the gun. He came into the private office and laid it under the window. We secured the gun and placed it in the private office before we got the cartridges from Cincinnati. When the cartridges came I gave them to Dr. Johnson and in my presence he filled the gun magazine with them. This took place in the private office of the Secretary of State. The reason we, Dr. Johnson and myself, ordered the steel bullets was, we had heard that Mr. Goebel wore armor and that he could not be killed with an ordinary bullet, and furthermore, Grant Roberts wanted that kind. The bullet used was a 38-35 smokeless steel bullet. On January 25th Dr. Johnson came to me, late in the afternoon, about five o'clock, and said that he certainly would have killed Senator Goebel that afternoon as he came out of the Senate chamber if it had not been for the fact that Goebel came out with the crowd, and he could not get a fair shot at him. He then told me that he wanted to have a message of some kind from Governor Taylor. I told him that I would go down and see Taylor that afternoon, if he desired it, and he said he did. I went to the mansion and had a talk with Governor Taylor. I told him that Dr. Johnson wanted to kill Goebel; that he wanted to shoot him from the window of the office of the Secretary of State and I told him that all the arrangements had been made. Governor Taylor did not object; he followed me out on the porch and told me never to tell a mortal man what had taken place between us. I went back and told Johnson exactly what Taylor had said and he was satisfied and said that Goebel would be shot the next morning. I never saw Johnson any more after that conversation."

After giving a vivid description of the Berry-VanMeter contest and the arrangements which were made by Culton, John Powers and others to have Representative W. H. Lilly make a fiery speech and that was to be the signal for a general slaughter of the Democrats by the mountain men and in that way give the Republicans a majority, but from some unknown cause the plan miscarried. Youtsey then told of the agreement on the part of the negro Hockersmith to do the killing which plan also miscarried, because John Powers had given him the wrong key to the private office and the negro could not get in. After that Hockersmith refused to do the killing unless Governor Taylor would sanction it, and when the matter was presented to Taylor he said that he could not trust the negro to do it. After all our plans had failed I went to Governor Taylor's private office and had a talk with him and on that occasion he dictated a letter to me to James B. Howard, Manchester, Kentucky. The substance of that letter was, that all arrangements had been made because he (Taylor) was liable to lose his office at any time and that he was to report to me and what I said about it would be all right.

Youtsey then told in detail, how Howard came to his office on January 30th, and told him who he was and Youtsey told him what he was expected to do and that they went to the private office of Powers, and Youtsey showed Howard the Marlin rifle which Howard examined and said it was all right and in a few moments after that they saw Senator Goebel with Col. Jack Chinn and Col. Eph Lillard coming up Market street towards the State house and thereupon Youtsey pointed out Senator Goebel to Howard and immediately afterwards left the room. Howard being the only occupant left in the room and he had the Marlin rifle in his hand when Youtsey went out of the glass door which leads into the hall. He closed the door after him and stood with his hand on the door knob until he heard the shot fired; after he heard the shot he ran down the steps which lead to the basement and out through the north entrance to the basement and around the northeast corner of the Executive building and came in at the east entrance, and he did not stop running until he had gained the private office of Governor Taylor, where he announced the fact that Senator Goebel had been killed. Youtsey testified on cross-examination, that on his trial in October, 1900, in his effort to mislead the court and jury he "threw a fit" in order to avoid being called to the witness stand and to excite sympathy among the jurors. He said that he lay on a cot and heard all the evidence in his case. His testimony in the case differed materially from the statements made by him at other times. The deposition of W. S. Taylor was read on behalf of the defendant, and Caleb Powers made an argument to the jury in his own behalf. This argument was very lengthy, covering some 138 pages (printed). It took up nearly every phase of the case, it showed considerable research and study and some ability. It was the strongest argument made for the defense in the case.

After about four hours in consultation, the jury brought in a verdict of guilty and fixed the punishment at death. An appeal was taken on the case and while it was pending in the Court of Appeals the election for Governor was held in 1907, at which time Augustus E. Willson was elected Governor. In a short time after he was inaugurated, the petition for a pardon was presented to him, after some delay the pardon was granted. At the same time the Governor also pardoned James B. Howard who was serving a life sentence in the penitentiary.

On April 23, 1909, Governor Willson pardoned W. S. Taylor, Charles Finley, John L. Powers, Harlan Whittaker, John W. Davis and Zack Steel, all of the other cases which were pending in the Franklin Circuit Court were filed away.

Governor William Goebel was a lawyer of considerable ability. He had been a successful practitioner for many years and had accumulated a considerable estate in the practice of his profession. Governor William S. Taylor was also a lawyer of more than ordinary ability. He had been Attorney-General of Kentucky and he made an excellent official, he was popular with all classes and under ordinary circumstances would do doubt have made a good Governor. About the time he was indicted he became a fugitive from justice. He sought refuge in Indiana where the requisitions from Kentucky could not reach him. Since his pardon he has remained in his adopted State, engaged in the practice of his profession.

Caleb Powers is also a lawyer of some ability. After his pardon he returned to his home in the mountains of Kentucky where he has since been repeatedly honored by his people who have elected him to the lower house of the United States Congress.

Among the remaining defendants who were charged with the Goebel murder was Henry E. Youtsey, lawyer and private secretary of the State Auditor; James B. Howard, Assessor of Clay county; Berry Howard, Representative from Bell county; Richard Combs, a negro from the mountains; Charles Finley, John L. Powers, William H. Culton, Whorton Golden, Green Golden and Captain Garnett D. Ripley, were all lawyers; Captain John W. Davis was "policeman on the square." The rest of the defendants were mountain feudists.

The Hargis-Cockrell Feud and the Death of Judge James Hargis.

The mountains of Kentucky have produced many excellent men. A more hospitable and generous people can not be found. They are active in their friendships and their hates; they are honorable and upright in their dealings with men and they are faithful and true to their friends, but they are intolerant and cruel to their enemies.

The average citizen of the mountains will compare favorably with the men of the Bluegrass or any other section of the State. In character, disposition and native shrewdness they are very much like the Scottish Highlander. One thing that has brought the mountains of Kentucky into bad repute has been the irresponsible newspaper reporter, who has sent out all kinds of false statements and malicious fabrications—many of them without any foundation. The worst evil with which the mountains have to deal is perjury. This crime is prevalent in all sections of the country but it seems to be worse in the mountain districts than it is elsewhere. Perjury has led to assassination and sometimes to feuds. Almost any one feels that he is justified in assassinating the man who has in person or by employed agent, tried to swear his life or liberty from him.

No section of the mountains has been more fully imbued with the feudal spirit than Breathitt county. There has scarcely been a time since the civil war when there was not an active feud in Breathitt. Following the war, was the Amis-Strong feud, in the midst of which occurred a fight in the court room while the court was in session and in which Bob Little, a nephew of Captain Strong, was killed and several other men were wounded. In a few years after the termination of this feud another broke out which was known as the Strong-Callahan feud and in which many men were killed on each side. Following this was the Jett-Little feud and succeeding that was the Hargis-Cockrell feud.

In 1878, Judge William Randell, Circuit Judge, fled from the bench and the county to save his life, he never resumed his seat on the bench. This condition of affairs was brought about by the assassination of County Judge John Burnett and his wife which occurred in their home at night.

The first local option law ever passed in Kentucky was when Breathitt county went dry in 1871. Since which time it has been, nominally a dry county.

The commencement of the Hargis-Cockrell feud dated back to the year 1899, when there was a contest over the county offices between the Republicans or Fusionist and the Democrats. Judge James Hargis was the Democratic candidate for County Judge and Ed. Callahan for sheriff. The Democrats were declared elected and the Fusionist, represented by J. B. Marcum filed a contest. Prior to this time James B. Marcum and O. H. Pollard were partners and they composed the leading firm of lawyers in Eastern Kentucky. Marcum and Pollard disagreed about this political contest and the partnership was dissolved; Pollard represented the Democrats and Marcum the Fusionists. Depositions for the contestees were taken at the law office of Pollard and the depositions for the contestants were taken at Marcum's office. Prior to that time Marcum had been the intimate friend and attorney for the Hargis brothers. While taking the depositions in Marcum's office the first open rupture occurred between them. Mr. Pollard was cross-examining a witness when there was a disagreement and the two attorneys nearly came to blows. Hargis and Callahan were sitting by. Pistols were drawn and all three of the men were ordered from Marcum's office. Warrants were issued by Police Judge T. P. Cardwell. J. B. Marcum appeared in court and confessed to a fine of twenty dollars. Hargis and Cardwell had been enemies for several years and Hargis refused to be tried by Cardwell. Tom Cockrell was at that time Town Marshal of Jackson and his brother Jim Cockrell assisted him in arresting Hargis.

J. B. Marcum's statement about the arrest of Judge Hargis was as follows: " Tom Cockrell went to arrest Hargis. Hargis refused to surrender and attempted to pull his pistol, but Tom beat him to it and covered him. Callahan, who was standing near covered Tom with his pistol and in turn Jim Cockrell covered Callahan. Hargis and Callahan saw that the Cockrells had the drop on them and surrendered. I sent word to Cardwell that I did not want to prosecute Hargis and I asked that he be dismissed, which was done, and the incident passed away without bloodshed." The first personal difficulty between Marcum and Hargis occurred in the same year at a school election. Marcum charged Hargis with trying to vote a minor and hot words were passed between them, Hargis said, " Marcum flew into a rage and pulled his pistol on me, but did not shoot. The trouble was patched up and we again became friends." Following this trouble the two families and their friends took sides and had frequent quarrels. Marcum charged Callahan with the assassination of his uncle, and Callahan charged that Marcum's uncle had assassinated his (Callahan's) father.

Tom Cockrell, who was not of age, and Ben Hargis, a brother of Judge James Hargis met in a " blind tiger " saloon in July 1902, and fought a pistol fight. Many conflicting statements were made in reference to the fight but it is sufficient to say that Ben Hargis was killed and the Hargis brothers became active in the prosecution of Tom Cockrell. Dr. B. D. Cox, the leading physician of Jackson had married one of the Cardwell women and he became the guardian of the Cockrell children, including Tom, who was not yet of age.

The Cockrells were also related to Marcum, who defended Tom Cockrell without fee for killing Ben Hargis. J. B. Marcum was also an intimate friend of Dr. Cox. In a short time after the killing of Ben Hargis, John Hargis, another brother, who was known as " Tige," was killed by Jerry Cardwell, a member of the Cockrell faction. Jerry Cardwell was a train detective and he claimed that Hargis was disorderly. Cardwell attempted to arrest him and in the pistol encounter which followed Cardwell was wounded and Hargis was killed. In a short time after that a half brother of Judge Hargis was killed in his own home, one night, while he was making sorghum molasses. He was shot from ambush and it was never known who killed him.

Dr. Cox, the guardian and kinsman of the Cockrells, and J. B. Marcum, their cousin, were intimate friends. Dr. Cox left his home about eight o'clock one night to make a professional call. He reached the corner of the street across from the court house and directly opposite the stable of Judge Hargis, when he was shot with small shot and killed. The assassin fired another charge into his body at short range and escaped. It was claimed that the shots were fired from Judge Hargis' stable. The Cockrells openly charged that Dr. Cox was assassinated because of his family relations to the Cockrells and his interest in the defense of Tom Cockrell. It was brought out in the evidence of Judge Hargis and Ed. Callahan, when on trial charged with the murder of Dr. Cox, that the two men, Hargis and Callahan, were standing in the yard in the rear of the shed from which the shots were fired.

The next man who became a victim of the assassin's bullet was Jim Cockrell, who was shot about twelve o'clock in the daytime July 28, 1902. He was shot from a window on the second floor of the court house. He had been very active in securing evidence for his brother's trial charged with the murder of Ben Hargis. Jim Cockrell was at that time the leader of the Cockrell faction and he was the Town Marshal of Jackson, at the time of the Jim Cockrell killing. Judge Hargis and Ed. Callahan were standing at the window on the second floor of the Hargis store and saw the shooting. This fact was brought out on their trial, charged with the murder of James Cockrell. At that time Curt Jett was a deputy sheriff under Ed. Callahan. It was generally understood and quietly said that Jett had done the killing. About a week before the death of James Cockrell, he and Curt Jett met in the dining room of the Arlington Hotel, at which time they had a pistol fight but in which neither of them was wounded. It was generally understood that Curt Jett and two other men were concealed in the court house at the time Jim Cockrell was killed, they remained there all day, and at night they were taken away by their friends on horseback, no arrests were made. The attorneys for Tom Cockrell, Mr. Vaughn and John H. Johns, filed some affidavits and moved for a change of venue in his case, they also moved the court, Judge Dave Redwine, to vacate the bench, which was done and Judge Ira Julian, of Frankfort, was appointed to try the case. On motion, he transferred it to Campton. Judge James Hargis and his brother Senator Alex Hargis, who had instituted the prosecution against Tom Cockrell, refused to go to Campton and thereupon Cockrell was dismissed. Judge Hargis said that he could never reach Campton alive, that in traveling over that mountain road, some of his enemies would kill him. In a letter written by J. B. Marcum to the *Lexington Herald,* dated, November 9, 1902, he said, "There have been over thirty killed in Breathitt since the 24th day of last December and the Lord knows how many wounded, etc." In a letter dated May 25, 1903, Mrs. James B. Marcum said there had been thirty-eight homicides in Breathitt county during the administration of County Judge James Hargis.

The most noted man who was killed during the progress of this feud was James B. Marcum, who was assassinated May 4, 1903, exactly nine years before Ed. Callahan was killed.

Marcum had incurred the enmity of the Hargis faction by reason of his position in the contest for the position of County Judge and for the further reason that he was the attorney for Tom Cockrell charged with the killing of Ben Hargis.

At the time he was shot, Marcum was standing in the front entrance of the court house at Jackson. He fell within a few yards of where Town Marshal James Cockrell was shot and killed in the July preceding. The assassins were stationed in the court house in each instance. As a result of Marcum's efforts and his sympathies with the Cockrell faction in the Hargis-Cockrell feud, he had for a year, been generally regarded as a "marked man." In an affidavit which he filed in the Breathitt Circuit Court, he declared that he was "marked for death." Various plots to assassinate him had been reported and sworn to. For seventy-two days he was a prisoner in his own home, he was afraid to go out on his own porch. The excitement attending the contest had abated, to some extent, and Marcum concluded to venture out and resume his law practice. He went to the court house in Jackson and filed some papers in the contest case. It was about eight o'clock in the morning; after filing the papers he walked from the clerks office to the front door of the court house, where he stopped and engaged in conversation with his friend Benjamin Ewen. The corridor at his back was full of men; he had been there perhaps thirty minutes when a shot was heard in the rear of the corridor, Marcum was seen to stagger and as he fell, another shot was fired. The first bullet entered his back to the right of the spinal column and passed through his breast and struck the floor in front of him. The next shot passed through the top of his head. The shots were either fired from the doorway in the corridor or from behind the door. Marcum's body lay for ten or fifteen minutes where it fell before his friends would venture to go to him. At the time of his death he was a trustee of the Kentucky State College and he was United States Commissioner for his district. He also represented the Lexington & Eastern Railroad and other large corporations. He had practiced law in Breathitt county for seventeen years. He had avoided feuds until he took charge of the election cases which involved the Hargis faction and prior to that time he had been friends and the attorney for both factions. For three months prior to his death he did not leave his home unless he was in company with his wife or carried one of his children with him for protection.

On November 14, 1902, he made the following statement, "I heard the rumor that Dr. Cox and I were slated to be assassinated; he and I discussed these rumors and we concluded that they were groundless, I went to Washington, D. C., and stayed a month. While I was there Dr. Cox was assassinated. I was attorney for Mose Feltner. On the night of May 30th, he came to my house in Jackson and stated that he had entered into an agreement with certain officials to kill me, and his accomplices were to be three men whom he named. He said that their plan was for him to entice me to my office that night and for him to way-lay me and kill me. He said that they had provided him with a shotgun and thirty-five dollars to give me. He displayed the gun, which had never been shot and he also showed me the money. I know that he did not previously have the money. A few mornings later Feltner took me to the woods and showed me four Winchester rifles, concealed there, and stated that he and his three companions had been leaving them there in the daytime and carrying them at night to kill me with. He said that the county officials had guaranteed him immunity from punishment for killing Fields, and he led them to believe that he would kill me, to secure their protection, all the time warning me of plans to kill me. He could visit me without arousing suspicion as he was my client and supposed to pretend friendship for me."

After the assassination of James B. Marcum business in Jackson became paralyzed, the residents of the town remained at home after dark and the streets were deserted. It was claimed at that time that at least forty deaths had resulted directly and indirectly from the Hargis-Cockrell feud during the two years prior to Marcum's death. He left a wife and five children ranging in age from seventeen years to fifteen months. He had three married sisters living in Jackson at that time. The only words uttered by him after being shot were, "My God, they have killed me." No one would accept the position of coroner and no magistrate could be induced to hold an inquest; consequently none was held. Governor Beckham offered a reward of five hundred dollars for the apprehension and conviction of the assassin.

At the time James B. Marcum was killed, Judge James Hargis and Ed. Callahan were sitting in the front door of the Hargis store just across the street from the court house. Each of them were seated in a rocking chair and they were on a direct line with the court house door and were in a position to see the shots fired and the victim fall, but according to the testimony given by them neither of them made any effort to locate or ascertain the identity of the assassin, notwithstanding each of them was a county officer at that time.

On May 25, 1903, Curtis Jett and Tom White were indicted for the murder of James B. Marcum and on June 12th, they were jointly tried for that offense. The Commonwealth was represented by Floyd Byrd, Commonwealth's Attorney and assisted by Thomas Marcum, brother of James B. Marcum, and Capt. William L. Hurst, father-in-law of Judge D. B. Redwine, and uncle of Mrs. James Marcum.

They were defended by John B. O'Neal, of Covington, Judge B. F. French, Judge Noble, Ben Golden, from Barboursville, James D. Black, J. T. Blanton and Rafferty and King.

Several companies of the State militia were present to maintain order and protect the witnesses. Judge James Hargis, Senator Alex Hargis and Sheriff Ed. Callahan were all present and assisted in the defense. The first trial was held at Jackson with Judge Redwine presiding. One juror saved Curtis Jett from the death penalty, eleven were for conviction and one for acquittal.

Judge Redwine ordered the cases transferred to Harrison county for trial and the prisoners taken to Lexington for safe keeping.

The second trial was before Hon. J. J. Osborne, Judge of that district, commencing July 27, 1903. L. P. Fryer was Commonwealth's Attorney. The facts proven were in substance as follows:

Capt. B. J. Ewen said, "I was standing beside Marcum when he was killed. His right hand was resting heavily upon my shoulder. Tom White passed by us from out of the court house and looked Marcum full in the face and turned around in front attracting Marcum's attention. Suddenly the shot was fired. The pressure of Marcum's arm on my shoulder half pulled me around to face the assassin and I turned the rest of the way. I saw the murderer and recognized him, it was Curtis Jett. He had his pistol in both hands and had advanced two steps. I thought he was going to shoot me. Marcum had fallen to the floor and I stepped out of the door to save my life. I heard the second shot, and a couple of moments later Jett appear at the side door facing the well. He placed a hand on either side of the casing and peered out each side of the door. He cautiously walked down the steps and turned into the crowd at the door.'' It was proven by other witnesses that Tom White was standing in front of Day Brother's store and was asked by Calloway Strong to take a drink, he responded that he was looking for a man and immediately crossed to the side door of the court house; he raised his hand and motioned for Jett to come to him and Jett responded. White walked into the side door of the court house and Jett followed him. White walked out of the front door beside the man whom he and the assassin behind him had conspired to murder. As he passed out he glared into Marcum's face to attract his attention, while Curt Jett fired the shot. He then walked out into the street and turned down the street a few steps to get out of the range of the bullets that he knew were coming. After the shots were fired he joined Jett at the jail and later walked down the street with him.

Before the shooting, Jett was standing on the court house sidewalk and appeared to be watching Marcum. Jett then went in the side door of the court house and in a minute or so later the shots were fired and Jett was seen to come from the side door of the court house. Tom White had come to Jackson a few days before that, to get a job, but he never asked anyone for work but Elbert Hargis. Jett and White were together before the shooting and they were together again immediately afterward. The only motive the Commonwealth attempted to prove, was that they were hired to do the killing. The defense was an alibi and an effort to impeach the evidence of the main prosecuting witness.

The defense completely failed to prove the alibi. The jury brought in a verdict against both Curtis Jett and Tom White and fixed the punishment at confinment in the penitentiary for life. Eleven of the jurors were for fixing the punishment at death but one juror persisted in the position he had taken and in order to prevent a mistrial the other eleven agreed on the life imprisonment verdict. Curtis Jett was twenty-four years old at the time of Marcum's death, he was the son of Hiram Jett, whose wife was a sister of Judge James B. Hargis and he was a cousin of the Cockrell boys. Curtis Jett had lived in Jackson, and was deputy sheriff under Ed. Callahan, when James Cockrell was killed. Several men swore that they saw and recognized him when he killed Cockrell. Jett had been twice accused of rape and he had frequently been in jail for shooting and wounding and disorderly conduct. He was also charged with the betrayal of a young girl. He was tall and had a bad countenance. He had deep set blue eyes, red hair, high cheek bones, thin lips and short chin. When he first went to the penitentiary he was stubborn and hard to control but after a time he claimed to be converted and he has since that time been a model prisoner.

Judge James Hargis in speaking of himself and Senator Alex Hargis, his brother, said: "We began our business twenty years ago, poor men, and we have accumulated wealth and position by dint of our industry. We own thousands of acres of land in this county and lands and stores in other places. We never had a difficulty in our lives and we had no motive to assassinate Marcum or Cockrell or anyone else."

In speaking of Marcum, in reference to Callahan, Judge Hargis said: "He was as intense a Republican as his uncle Bill Strong and he was willing to go to any extremity to further the interest of his party. He was the enemy of Ed. Callahan, because of the Strong-Callahan feud and he accused Callahan of having a hand in the death of his uncle. Callahan's father was also ambushed; but Callahan never had anything to do with the ambushing of Bill Strong.

The Hargis-Cockrell feud was like nearly all the other mountain feuds; it was a family difficulty. Senator Alex Hargis' wife was a sister of J. B. Marcum. Curtis Jett's father was a brother of Tom and Jim Cockrell's mother. Curtis Jett's mother was a half sister of Judge James Hargis and State Senator Alex Hargis. Dr. B. D. Cox married a daughter of State Senator Thomas P. Cardwell and she was a sister of T. P. Cardwell, Jr., the police judge of Jackson.

Ed. Callahan, one of the most noted leaders of the Hargis-Cockrell feud, was assassinated Saturday, May 4, 1912. Callahan was shot from ambush about nine o'clock in the morning through the window of his store at Crockettsville, a small village in Breathitt county about twenty-five miles from Jackson. One steel bullet entered his leg just above the knee and another struck him in the breast.

Callahan was shot through the front window of his store. which is a short distance from his residence. He had just hung up the receiver of the telephone and when passing the window in going to the opposite side of the store a volley of shots came from the hillside across the creek; ten or twelve shots were fired, but only two bullets took effect. The shots were fired from near the same place from which Callahan was severely wounded about one year prior to the killing.

Ed. Callahan was one of the most prominent men of the mountains. He was elected sheriff of Breathitt county at the same election that Judge James Hargis was elected County Judge. It was the contest over these elections which originated the Hargis-Cockrell feud, in which it was claimed that more than a hundred men were killed from 1902 to 1912.

Callahan operated at Crockettsville one of the largest

general merchandise stores in the county. He had been enterprising and prominent in business and had accumulated considerable wealth. He was a substantial citizen and a deacon in the church, but he was regarded as the leader of the old Hargis faction in the Hargis-Cockrell feud. Ed. Callahan and Judge James Hargis were indicted for murder five times, they were tried in Lexington, Beattyville and Sandy Hook. These indictments for murder grew out of the assassinations of James B. Marcum, Dr. B. D. Cox, Jim Cockrell and others.

Curtis Jett, Mose Feltner, John Abner and John Smith, all of whom confessed to having participated in the assassinations and they implicated Judge James Hargis and Sheriff Ed. Callahan and they claimed that these two men had planned the murders and designated the time in which they should be carried out.

Though Hargis and Callahan had escaped conviction on the five trials for murder, Mrs. Marcum, the widow of James B. Marcum, secured a judgment against the two men for being instrumental in killing her husband; the judgment was for eight thousand dollars which was paid.

Following the confession of John Smith, who was subsequently dismissed by the prosecution, he became the bitter enemy of the Hargis and Callahan faction and some of the Smith faction were arrested and charged with the attempt to assassinate Callahan two years before he was finally killed. After the first attempt on his life, Callahan built a stockade around his home and yard and so arranged that he could go from his home to his store, without anyone from the outside seeing him. He took this precaution because he said he had premonition that it was only a matter of time until his enemies would " get him."

Callahan fell when he was shot, but with the assistance of his family he was enabled to find shelter in his home.

The circumstances of the shooting were almost identical

with those of the attempted assassination of Callahan on May 3, 1910, just two years and one day prior to the killing. He was standing almost in the same spot and the bullets were fired from the same place.

Beach Hargis shot and killed his father Judge James Hargis. The indictment for murder was returned against him on February 18, 1908, and on a trial before a jury he was found guilty as charged; his punishment was fixed at confinement in the penitentiary for life.

The facts which were given on the trial of the case and which are set out in Kentucky Reports, Vol. 135, page 589, are as follows: On the night before the homicide, Beach Hargis had gone to his father's store and asked one of the clerks to let him have a pistol. The clerk declined to give him a pistol out of the stock, but told him that his father's pistol was there in the drawer of his desk, and he could take that. The defendant got the pistol, but said nothing to his father, although he was then in the store. The next morning between nine and ten o'clock the defendant was sitting in a barber shop. His face was swollen. He told the barber his father had hit him in the mouth and hurt him there. A man who looked like his father then passed by. He raised up in the chair, threw back his hand, and said, "I thought that was the old man." About an hour later he drank a bottle of Brown's Bitters, and said to a bystander, "Did you hear about the old man mashing my mouth," and added, that it was hard to take. Some two hours later, he appeared at a drug store kept by his brother-in-law, Dr. Hogg. There he drew his pistol, and was waving it about, pointing it in the direction of a bystander and his brother-in-law. From this drug store, after a few minutes, he went to his father's store. It was a double storeroom. His father was in one room and he entered the other and took a seat in a chair not far from the front door. While he was sitting there in the chair, a man in the other room asked his father where he was, his father pointed him out to the man and said: ' There he sits, I have done all I can for him and I can not go about him or have anything to do with him.'' A few minutes later, his father said to another man who was in the room, '' I don't know what to do with Beach, he has got to be a perfect vagabond, and he is destroying my business, and if Dr. Hogg lets him stay there he will ruin his business.'' After saying this to the man, the father walked in the direction of where the defendant was sitting. There were a number of persons in the store. As his father approached, the defendant got out of his chair and walked around behind a spool case that was sitting on the end of the counter, no words were spoken. The first sound that anybody heard was the report of a pistol. His father was then about three feet from him. A struggle ensued between them, during which the pistol was shot four times more; all five of the shots taking effect in the father. Persons in the store ran up, and when they got to them, the father had the son down and had the pistol, which he handed to one of them saying, '' He has shot me all to pieces.'' The father died in a few minutes.

The proof for the defendant was in substance, that the father came up to him, struck him in the face and began choking him. When he felt his eyes bulging out, he drew his pistol and shot him, and his father continuing to choke him, he fired the other four shots in the struggle; the last two being fired from the floor. The proof for the defendant also showed that the father was drinking.

The court said: '' Taking all the evidence, we think it is reasonably clear that the father was unarmed and that he was shot by the son while he was approaching him, and before he had touched him. Two witnesses who were on the outside of the store were looking through the window, and their testimony as well as the testimony of the persons in the store confirm this conclusion. We think it is also reasonably clear from the evidence that the son was maudlin drunk and but for this the unfortunate homicide would not have occurred. He showed that he was under the impression that his father had left the store and that he went there to meet his uncle, but expecting no difficulty. He also showed, that about a week before his father had beat him unmercifully with a ram rod, that previous to this he had whipped him with a rope and on the last occasion had struck him in the mouth with his fist and had got upon him on the floor and churned his head against the floor; that he had taken his pistol from him and had threatened to shoot him with it, but had been prevented from doing this by the interference of a bystander, and that he had then declared that he would kill him. There was also evidence that the son had said that the old man had beaten him up, but he wouldn't ever get a chance to do it again; also that he had declared, when his father had taken a pistol away from him when drunk, that every time he got drunk and was having a good time they had to do something to him, and that he aimed to kill his father and certain other persons whom he named. The defendant offered to prove by his grandmother and others that his father had taught him to carry a weapon, encouraged him to drink whiskey, and had caused him to associate with disreputable men, thus rearing him in a manner calculated to bring about the result which followed.

"The court did not allow the defendant to prove that about two hours before the killing he met James Isom and told him that he would kill the defendant before night, and that he was done with him forever. The defendant showed by several witnesses, that his father, a week before had pointed a pistol at him and threatened to kill him."

The court said: "The fact is the defendant had his father's pistol. The father was unarmed. The shooting was done before a word was spoken and when the father was at least three feet from him. The storeroom had a number of people in it and it is hard to believe that the defendant, if he had been sober, could have thought that he was then and there in danger of death or great bodily harm at the hands of his father.''

The judgment of the lower court was affirmed. The defendant Beach Hargis was in due time sent to the penitentiary. Some unsuccessful efforts have been made to secure a pardon for him.

The prosecuting attorney represented the Commonwealth and the defendant was represented by Governor William O. Bradley, A. W. Young, D. B. Redwine, J. J. C. Bach, Sam H. Kash and Thomas L. Cope.

A

Allen, Alfred 163 177
Allen, Jack 183
Allen, John R 284
Allen, W B 191-194

B

Bach, J J C 336
Baker, Francis 34-43
Barron, James 28
Bean, John E 248 254
Beauchamp, Jereboam 44-56
Beckham, J C W 302
Bell, T C 191-193 237 243
Berry, A S 276
Bibb, C S 48
Bibb, George 7-15
Bickley, Captain 36
Black, James D 328
Blackburn, J C S 237 276
Blair, Francis P 32
Blanton, J T 328
Bradley, R M 192
Bradley, Solomon 259
Bradley, William O 192, 245 298 303 305 336
Bradshaw, Nancy 189
Bramlette, T E 192 195
Breckinridge, John C 28 179 181 277
Breckinridge, R J 181
Breckinridge, W C P 211-220 305
Bridges, John 436
Brooks, C R 253
Brown, John M 60 61 179
Brown, Samuel M 63
Buford, Mary E 206-209
Buford, Thomas 205-223
Bullock, Edward J 68 77 78
Burbridge, General 180
Burks, Benjamin 60
Burr, Aaron 7 28
Bush, W P D 208
Butler, Noble 163
Butler, William 224-230
Butler, Wm H G 163-179

C

Caldwell, George 163
Caldwell, Isaac 227
Callahan, Ed 321-332
Cantrell James E 236 243
Cardwell, Jerry 323
Cardwell, T P 321-331
Carlisle, John G 278
Carpenter, R B 163 169 170
Carroll, William 212
Catlet, Hanson 19 20 25
Chambers, James 7-15
Chinn, Jack 234-241 293 306 317
Chinn, Kitt 293
Clark, Hector M 186 187
Clark, J C 59 60
Clark, James 35
Clark, Leonadus 186
Clark, Marcellus Jerome 180-190
Clay, Cassius M 290
Clay, Henry 28 219
Cockrell, James 322-324
Cockrell, Tom 322-325
Cockrill, Jeff D 254
Colson, David 292-300
Combs, Richard 308-319
Cook, Ann 45-56
Corneilison, John J 246-256
Cox, B D 322-332
Crabb, W L 212
Crittenden, John J 28 44 45 60 163 171-179 224-232
Crittenden, R H 224-232
Crittenden, Thomas 224-232
Culton, William H 308-319
Crozier, Eliza 68 79
Crozier, John 12-14
Covington, John 52
Cunningham, Charles M 69
Curtis, George M 211
Custer, George 232

D

Darby, Benjamin 45-56
Darsie, George 246
Davis, Garrett 179
Davis, J B T 192
Davis, John W 308-319
Davis, Samuel 69
Davis, Walter 233-244
Daviess, Larue 192-203
Daviess, Theodore H 191-203
Day, B F 253
Decatur, Stephen 28
Dejarnell, A D 210
Demaree, Luther W 292-300
Denny, George 236 243
Denny, James 48
Desha, Claude 279
Desha, Isaac B 34-43
Desha, Joseph 28 35 38-43
Dickinson, Charles 16-26
Donelson, John 16

Dudley, Benjamin 43
Durham, M J 191
Duvall, Alvin 208

E

Edelen, T L 305
Elliot, John M 205-223
English, Samuel 63
Ernst, Richard P 279
Ervine, Joseph 18 26

F

Fillmore, Millard 231
Finley, Charles 308-319
Fisher, Al 165
French, B F 328

G

Gaitskill, S S 253
Gambill, W S 22
Gibson, T W 163 170 172
Gilmore, J J 167
Goebel, William 272-281 301-319
Golden, Ben 292 328
Golden, F W 308-319
Golden, Green 308-319
Gooden, Sam 258
Goodloe, William Cassius 282-291
Gordon, Thomas 211
Graves, Rice E 187
Graves, William J 28
Greenup, Wilson 27-33
Grubbs, J B 21 22

H

Haggin, James 61
Hall, N H 63
Hallam, Theodore 211 278
Hamilton, Alexander 7 28
Harbison, Mat 279
Hardin, Ben 68 77-79 126-162 192
Hardin, C A 191-192 234-243
Hardin, P W 191 257 301
Hargis, Ben 322-332
Hargis, James 246 321-333
Harlan, James 179
Harlan, John M 179
Harris, Sylvester 163 170
Harrison, William H 231 290
Harvie, W P 198
Hays, J W 163
Hays, R B 163
Hazelrigg, J H 249 253 255 305
Helm, Frank P 272
Helm, John L 163 164 170
Hendricks, John K 257
Hendricks, William 253 273
Hines, Thomas M 205
Hobson, J P 305
Holloway, L B 211
Holman, Jacob 27-33
Howard, Berry 308-319
Howard, James 308-319
Hubbard, Thomas 12-13
Huett, J M 60
Hume, Dr. E E 296 307
Humphreys, W C 257-261

J

Jackson, Andrew 16-26
Jackson, Rachel Robards 16
Jackson, W L 210
Jacobs, R P 237
Jett, Curt 324-330
Jett, W L 212
Johnson, Francis 60
Johnson, Frank 68 74 97 103
Johnson, L F (Author) 309
Johnson, M C 179
Jones, Joshua 39
Julian, Charles 292-300
Julian, Ira 210

K

Kehoe, J N 295
Keller, W E 192
Kendall, Amos 40
Kinney, W R 211 227
Knott, Proctor 203 257 267
Kohn, Aaron 305
Kyle, John J 192

L

Lacy, J 48
Laffon, John 63 64
Landrom, Reuben S 64
Leathers, T P 277
LeCompt, Joseph 61
Lewis, Joseph 13
Lillard, Eph 306 317
Lindsey, William 253
Lindsey, D W 237
Little, Bob 320
Logan family (Rowan Co.) 257-271
Loofborro, Thomas 31
Lowe, John F 47

M
Magoffin, Beriah 193
Magruder, Billy 182
Major, P U (Dedication) 210
Major, S I M 209
Marcum, J B 321-332
Marks, Nathan 184
Marshall, Humphrey 28 277
Marshall, John 302
Marshall, John J 31
Marshall, Thomas 60 163 169
Martin Family (Rowan Co.) 257-271
Mayo, J C C 294
McChesney, W S 284-287
McCreary, James B 208 297
McEwan, Harry 292
McHenry, W D 60 61
McKee, H Clay 253 255
McKee, Lewis 264
McManama, O D 210-212
McQuown, Louis 305
Meaux, Richard 191
Meeks, Alexander 69 74 79 102
Menifee, Richard 28
Mitchell, R A 253 255
Monroe, B 179
Montgomery, Warren 210
Morehead, Charles 67 179
Morgan, John Hunt 189 277
Morton, Jerry R 236 243
Morrow, Moses 63
Mosby, Rose 224-232
Muir, P B 227
Mundy, Marc 227
Mundy, Sue 180-190
Murdaugh, John 68-162
Myers, Harvey 278

N
Nelson, R W 310
Nicholas, Henry 227-230
Noel, Silas M 29 33 65
Nuckols, J P 208

O
O'Hara, Theodore 29
O'Neal, John B 328
Osborne, J J 328
Overton, Thomas 18 21-25
Owens, W C 236 243 309

P
Patterson, W R 253
Paxton, Richard 293
Perry, J W 211
Phelps, Jack 305
Pollard, O H 321
Pope, John 48
Porter, Thomas P 179
Poston, O S 191 192
Powers, Caleb 308-319
Powers, John L 308-319
Prentice, George D 167
Prentis, Sargent S. 68 77-125
Pryor, W S 205

Q
Quinn, Esquire 210

R
Randell, William 321
Randolph, John 28
Redpath, C D 292 296
Redwine, D B 328-336
Reid, Davis 246
Reid, Richard 246-256
Richards, A E 249
Richardson, John C 61
Richardson, Samuel Q 48 58-67
Riddle, Judge 248
Riley, T W 163
Riley, Thomas 275 280
Robards, Lewis 16
Robards, W F 203
Robbins, B S 236 243
Roberts, Joe 29 33
Robertson, Colonel 69 77
Robins, Judge 59 62-64
Rodman, John 179 208-213
Rodman, Hugh 211
Rothwell, John 69 73 74
Rowan, John 7-15 68 77 78
Rupell, Felix 63

S
Saunders, Jr. 60 61
Scott, E D 292-300
Scott, James A 305
Scott, M T 287
Sebastian, Benjamin 7 14
Settle, Evan E 211
Shannon, George 39
Sharp, Eliza 49 56
Sharp, Leander 49 56
Sharp, Solomon 44-57
Shaw, W McD 279
Shelby 283 284
Shipp, G B 229

Shuck, Finley 236 243
Smith, Green Clay 210
Sneed, W H 210
Stanford, John L 272-281
Stevenson, J M 179
Stone, H L 253
Stone, W J 301
Sweeney, W H 305
Swift, H C 285-287
Swope, A M 282-289
Swope, George 185

T

Taylor, James 69
Taylor, W S 302 309
Thompson, D D 166
Thompson, Davis M 192-203 233-244
Thompson, J B 191-204 233-244
Thompson, John B 69 78
Thompson, P B 191-203 211 233-245
Thorne, W P 253
Tolliver Family (Rowan Co.) 257-271
Tony, Sterling B 303
Transylvania University 65 290
Trimble, John 38
Turner, Charles C 253
Turner, Thomas 253
Tyler, M S 253
Voorhees, Daniel W 237

W

Waits, David 61
Wallace, Annie O 206
Ward, Matt F. 163-179
Ward, Robert J 163-178
Ward, William 164 168
Waring, Francis G 27-33 65
Waring, John U 33 45-47 58-67
Whalen, John 303
White, Tom 327-330
Whittaker, Harlan 307
Wickliffe, J C 193-202
Wigginton, M R 62
Wilkinson, Benjamin D 68 162
Wilkinson, Edward C 68 162
Williams, Andrew 61
Williams, John S 180
Willson, A E 309
Willson, James C 198
Wilson, John 239
Wilson, J C 192
Wintersmith, C G 163
Wolfe, Nat 163 170 178
Wood, A T 253
Woodford, Henry 253

Y

Yost, W H 305
Youtsey, Henry 308-319